365 Dates of Travel: The SECOND six months

Fran Heap

The information in this book is the author's personal experiences, memories and opinions on the situations that occurred. Memories are not always accurate years later. Any discrepancies are from faulty memories rather than a deliberate altering of the events. Updates or corrections that may surface will be acknowledged on the author's website.

First published by Frances Heap contactable at fran@franheapwriter.com

Copyright © 2023 by Fran Heap

All rights reserved.

ISBN: 978-0-6457056-2-1   (paperback)

ISBN: 978-0-6457056-3-8   (ebook)

The right of Fran Heap to be identified as the author of this work has been asserted.

No part of this book may be reproduced or transmitted by any person or entity in any form or by any means, electronic or mechanical, including photocopying, recording, scanning or by any information storage and retrieval system, without written permission from the author/publisher at fran@franheapwriter.com

 A catalogue record for this book is available from the National Library of Australia

Cover design uses elements from Canva by Macrovector; Hiran Roy; aaf from Art and Funny; sorembadesignz; RESA from sketchify; and sketchify.

Created with Atticus.

Contents

Introduction	V
How to read this book	VIII
Getting to know me!	X
1. May	1
2. June	35
3. July	100
4. August	166
5. September	216
6. October	269
7. November	323
About the Author	332
Index	335

Introduction

I set myself a challenge. Have I been travelling on every date of the year? An interesting thought which produced a wonderful trip down memory lane. (Spoiler alert: I made every date of the year twice over!) I started with the day my adult travelling life began. For this trip, I had multiple sources with which to build a detailed picture: a diary; trip scrapbook; photo album; original guidebooks and snippets of memories. I wish I could say the same for every trip. This first trip remains my all-time favourite and I would love to re-live it.

This book is the second half of the year, starting where the first book finished in May. If you want to read from the beginning, you will need to start with *The first six months*. I did not like splitting the book into two, but the volume would have been too thick for a first-time writer and a travel memoir.

Make the most of the interactive properties with photos, indexes and podcasts available to enhance your experience.

The QR codes at the start of each chapter will take you to my website and the corresponding photos for that chapter.

The index at the back, and other indexes on the website, will allow you to choose the stories you read and in what order. They cover both books.

The podcast adds background to the stories, and you can hear my voice.

I've tried to be as accurate as my memory allows. Names are real unless specified to the contrary.

Read the *How to read this book* and the *Getting to know me!* sections for more in-depth information.

**Travel photos are
available for viewing on my website**

https://franheapwriter.com/photos/

Each chapter has a QR code with a link
to the specific photos from that chapter.

Any **incomplete trips** from either book, will be finished
in future podcast episodes.
(And extra unmentioned trips.)
Check out:
365 Dates of Travel with Fran Heap
wherever you get your podcasts.

Countries visited (in the second six months)

Europe

Denmark
France
Germany
Holland
Ireland
Italy
United Kingdom

Africa

Kenya
Mali
Rwanda
Tanzania
Uganda

North America

United States (USA)
Jamaica

South America

Peru

Oceania

Australia
New Zealand

How to read this book

You choose your own adventure!

This book is not a diary, rather a collection of stories characterised by the date on which they occurred. There's a story for each date of the year allowing you to use it as daily travel inspiration should you choose. I use snippets from my original diaries but it is not a year long diary.

Get to know me by reading the following section, and listen to Episode 1 of my podcast titled "That Time In The Beginning", to hear me talk about my life preceding my travel to America in 1992 and other background stories. You'll hear my voice to help increase your understanding of my character.

Check out the trip photos on my website to see me and the places you'll read about. There's a QR code to scan at the start of each chapter, taking you to the corresponding photos.

Once you know what I look and sound like, you can put me in the stories as you read; hear my laugh when I've done something funny; and see my Cheshire cat smile when I'm marvelling at Roman ruins.

I've included a chronological index covering both books. And also links to various themed indexes to help you chose what to read and how to read. You can choose from chronological order, train stories, packing information, or individual countries to Lottie the Arkana, plus more.

It's okay to skip sections or move backwards and forwards. No one will enjoy every story. Or like every country. Not everyone will be interested in the costs or how I packed. I expect people to skip the bits that do not entice them.

There's nothing wrong with reading from start to finish or one per day, as in one story for each date of the year.

For an immersive experience, open the photos while reading and listen to the podcast either before or after reading a chapter. Each chapter has two podcasts: one with stories behind the stories; and the other direct readings from the book with a one or two sentence introduction to each date read.

My intention is to elicit laughter regarding my comical collection of receipts and assorted memorabilia. I expect you to react by shaking your head or rolling your eyes as I confess the items I have held onto or the dust-able souvenirs I have purchased. And for you to react to my spending habits, whether it be my frugal tendencies or extravagant indulgences.

There is no story arc to follow. You chose where the beginning, middle and end lie. Though the first date (from *The first six months*) and the last date (of *The SECOND six months*) have a certain symmetry.

I wasn't finding myself or repairing myself or reinventing myself or looking for love. I was living my life around the world.

I include details I find lacking in other travel books. I want to know what it was like day to day. Was transport hard? Navigating hard? How does the public transport system work? How long did it take to get there? How did you communicate in a foreign language? How long did you spend at places? What did it cost? If you are not interested in these details, skip them.

Being shy, I don't seek people. Travel books often mention the people met. That's my worst nightmare. Small conversations are fine, but I don't want to do it every day. I don't *need* contact with people when travelling on my own. I'm happy in my own company, though I have made some lifelong friends along the way.

Learn more about me in the next section!

Getting to know me!

When I started travelling, I was a naive 18-year-old with high expectations and low funds. My obsession with the television show *Beverly Hills 90210* was my motivation. In later years, I'm a scaredy-cat with a Cheshire cat grin fuelled by my multitude of interests. My once fiery, vibrant red hair contains white streaks of age creating a "sugar and spice" colour palette.

Being shy, self-conscious, sensitive and insecure, I prefer solitude, hence why comment on having places to myself. With no one around, there's no scrutiny. I constantly feel judged, especially about being alone. I've been single long term, mostly unhappily, but now content with that status, and no desire to alter it.

I don't drink coffee or alcohol, which by default makes me anti-social. I don't need to frequent cafes during the day or bars at night. I drink tea in the mornings and hot chocolates in the afternoons and evenings. Both of which can be made in my hotel room.

I am passionate, though my passions change. My interests include trains (not engines); space exploration and astronauts; ancient ruins (or any ruins); social history (especially Victorian and during World War II); baroque architecture and design; deserts and vast scenery; snow and mountains; animal safaris; and codes and code breaking, to name a few.

My giggle is unique and led to the nickname "Scooby" more than once. Another nickname was "Fran-tic" because I rushed about the place. And like every Australian redhead, I'll answer to Blue or Bluey. But not carrot top.

My two careers have been nannying and nursing but also worked as a cleaner, dishwasher, kitchen hand, retail assistant and a school lunch lady!

People consider me brave, but I am not. I'm frequently petrified, and that's the motivation behind the quirky data collecting because knowledge alleviates fear. This is also the reason behind the extensive planning. With my perfectly crafted travel bible, I just follow instructions. Easy.

I choose accommodation that allows me to walk to sights. If I need public transport, I watch YouTube videos on how the ticket machines and entry gates work. This identifies the buttons to press, and whether it has an English option. I learn how to insert or tap my ticket, so I don't appear foolish before the locals or scream tourist. I feel safer if I look like I belong.

These details form my travel bible, my personal guidebook. Further public transport details include what line to catch, the number of stops and how long it will take. I note which exit to use and landmarks such as a chemist on the corner or a park to the right.

Whenever possible I choose hotels with restaurants. Room service is the best option. I hate eating in restaurants by myself. I prefer an included buffet breakfast, so I have at least one proper meal a day.

I search for supermarkets and write directions to them in my travel bible for food supplies. They are easier than bakeries or cafes, for example, as I help myself and don't need to talk to anyone. I choose from the shelves; take my own bag and make it obvious so they don't ask if I want a bag which I won't understand and be embarrassed by not understanding; and pay by credit card so I don't have to translate the amount and count it out in cash. Tap the card and I've paid. The early travel days in youth hostels made food easier with kitchen access.

I've grown into more of a chicken as become older. The confidence of youth has retreated. But I make it work. And I have travelled the world!

Now choose your own adventure!

May

9th May (2019) North Island, New Zealand

After a work conference, I stayed an extra day in my surprise upgraded room with views of Auckland. I had one day to experience New Zealand, so booked a day trip to cover more ground. My primary goal was seeing glow worms.

    I indulged in a room-service breakfast of scrambled eggs, sausages, bacon, tomatoes and the cutest baby hash browns. Because of my shift work and time zone adjustments, I had an early schedule allowing time to savour my breakfast despite a 7:30 am tour.

    I met two fellow nurses from South Africa and Hawaii at the tour departure point around the corner. We spent the day together.

    The streets of Auckland soon gave way to rolling green hills, so lush you could imagine being in the English countryside.

    Our first stop was the glow worms in Waitomo, which filled me with child-like excitement. No photos were allowed as camera flashes affect the worms' glowing behaviour. No talking either. The idea is to glide in slow-moving boats in silence, marvelling in the greenish, blueish glow above you. Magical. Ethereal.

    Next we visited a sheep dog and shearing show. I saw my first kiwi fruit plant on the farm tour afterwards. The kiwi plants were laid out in a grapevine style. We sampled the kiwis straight off the vine.

We continued to the strange town of Rotorua with geothermal activity everywhere. Steam rising out of front yards is not a normal occurrence for me. It almost has alternate universe status.

We went to Te Puia for the cultural displays, followed by the geysers and mud pools. I could spend the entire day watching the big geyser erupt. Such power and energy, and of course smell. The sulphurous scent follows you as you wander around the various sights.

One such sight is the Kiwi Conservation Centre, where the native kiwi birds live. Alas, they were sleeping, only glimpsing them via the cameras in their burrows. Does that count as seeing a kiwi?

We finished here around 5:00 pm and began the three-hour drive to Auckland. A long but good day. The tour was better than hiring a car and driving myself, which I'd considered during my planning.

I flew home the next day and travelled to America the following week.

10th May (2004) Perth to Merredin, Western Australia (WA), Australia

My sum of information is sixteen diary lines on the first day; seven photos; a packing list; a food shopping list; and five pages of a mini notebook with scribblings on diesel fill ups, managing two tanks, and kilometres driven. I wish I had more.

My new-to-me car was a modified Toyota Arkana. It's a rare Toyota model most people don't know. This specimen had been enlarged, and in its heyday, luxurious, for its role of transporting mine managers in style. Now it oozes faded grandeur. If you picture a Toyota Troop Carrier, or Troopy, this car was longer, wider and taller. I could stand upright in the rear, which held ten forward-facing seats. With the seats removed, it's perfect as a camper van for my trip across Africa. But I had to get it to Melbourne first. After an engine overhaul, it was now ready to drive.

I flew into Perth a few days earlier, collected the car, and caught up with friends. Now I had to leave the safety of Perth and drive my new car home. I had five days to drive 3000 km.

The packing list I found included a doona and pillows. I needed these items as planned to sleep in the car. Did I take the doona on the plane? The car's back seat spanned the width of the vehicle, and I could stretch across it. With a bed, I did not need camping gear for this inaugural trip.

I spent $100 at the supermarket and bought items from Bakers Delight. I'll assume I ate the bakery items while fresh.

I'd been told the car had two 70 litre diesel tanks. I filled both till the pump cut off, totalling 97.43 litres. It cost $95.38, meaning around 98 cents per litre. I wish I could pay that price now.

I was stocked, ready, and very nervous. City driving would be the hardest to navigate. I had never driven in Perth. I did not know the city well, and driving a car I didn't know, including it being a manual, or stick shift, which I'd only driven once since passing my manual driving test in London in 1998.

I had photocopied pages of a Perth Street Directory which was available to view, but not borrow, at my local library. No GPS. No navigator in the passenger seat. A few photocopied pages with a highlighted route and me. I needed to get through the city and onto Highway 94, the Great Eastern Highway.

I left at 1:30 pm managing 264 km. I parked at a campground on the outskirts of Merredin for the night. $12 allowed me to enter and use the facilities.

I don't know what time I stopped driving, but I wrote my diary entry at 7:30 pm.

> Here I am in Merredin. My first night in the car. It's so cool. All the lights work etc. and plenty of space. I love it. I probably should

have parked up sooner, but at least I'm in a proper caravan park here and I've had a shower and all I need. I drove in the dark, but it was fine. No kangaroos yet, so I was lucky. Only did 264 km today. Hoping for a much better day tomorrow mileage-wise, but at least it's better than still being in Perth and leaving tomorrow. The car drives perfectly. No problems at all except maybe oil. There's a gauge in the car and not sure if that means how much oil there is or temperature, but will buy some oil just in case in Coolgardie, or next petrol stop, so I can top it up if need to. I'm tired. So early to bed tonight and up with the sun to start the day.

Not sure what the oil gauge comments mean. Did I have any idea what I was doing? Probably not.

I moved my belongings to between the rear two rows. This created a generous sleeping bay where I comfortably curled up. Although simple, it was a decent setup and easier than pitching a tent. With no window coverings, I would be awake with the sun.

As promised, I messaged my flatmate to inform her of my whereabouts. I made it a habit each night to serve as a reference point in case I went missing. Travel was changing with this my first trip with a mobile phone.

11th May (2004) Merredin to Caiguna, WA, Australia

I left Merredin at 7:30 am. Breakfast in the car comprised Sultana Bran with UHT milk and a banana.

I wished I'd had time to detour to Kalgoorlie, but I had a huge drive to do in five days. I reluctantly drove past the Kalgoorlie signs.

I switched to tank two after driving 427 km. So straightforward. I moved a switch from left to right and the fuel gauge said full. In Coolgardie I filled tank one with diesel until the tank overflowed. It took 61.7 litres to achieve the 427 km, meaning I switched early. Useful data to know. The diesel cost more at 103.9 cents a litre.

After Coolgardie, Highway 94, which has been heading east, turns south for 166 km until Norseman. Here you turn onto Highway 1, the Eyre Highway, heading east again. After 200 km on the Eyre Highway, passed the town of Belladonia, I begin crossing the Nullarbor Plain, a 90-mile stretch of straight road, the longest in the world. No bends or curves for 90 miles, or 146.6 km. There is nothing in the landscape. Nullarbor is Latin for "no trees". Only desert and low-lying shrubs to the horizon. Some consider it boring. I found it mesmerising.

On this trip, I learnt the importance of having your driving lights on during the day. You notice cars in the distance sooner if their lights are on. This is important for single lane highways containing trucks and road trains. I turn my lights on now whenever driving on country roads regardless of the time of day.

I had received instructions on sharing the road safely with the great Australian road trains. My memory is fuzzy, but I think I'm close. You stay far enough back that the road train driver can see you in their mirrors. If they perceive you intend to overtake and the road is clear ahead, they use their hazard lights and manoeuvre to the right. They are telling you to overtake. They can see for miles in the flat, straight terrain. Your view from behind is limited. An incorrect decision can have serious consequences if you pull out into an oncoming road train.

It sounds intimidating at first, but once the system has worked a few times, it becomes the norm. I had planned on not overtaking but even in my old Toyota Arkana and my nervous driving, sometimes you needed to. One or two toilet stops, and you're behind the same road train and have to overtake again.

DON'T follow this advice. In my first search, I found nothing online to confirm this information. I wasn't sure if specialised insider knowledge, or no longer the case. Everything I read advised to pull over, no matter what direction the road train was going. Otherwise, follow the usual precautions. I know there was a system in 2004, and it worked then.

On further research, I discovered it was not hazard lights but the right turning indicator used to signal clear. I read multiple stories and warnings of how this created misunderstandings and accidents. Consider the scenario where the truck signals a right turn, entering the left lane to enable said turn. And you accelerate to pass as the road train slows to make the turn. You can imagine the accident potential.

Do not assume the truck is signalling you. Overtake if safe based on your own checks. If you have a CB radio in the car, contact the truck to inform them you want to pass. That alerts them to your presence and movements, and they can inform you if unsafe. Do not take risks. It's not worth it.

I wish I'd taken more photos. I didn't appreciate the experience. Not sure why I didn't treat it as an adventure. I loved every bit of the drive, but it was just a drive. I didn't even stop at the sign showing the start of the record holding straight section. Such a shame.

Food-wise I finished a Chives and Garlic Twisted Delight that I must have started yesterday; had two apricot jam sandwiches; rice cakes; a fruit cup; and an apple. Drinks-wise, I had three water bottle refills, a bottle of cola and three cups of tea. I'm unsure where I got those cups of tea, as don't mention paying for them. Did I make them myself after buying a camping stove before leaving Perth? I have a camping stove, but I cannot recall when I bought it.

My notebook records six toilet stops; two petrol stops; a lunch stop; a text stop; and a tea stop. I mentioned being dark by 5:00 pm, and I stopped driving at 6:00 pm, at Caiguna.

It cost $12 again to park my car at the Truck Stop. I believe one of my clearest memories of this trip occurred here. I pulled in and jumped out of the driver's seat. It's a drop to the ground. A truck driver noticed me. I locked the car and walked away. The truck driver's head did a double take back to my car. He was expecting someone else to get out and became perplexed when no one did. I took that as a compliment. He thought I couldn't drive the car on my own, but I did. Go me. I can see his expression when he realised I was alone.

After beef stroganoff from the Truck Stop restaurant for $15.50 and a shower, I headed to bed in the back seat.

Diesel management-wise, tank two showed empty after 439 km. I refilled in Caiguna, squeezing in 71.38 litres. How can that be? Maybe it was a 75 litre tank? The cost rose to 135.9 cents a litre. I covered 833 km, much further than yesterday.

12th May (2004) Ceduna, South Australia (SA), Australia

I started driving at 7:00 am. I reached the Great Australian Bight, stopping at three viewpoints with no expectations of what I'd find at the first one.

What I saw astounded me. You drove almost to the edge and then nothing stopped you from walking further. No barriers apart from your nerves. Such a surreal experience perched on a cliff edge with the isolated barren desert behind and a vast ocean ahead. And not another soul.

You view the Bunda Cliffs which stretch for 200 km and are around 70 m high. The jagged cliffs jut at varying distances. I stood at the bottom of a U-shape with undulating cliff faces on either side. Exhilarating. You can understand how jokes and advertising campaigns changed it into the Great Australian "Bite". It looks like a giant mouth has taken a "bite" out of the land, leaving jagged tooth marks along the coast.

This natural wonder goes unappreciated because of its remoteness. I pondered on why no one had delivered more visitors here. The only infrastructure being the Truck Stops. But then I realised part of its beauty stems from its isolation.

More people visiting would ruin that. I felt privileged to experience this sight and glad I stopped.

Based on online photos from more recent trips, there may now be barriers keeping you from the edge. I can't be sure. Maybe more people do visit now.

In the day's practicalities notes, I stopped counting toilet stops with my notebook stating:

> Loads of toilet stops.

I learnt if I drank water while driving, I'd have to stop for the bathroom. This negated the need for rest stops of twenty minutes or more every two hours, as recommended. I stopped more often but for shorter periods of time. I have continued this pattern on my long distance drives since.

For breakfast, I had Sultana Bran and fruit. Over the day, I ate two bananas, two apples, grape tomatoes, cashew nuts, three jam sandwiches and potato chips. Somehow I had four cups of tea. As well as cola and water. No wonder I needed loads of toilet stops.

I am guessing I had forgotten about not taking fruit interstate, and bought too much in Perth. It sounds familiar, thus possible, I stopped to eat my fruit before it was taken off me when crossing into South Australia.

I used the Truck Stop's laundry facilities, and ate cold tinned spaghetti from the can, while sitting in bed. Tinned corn and apple juice rounded out dinner.

Diesel-wise, tank one showed empty at 378 km on the odometer. I waited until it read 400 km, then switched to tank two. Tank one needed 65 litres at a reduced price of 112 cents a litre. Tank two needed 72.41 litres after travelling 411 km. They have to be 75 litre tanks based on the collected figures. The price dropped further to 102.9 cents a litre at the second stop.

I travelled 854 km.

13th May (2004) Berri, SA, Australia

From Ceduna you can take the coastal Flinders Highway, or continue on the Eyre Highway, as I did, for a more direct route. The wide open country gave way to built-up areas as I edged closer to South Australia's capital, Adelaide.

Driving through the Adelaide Hills and Adelaide city made me nervous given I'd arrive during peak hour. I studied my map, deciding on a different course. I enjoyed the country roads and was not ready to lose that freedom.

I headed to Berri, South Australia. This had me east of Adelaide, but further north than needed. When checking in at the Berri camp site, I confused the manager when said I'd driven from Perth and heading to Melbourne.

"What are you doing up here? Aren't we out of the way?"

I said I wasn't ready to hit the city. I think he thought I'd taken a wrong turn. Well, I did, but on purpose.

I pushed both tanks further, getting to 445 and 450 km before switching. 852 km driven, which appears to be the daily potential average.

14th May (2004) Berri to Home, Victoria (VIC), Australia

I crossed the border into my home state and everything became more familiar. The hard drive was behind me. An easy 720 km for the day.

I pushed the tanks, not switching until 485 km. So I might get 500 km per tank, meaning a 1000 km range. Incredible. No jerry cans required. Built in tanks is easier than fiddling with jerry cans and funnels, as with Lucy in Africa. This car is better than Lucy already. Not that she's hard to beat.

Diesel became cheaper as I got closer to home, at 101.5 cents.

From Perth to home, I drove 3323 km over five days across Australia by myself. I spent $505 on diesel.

After re-living this trip, I wanted to jump in my car and do it again. Not sure how my twenty-year-old Toyota Corolla hatchback would cope with it. But what a delicious thought.

15th May (1998) Kayes, Mali

We chose our free camping spot last night, expecting not to be disturbed. We set up away from town, near the railway track. The guidebook said trains pass through once a week in either direction. We were optimistic about not encountering a train after hearing one had been through recently. However, it seems the trains had become more frequent or our unlucky night.

The first train arrived at midnight. We heard a rumbling noise in the distance for ten minutes. Then a roar. Out of the night, bright lights appeared as a freight train thundered past two metres away. A surreal experience. Another screeched by a few hours later. Not conducive to sleeping.

16th May (1998) Chutes du Felou, Mali

The sweltering heat had persisted for an unbearable duration, prompting us to strip and jump into our discovered rock pool and rapids. Swimming naked in the cool water was glorious. This led to another bout of peeling sunburn. Not that it crossed my mind today. I would later express it being worth it.

If you swam away from the rocks, it was magical. You became a tiny speck in the middle of the massive Senegal River. For days we'd been asking if it held water. People said it might be empty. How could this amount of water disappear? Its width was too great to swim. Surely it always contained water. Emerging from the protective rock pool into the river's vast open expanse was intimidating. I could not stay for long. You were too insignificant to be safe. My exact sentiments:

It was frightening, yet exhilarating at the same time.

We found a spot above the rock pools to camp, staying for two nights. A large building complex with high gates sat to our right. Nobody came or went, thus no one bothered by our presence. It was an electricity plant which proved useful as well lit at night.

We made dinner utilising the light. I helped, but everyone told me to sit and rest. I'd grown unwell throughout the day. Most likely from too much sun. My memory says we had macaroni cheese for dinner. We had this yummy cheese sauce powder mix you added water to. An easy, delicious dinner after a long day. We ate this often.

As we packed up dinner, a storm brewed out of nowhere. We made it into the car, Lucy, just in time, and waited the storm out in there. A ferocious wind blew dust around, but also held rain. Anna played in it for a few minutes. Sarah joined her when it became more rain than dust. I loved our wild weather encounters on this trip.

We exited Lucy once the storm subsided enough to set up the tent. I elected to sleep in the car, finding it comfortable. With the windows down, a cool breeze blew over me. The storm remained throughout the night.

17th May (2019) In transit to the United States of America (USA)

I took the evening flight to Los Angeles, not my preferred departure. As a night shift worker, I find it easier to sleep during the day, then pack and organise overnight, heading to the airport once ready for the morning departure. That is more relaxing than packing, sleeping, and setting the alarm to get up and head to the airport. That's when last-minute items get forgotten. It's easy to do everything at once and then leave.

My diary starts with:

> I couldn't help myself from sleeping. Looks like I have no choice now but to sleep on planes. I didn't sleep well during the day–maybe that was it. Anyway, I managed a full movie awake–*Mary Poppins* then slept through some of *Aquaman* and [*Welcome to*] *Marwen*. Maybe all of *Second Act*. Then no time left to watch anything else so started a tv series I may watch on my way back if no new movies. Quite disappointing in movies, really.

For most of my travelling life, I could not sleep on planes. I resigned myself to that years ago, stopping even trying, focussing on movie watching instead. It was disappointing to miss movies while sleeping. I have now given in to my new ability to sleep on planes. I'm content with a movie or two at the beginning, and a movie at the end.

Our Dreamliner flight was full. I had an aisle seat, allowing space on one side.

I arrived in Los Angeles three hours before I left Melbourne, which gives me a kick each time.

No problems with immigration other than baffling the officer with my storm chasing plans. But he let me in so I could chase.

A twenty-minute wait for a hotel shuttle didn't impress me. Arriving at 6:15 pm local time, I slept at an airport hotel to continue my domestic travel the following day. I noted every other airport hotel shuttle came round more often than mine.

A long check-in queue greeted me, but made it to bed by 9:00 pm after putting my breakfast order on the card and placing it on my room's door handle.

18th May (2019) Norman, Oklahoma (OK), USA

I slept well after taking melatonin. I woke later than expected, jumping out of bed in a rush at 7:00 am, thinking they would deliver breakfast any second. Alas, ordering breakfast via a door menu did not work at this hotel. I couldn't even make myself a cup of tea, as had no milk. I wouldn't choose this hotel again.

On arrival at the airport, I was starving. I bought a bacon, cheese and egg bagel with an apple juice. As I ordered, I noted cups of Half-and-Half at the coffee station. I added a mug of hot water to my order. I had tea bags but needed water and milk. A free, delicious and large cup of tea. I love the land of Half-and-Half, half milk, half cream. It is thick, sweet and creamy. Perfect for my cup of tea. I had to change to full cream milk at home after getting accustomed to Half-and-Half in America.

Despite sleeping well, my eyes were sore, and I developed a headache. I took ibuprofen with breakfast, noting in my diary I often get headaches after taking melatonin. I have since discovered if you take a higher melatonin dose than is required, headaches can develop. Unbeknownst to me, whatever dose I'd taken was too high.

My diary notes it didn't take long to get through the formalities despite being busy and lines for everything, including the elevators and a sniffer dog section. I travelled in first class for this domestic flight, but it didn't come with fast-tracked security. The bag drop, though, contained special access and welcoming staff.

As I explored airside, I noticed a lounge for One World Sapphire guests. That would be me once this trip's status credits were added to my Qantas Frequent Flyer account. I looked forward to being Qantas Gold, One World Sapphire, and the ensuing lounge access.

I met a fellow storm chaser at the Oklahoma City airport as arriving at similar times, thus sharing a transfer. With his flight delayed, I had to wait. I used the time to insert a pre-bought SIM card into my iPad to test it. I'd ordered a card from an online company. It was easy, and it worked.

Changing my SIM card and losing access to my phone number made me nervous after my father passed away while overseas in 2016. What if they couldn't contact me and I found out after I returned home? I wanted direct access to my Australian phone number, and have internet without relying on free Wi-Fi. I put the SIM card in my mini iPad and created a hotspot for my phone without losing my phone number. Perfect. It was revolutionary for me. Technology has changed and improved since 2016 and 2019.

Once we checked in at our hotel in Norman, Oklahoma, they informed us of a 10:00 am briefing the next day. Our two-week storm chasing tour would begin with a drive day followed by an action day. My anticipation built. I have wanted to do a storm chasing tour forever. I love wild weather.

I didn't appreciate our starting hotel.

> Hotel pretty ordinary. I definitely have high standards these days.
> I'd better do all my rough travelling asap.

I explored the Walmart behind the hotel.

> It really does have everything, including guns! Oh, and PG Tips! Will buy some on the way home! Then I had McDonald's for dinner–inside Walmart.

Having McDonald's, guns and PG Tips tea bags is the true definition of everything. I would enjoy multiple visits to Walmart throughout this trip.

I travelled with a company called Cloud 9 Tours. They are the oldest chasing tour company in operation. They must do something right if operating since 1996. The well-travelled Australian couple in Turkmenistan recommended the company. They have taken this tour. Brilliant advice. Unfortunately, 2022 is the company's last year. They missed two seasons because of COVID in 2020 and 2021. I am glad they had one last season, but sad I won't be able to repeat my experience with them. A last-minute takeover bid may offer a reprieve, but nothing's been confirmed.

This is no ordinary tour with no itinerary or sightseeing list. They plan each day the night before based on weather forecasts and may change multiple times throughout the day. No accommodation is pre-booked. Everything is unpredictable. You follow the storm and maybe the storm turns and takes you in the opposite direction from where you expected, leaving you miles from your booked hotel. They tried to estimate where we might be and ring ahead in the late afternoon when possible. It's difficult getting twenty rooms at short notice. We stayed wherever rooms were available.

Here are some notes from my travel bible compared with the reality:

- *free 'hotspot' for internet in van*   [It never worked on my trip]
- *stay Motel 6's mostly*   [Cheap hotel chain]
- *max 18 guests*   [Not true]

- *early mornings* [Not really]
- *long drive days* [Yes]
- *close quarters in cars* [Not in the front seat]
- *lunch may be main meal as storms in arvo/evening so may not stop till 9 pm or later (take snacks)* [Snack supplies essential]
- *will see "supercell thunderstorms"* [Absolutely]

19th May (2019) Childress, Texas (TX), USA

All names changed

I slept well, helped by melatonin, but awake early, making our 10:00 am meeting hours away. I watched television to fill in time.

I found the hotel floor to be too dirty for bare feet. I didn't sit on the chair, as it also appeared dirty. A weird scent wafted through the room. I considered returning to Walmart to buy air freshener in case other hotels were similar.

Our 10:00 am meeting didn't happen until later. Everything appeared messy. Vehicle choosing was disorganised. Chaos might be a better word. As usual, I stuffed up the seating arrangements. A mad rush and fight occurred for the so-called main van where the decision making occurred. In this van, you could see the computer data used to inform decisions. If you wanted technical stuff, you wanted that van. Also, as they led, you arrived first, catching a cell before it dissipated. There was also someone to avoid.

Three fellow Aussies asked if I wanted to join them. Great. But that plan fell apart. The organisers only realised now they'd overbooked, meaning not enough seats in the vans. They solved this by asking one of the regular chasers if he'd drive his car throughout the trip, taking three passengers. He said yes. The three Aussies jumped in, leaving me to find a new home.

Like every other trip of my life, I got the leftover seat. I ended up with the person the repeat clients actively avoided, Malcolm. We first timers, did not know about this. Malcolm had, amongst other issues, a skin condition requiring him to put lotion on every morning. Most people would do this before getting dressed. And most people would rub it in. Not Malcolm. He waited until sitting in the van. His concept of how much lotion to use was not ideal. He splashed lotion everywhere which grossed me out.

After a couple of minutes, I realised the front seat was free and moved. I knew I could not rely on sitting there every day, though, so planned to pack a towel in my daypack for the following day in case I had to sit next to Malcolm. Then Carl arrived with the only free seat next to Malcolm. He was not happy. It turned out these two were complete opposites, creating tension in the front row.

In summary, I got the second last seat, and Carl got the worst seat.

My memory is losing the details. I believe we had eight in our van. A single in the back amongst the luggage; three rows of two; and myself in the front. Nine with the driver. The official tour numbers should be eighteen plus three drivers. We became twenty-three plus four drivers. If my numbers are correct, we totalled twenty-seven. Someone lost count during the booking phase.

By pure chance, we had international newbies in our van. Only Malcolm and our driver, Jeremy, were American. We had a father and son from Holland; a guy and a girl from Finland; a girl from Sweden; Carl from Canada; and myself from Australia.

Once bags loaded and seats chosen, it was lunchtime. We ate at a venue next door called the Golden Corral Buffet and Grill. The regulars guided me through the options being my first time. There was a menu for individual dishes or two levels of buffet choices. I tried the extended buffet for $17.70 with multiple stations, including dessert. I enjoyed everything I ate.

After lunch, our four vehicles drove through Tornado Alley. This refers to an area from Texas in the south, to South Dakota in the north and everywhere in between. We could be anywhere in this alley over our two weeks. Today we travelled over 200 miles and crossed the Texas state line, positioning ourselves for the following day's forecasted activity. Expectations were high, making even the experts nervous.

I delved into my Walmart snacks while relocating. I discovered my new favourite snack in Chocolate Chip Cookie Dough Bites. How did I not know about these? I'm hooked for life.

We drove for three hours with one bathroom break. My ability to sleep has extended to all travel modes, having a couple of naps. The scenery was lush, with colourful wild flowers by the road.

We ate dinner at Pizza Hut but I ordered pasta. A group of twenty plus people arriving unannounced is not ideal for any restaurant. It took time for everyone to get their food.

I was happier with tonight's hotel room being more stylish and cleaner than the previous one; Super 8 by Wyndham in a town called Childress. The photos on my hotel wall reminded me we were in Texas.

20th May (2019) Clinton, OK, USA

My Facebook post for today.

```
Our first chase day. Our first tornado.
Beautiful clouds and incredible lightning.
```

The predictive models labelled today as high-risk, with a greater than ninety-five per cent probability of numerous violent tornadoes. Schools closed and a nearby Air Force Base evacuated. Alas, the models got it wrong. Tornado prediction is not an exact science. We experienced little activity and nothing close to violent. Large numbers of chasers came out ready for the storms, with most seeing none. We spotted two. Not bad for our first day.

Paducah, Texas, became the sweet spot. Human emotions, expectations and weather phenomenon filled the air. The tornado warning sirens creating the perfect soundtrack. Nerves and excitement built. Would we witness a tornado on the first day trying?

A cloud breaks away, and you cross your fingers and toes. A sensation in your stomach rises in anticipation. Are the factors aligning? Is there the correct mix of temperature and wind? Atmospheric conditions can change or fail to cooperate. The cell can break up the moment it looks promising.

Then touchdown. The funnel reaches the ground and we have a tornado. Did the anticipation we put out into the air manifest it? Who knows? Who cares? We saw a tornado.

Between activity, you enjoy the clouds and moody skies. It is not only about funnels and tornados. The colours and light you experience can be ethereal. The darkness or greyness of the clouds; blueness of the sky turning to white; the green grass; and the brown of turned fields can create picturesque scenes.

Mother Nature's hail creations can be intoxicating. The individual pieces the size of your palm; crystal shaped, or maybe like snowflakes, each a distinct form.

And there's lots of waiting. In the middle of nowhere, we pull over and wait. People discuss cameras, photos and tornadoes from previous years. These are a seasoned group of storm chasers. Some have done this trip every year for twenty years, creating endless stories.

We were not alone. Whenever tornado activity is predicted, the cars follow. Other chasers litter the road in kitted out vehicles and with varying levels of knowledge and information. We tried to break from the crowds via side laneways to get ahead of the storm and watch it approach.

An app sends notifications when a tornado touch down is reported, along with hail and other cloud formations noted. Follow the app, follow the technical data, throw in expert knowledge, and you can find the next weather cell to follow, to chase and to watch and hope.

Chicken tenders and chips formed dinner, after starting the day with French toast and bacon—delicious. No official lunch, just snacks.

Motel 6 in Clinton, OK, became our home for the night. We had an incredible lightning show from the carpark. My fellow tour members and I tried to capture the show on camera. I was an amateur, thus less successful than the others. The rain didn't stop us from watching. The storm grew smaller in the distance and sleep beckoned. Tomorrow would be another chase day.

21st May (2019) Newton, Kansas (KS), USA

McDonald's for breakfast–sausage McMuffin, hash browns and apple juice. I stocked up for the day ahead.

Our chase day became a driving day. The storms were not strong enough for activity. We drove grey roads with yellow and white markings. Green fields sat on either side. A blue sky housed a smattering of clouds in the distance. The other three vehicles lay ahead of us.

Our convoy comprised a second van holding seven passengers, a driver and Charles, our expert leader; a station wagon carrying four passengers and a driver; and the passenger turned driver, Sean, with the three Aussies, rounding out the twenty-seven.

We enjoyed sunshine, then rain, and wind turbines every which way. We saw rain that didn't reach the ground. It evaporated in the sky because of the air temperature. It was fascinating to watch as an unknown phenomenon to me. You saw the sheets of rain, but it petered out before touching the ground.

Moody clouds followed us to dinner, where I ate pulled pork, macaroni and cheese, and fries.

We crossed into state number three, Kansas. Thus far, we have driven 794 miles.

22nd May (2019) Somewhere in Tornado Alley, USA

I ate French toast and bacon for breakfast from IHOP. We ate here often. It took me a few visits to realise IHOP stood for The International House of Pancakes. I thought they were different chains. They wanted to shake off their pancake image and expand the menu, so contracted their name.

We drove along the famous Route 66. Driving the full length is on my bucket list. We had a rest stop in Arcadia, Oklahoma, an iconic Route 66 stop. Here you'll find Pops, a landmark diner with hundreds of different flavoured soft drinks, or pop, and a gas station. Coloured bottles containing varying flavours covered the walls. Out the front stands a 66-foot pop bottle with a straw. It was white during the day but lit in multicoloured lights at night.

We explored the shop. They had more flavours of M&M's than I have ever seen, including coffee nut, pretzel and caramel. And merchandise such as T-shirts and hats being a Route 66 icon.

We filled the cars with gas, our stomachs with food and drinks as we waited for information to guide us on when and where to move. We had to be ready at short notice. When told to get in, you hustled. Otherwise, we might miss the storm.

Once at a storm location, you jumped out fast to catch it. Unfortunately, today I got stuck in the van in everyone's eagerness to alight. The van's back door swung open to the right. When fully open, it prevented my door from opening.

Malcolm threw the door open. Everyone ran to catch the action without closing the door. I was stuck. From his window, Jeremy had a superb view of the tornado to the left. I peered through Jeremy and his side window. Not ideal.

The first car to arrive got the best views, saying a tornado sat 50 metres in front of them. I don't think anyone in our vehicle experienced anything that close and I saw nothing.

Someone returned to fetch extra camera gear and closed the door upon request, allowing me to hop out. But it was over. The clouds remained, but the tornado had dissipated. It only takes a few minutes to form and disappear into a cloud free blue sky. Everyone was enraptured by the scene, but I missed it. This occurred near Okemah, OK.

When observing at a stop, we must obey instructions. We must hurry if told to get in. The storm may either head our way or a more favourable event lay ahead. The potential of better makes everyone move fast.

We made a plan with Malcolm. He'd open the door after Jeremy or myself said "go". I needed a second to open my door first. I can get out if the two doors are ajar. If I'm one second behind, forget it, without scratching both doors. Who knew the front seat had a downside?

There was no switching of vehicles, only rearranging of inside seats. Every morning, I'd stand back and wait for people to board. I'd check if anyone wanted the front seat. Everyone was comfortable where they were, so I got the front seat every day. Our car never rotated seats as no one wanted to sit next to Malcom. The moment we started rotating, we knew we each may end up next to him. Poor Carl was desperate to change. I can sympathise.

As we moved on, we drove through a hailstorm. I loved the sound of the rocks on the car's roof. Of course, the driver wasn't having fun as worrying about the windscreen breaking. Without the responsibility of driving, or it being my car, I relished the experience and wore my best Cheshire cat grin while doing so. I have video with the sound of the thud, thud, thud.

Today we partook in "punching the core", or driving through the storm's centre. This is the most direct way to get ahead of the storm. Once in front, you positioned yourself for a potential tornado, meaning wild weather, and that's what I wanted. I wish we punched the core every day. Some feared it, though, including Malcolm.

The water had nowhere to go in the saturated ground. This created flash flooding and ridiculous amounts of water over the road. The waves created by our cars were amazing. Again, it's easier to enjoy when you have no responsibility. I trusted Jeremy's driving. He was a firefighter paramedic.

Everyone had downloaded a tornado warning app, making the phones alarm at once. The app gave off this deep barr, barr, barr, barr sound. Everyone got animated over what was next.

At various points during the day, we have stops where we are "staging". This is arriving near a potential storm (somewhere with amenities) and wait for further information. Sometimes these stops are a quick ten minutes for a bathroom visit and snack purchases; or longer if filling up the cars and cleaning the windows; to two or three hours if waiting for the weather to declare itself.

Once today we tried to have a break but weather warnings had been released, making shops close. We wanted a toilet break, but they were locking the doors. They opened for us, inviting us to join them in their shelter. A decision had to be made. With the doors locked, we'd be unable to leave until the storm subsided.

We chased the storm instead.

It's a tradition to eat a celebratory steak dinner after a tornado encounter. No steak allowed on other nights of the tour. So tonight we had steak, with vegetables and a baked potato, for the sum of $47.84 at Charlestons.

We had a late night getting to our hotel at 11:00 pm and to my room at 11:40 pm. With so many rooms, check in takes forever. No chance of early nights on this tour. Catnaps in the car helped keep tiredness at bay.

The official count for today was four tornados, but that number didn't apply to me. We added 470 miles to our tally.

23rd May (2016) Naracoorte, SA, Australia

My father's funeral was done. I had a week before returning to work and needed to escape. I was meant to be in Uzbekistan. So I planned a mini getaway, packed a bag and hopped in the car. I only made it a few hours away to Ararat on the first day.

I left Ararat this morning driving over 200 km into South Australia and the Naracoorte Caves. I arranged two tours.

A quiet weekday visit meant five of us took the Alexandra Caves' tour, during which I learned about the formations as we walked through the stunning caves.

The second tour revolved around bats. With no one else joining, I had a private tour. It was interesting seeing the command room, otherwise known as the Bat Observation Centre. Infrared cameras in the caves send footage to the observation centre so they can monitor and learn without disturbing them.

We toured a cave often frequented by bats based on the information gleaned from the cameras. I am not frightened of bats or dark caves, so surprised by what I experienced.

The guide and I walked to the rear. It was dark. He says to look up. I observe lumps and curves in variations of colour without comprehending what I'm seeing. The guide explains around seventy bats are sleeping above my head. I stare at the bumps and one bat opens their eyes. I see them now. Then another wakes. And bam, I'm scared.

It's fine while they're asleep and don't move, but your imagination is picturing them opening their eyes together and flying off at once. The guide asks if I want to move further away and I jump at the chance. I didn't expect to be scared, but I was. I tried to pretend I wasn't, but maybe the guide recognises the signs.

I spent the night in a local hotel.

24th May (2016) Warrnambool, VIC, Australia

I wanted to spend as much time as possible on coastal roads. I turned off the main highway in favour of driving the smaller local roads.

Nelson was my first town back in Victoria and on the water. As a teenager, I'd chosen Nelson as the town where I wanted to live. Not that I'd ever visited. I was living in Hamilton, but wanted somewhere smaller, by the beach and far from Melbourne. After Nelson, the road no longer followed the coast. Never mind.

I visited the Cape Nelson Lighthouse, outside Portland. While driving with a view of the lighthouse, a wallaby jumped onto the road. He turned at the last second, as did I, but I heard a thud. I was mortified. I had never hit an animal before. It was a narrow road making turning around difficult, but eventually I could and tried to find whatever I had hit. There was no evidence of an injured animal. I believe I made contact, but due to lack of evidence, I have to assume he hopped away. I felt uneasy for hours, worrying whether I'd done the right thing. If I'd found him injured, I would have called the Help for Wildlife number posted on signs at regular intervals on these roads. I took a photo of the sign for future reference.

After visiting the lighthouse, I drove slowly along the road, searching again for a hurt animal. But found nothing. I have to assume it was alive somewhere uninjured, apart from minor bruising and embarrassment.

I continued driving to Warrnambool finding my pre-booked part-ocean-view room. I explored the nearby walks by the breakwater and surrounding cliffs. Such a perfect place to enjoy nature and wash away the cobwebs from dealing with my father's funeral and cancelled overseas plans.

I enjoyed this hotel and location staying here again. They have mineral dense hot springs. On my first visit, it had one small pool inside the hotel. Now it's a full hot springs experience with multiple outdoor pools of varying designs and temperatures. I prefer the indoor springs when I visit.

25th May (2016) Great Ocean Road, VIC, Australia

From Warrnambool, I drove home via The Great Ocean Road. Seeing as most visitors drive from Melbourne towards Warrnambool, the sights are quieter and less traffic on my side of the road in the mornings.

From this direction, you reach the rock formations early in your drive rather than towards the end. The day trippers are yet to reach this section. You turn right into all but one sight, but that wasn't a problem.

I stopped at London Bridge, remembering seeing the news when it collapsed in 1990 as a teenager. It's no longer attached to the mainland. As a child, we visited here and I believe I walked over London Bridge when intact. Every time I visit, I strain to recall my childhood memories and wonder if they are real.

It's interesting watching the changes in the rocks over the years. The Twelve Apostles have eroded away in my lifetime. It makes you wonder what may be left in the future.

A brilliant day weather-wise, with a storm following me throughout the day. Sometimes it was closing in through the rearview mirror, and at times I drove through it to my next destination. It added an extra layer of atmosphere to the experience and the photos.

The weather produced a once in a lifetime encounter. I wish I caught it on camera. I can read in people's faces they don't believe me when I tell them this story. But I promise you this happened.

With the stormy rain coming and going, rainbows appeared. At one stage, when driving through the Otways, a rainbow lay ahead of me. It was full of colour and hard to remove my eyes from it. Ahead, the road zigzagged back and forth. I realised if the road turned in a particular direction, I might drive straight to where the rainbow sat. How close can you get to a rainbow?

It got closer and closer as I rounded the bends. With no cars behind me, I slowed to enjoy the view. The road turned at the perfect moment. I drove right through the rainbow. Unimaginably magical and ethereal. For a moment or two, a colourful mist surrounded me.

I drove through a rainbow!

I know it sounds ludicrous, but it happened. Even I was in disbelief, but it happened. It's a moment I will never forget.

I drove through a rainbow!

26th May (2019) Somewhere in Kansas, USA

Breakfast comprised scrumptious strawberry crepes, hash browns and bacon with orange juice. We ate big at breakfast, never knowing when we'd eat again. We had two meals a day, twelve hours or more apart, depending on the weather activity.

I bought a map book to follow as we drove. Not even the driver knew the destination. Being the last car, we just followed. We had radios to communicate through if needed.

The radio signalled the end of the day's chase. Until the last proclamation, the possibility to chase remained, regardless of the time. One frequent chaser had a unique method to announce the end. Over the radio, we'd hear Bill Paxton's famous line from the movie *Aliens*.

"That's it man. Game over, man. Game over."

The chase had finished, and we were driving to our hotel, either nearby or where we needed to be for the next day's events. We knew we wouldn't alight the van until dinner or bed.

We hit our fourth state today, Colorado. We waited and hoped in Cheyenne Wells for awhile. But the temperature had dropped, becoming too cold for tornado production.

No tornados, but we saw rainbows, crops dancing to the wind, and the power of clouds to change the day into night and back again. Night skies surrounded us with daylight ahead.

A few times, we pulled over for emergency vehicles, or so we thought. We'd realise later they were storm chasers with red and blue flashing lights to get ahead. I think that's disgusting. So too did the firefighter paramedic driving our car. It's illegal but good luck catching them.

Real police officers appeared whenever big chaser crowds formed. They urged people to be careful, and preferably to leave, but stupidity was everywhere. People stop and park in places they are not meant to. They focus on the storm and forget they are on a road, stepping out into traffic in their excitement. Police hate chasers. I don't blame them. Being a tour company, we were more respectful than individuals. If a situation looked dangerous, we'd find a side road or try the opposite side of the storm. No storm is worth an injury or your life. Or your business.

Dinner was a garlic steak burger with fries and a Sprite. We didn't witness a tornado, but I don't think a burger counts as steak.

512 miles driven.

27th May (2019) Salina, KS, USA

I started the day with cannoli for breakfast.

The radar showed nothing of interest, so we caught up with laundry. Nothing like twenty-seven people arriving at the same launderette. Everyone scrambled for change. It was here I discovered laundry pods. Like dishwasher pods, tabs or tablets, you can get ones for your washing machine. They are perfect for travelling compared to bringing washing powder or liquid. I bought a packet on this trip for future travels.

I did a supermarket shop to bolster my snack supplies while waiting for the washing machine. I bought water, blueberries, dried apricots and highlighter pens. We passed a Walmart where I bought four packets of Cookie Dough Bites.

The afternoon started with a show of massive rotating clouds over our heads. We stared into these swirling clouds. An imminent sense of being engulfed by them washed over me. If they'd become tornadoes, we'd have been in the middle of them. I'll assume the experts knew the conditions weren't right for that. The power, the fury and the possibility were exhilarating. It was a monstrous structure crossing overhead. It rotated with smooth edges like a hovering spaceship in a movie. I thought I'd captured it on video, but I can't find it. Disappointing.

After 9:00 pm, we had a lightning show. The entire sky glowed. Lightning bolts coming out everywhere and anywhere above us. They weren't CGs, meaning bolts from the clouds to the ground, but a magnificent show of what Mother Nature can do. We had a lengthy stay, allowing for the professional photographers to set up their tripods and organise their camera settings for the night sky. I did not have a tripod.

I played with a new app downloaded on the advice of my fellow chasers, called iLightning Cam. You open the app, direct the phone or tablet towards the night sky and it senses when lightning is coming and takes a photo. I found it a bit hit or miss, but I have the free "lite" version, so it may improve if you pay for it. It's an interesting concept. It's difficult to predict when lightning will strike. The app increases your chance of getting a photo. Some chasers have lightning triggers attached to their cameras. Who knew all this technology existed?

The storm entranced us way into the night. Thank goodness I'd bought snacks earlier in the day. I had a small dinner of fries and a hot chocolate at 12:30 am. It was too late to eat anything more. We arrived at our hotel at 2:00 am. A long day.

We didn't travel far, only driving 318 miles today.

28th May (2019) Wichita, KS, USA

I bought something I didn't know existed but think is cool. Forever Stamps. These are stamps without a price. I can use these stamps in ten years' time, paying no price difference. What a handy idea! I needed one stamp, but could only buy a pack of ten Forever Stamps. The rest may never be used, but if needed, I have them without adding extra postage.

I can tell we drove through Newton, Park City and Bel Aire today based on my photos of town water tanks. I love these structures. They are everywhere and each unique. I never tire of seeing them. We had rainbows and cloud formations to occupy our imaginations as we travelled.

Storm chasing is fun and games until something goes wrong. Another storm chasing tour came too close to a tornado, flipping their vans. While chasing a supercell near Lawrence in Kansas, they got caught in a rain wrapped satellite tornado. Two vans rolled. Only minor injuries were sustained. They were two miles from a forming tornado, but satellite tornadoes can pop out of nowhere and that's what hit them. They had a four vehicle convoy with two affected. If the vans had maintained a greater following distance, the satellite tornado may have passed between without causing harm.

People on our trip knew one of the injured. We heard a firsthand account from this chaser in a flipped van. She said it happened without warning. The tornado hit them with a "thunk" causing the van to roll three or four times, ending upside down. She crawled out via the window. The van landed in a ditch with a stream and belongings floated away. Climbing back in to retrieve personal items, she discovered most had sustained water damage.

The second van was in front of theirs and lifted over a fence. She later discovered she'd been non-coherent, which she doesn't recall. By the time the ambulance arrived, she had improved. It thrilled her to have been inside a tornado. It didn't diminish her love of the chase.

Another late dinner with slow service. I have photos of a hangry Swede wanting food at 11:46 pm. He was last to eat, with some finished by the time his food arrived. It's frustrating to receive your food last at this time of day.

I'm not sure what time my cheeseburger and hot chocolate arrived.

Another low mileage day reaching 364.

29th May (1998) Timbuktu, Mali

I have no diary entries for a few days relying on memory and photo descriptions. The finer details are impossible to remember. Forgive me if I'm vague or muddled.

We spent last night in Mopti, a staging town for people heading to Timbuktu. We had organised a guide, Ibrahim, to direct us across the desert to Timbuktu and on to hike through the Bandiagara escarpment or Dogon Country.

Lucky we were four people again. Vinnie was not with us. I'm not sure what would happen if we'd had five in the car. Joe drove with Ibrahim in the front seat, guiding. Us girls, Anna, Sarah and I, sat in the back. No room left for Vinnie.

You begin on the main road, then turn left, leaving behind signs and markings. You drive on sand with the odd shrub or tree. I don't know how the guides do it. I'm glad we had one with us.

We drove all day. We were close to Timbuktu, but told best to wait till the morning to catch the ferry across the Niger River. Once across the ferry, it was a further eleven kilometres. I was jubilant. I could soon forever say I have been to Timbuktu or Tombouctou, as known locally.

30th May (1998) Timbuktu, Mali

This morning, we drove Lucy onto the small ferry for the short ride across the Niger River. Width-wise, the ferry held three cars packed together and not much more in length, and open to the fresh air. We alighted Lucy to enjoy the view of the river surrounded by desert.

After a short drive, we arrived in Timbuktu, or Tombouctou. The town is not paved in gold, as fabled. I can't even call it faded grandeur. Crumbling mud-brick houses don't have a sense of old charm.

Ibrahim recommended a hotel where I had a moment I'll never forget. I can see it clearly as if it happened this morning. The daily heat, combined with the lack of electricity resulting in an inability to access cold drinks, was getting to me. Throw in a lack of flavour, and I was going insane. We arrived at the hotel and I spotted a chest freezer. Not all freezers in Africa work. We have been disappointed before. I rushed over and opened it. It was plugged in and cold. Utter bliss!

When the light comes on and frigid air wafts out, it mimics the scene in *Pulp Fiction*. There were a few drinks, but the shining glory was the one bottle of grenadine flavoured soft drink. This is the equivalent of a raspberry lemonade outside Australia. Heaven. Cold and flavour. I grabbed it and devoured it. I didn't care about anyone else or what it cost. It was mine, and no one was stopping me. Ahh, the flavour.

We had to check in with the police. We left the car and walked the streets of Timbuktu, with Ibrahim guiding and explaining. We were the talk of town within seconds of arriving. Few tourists visit. Our arrival was the most exciting thing happening in town. By the time we got to the police station, we'd amassed a following. Everybody wanted to say hello and welcome.

They stamped our passports. I have tangible proof I have been to Timbuktu. Many people don't believe me. People think it's a fictional place, so I couldn't have visited. It is an actual place, and here's the passport stamp to prove it. It's a brilliant story to wow even the most experienced travellers. My claim to fame in the travel realm. I hated renewing my passport on expiry, losing my convenient proof.

It saddens me what has happened there since my visit. Bandits have taken over at various times. ISIS has moved through destroying buildings and ancient books. It's a shame a revisit is improbable. I'm fortunate to have seen it before it disappears into the sand.

We spent the afternoon on a camel safari. A girls' trip. We negotiated being taken into the desert and left for an hour. I've ridden camels before, so not a new experience, but it felt appropriate to indulge in one here. It was relaxing being left in the dunes with nothing but sand. With barely a scrub, we experienced the serenity as we lay in the dunes.

We were a teeny bit worried they wouldn't return to pick us up. But they did.

31st May (2019) Norman, OK, USA

You can't have a bad day when it starts with French toast. Today it had a different slant as a French toast wrap with turkey, ham and cheese. That's new and worth a try. Two breakfasts at once. I washed it down with a hot chocolate and orange juice. You can't focus on the calorie count in America.

We drove to the starting hotel in Norman, OK. We covered 4391 miles over our thirteen days of chasing storms, or 7066 km. An average of 543 km per day. A significant effort.

Earlier in the trip, one of the group showed me a phone app called Polar Steps. It tracks your movements and produces a summary map. It was fascinating watching the backtracking and weird directions we took daily. I took a photo to summarise our movement at the end of each day. I'm glad I took the photos as the app will no longer give me a daily view. It has the final interesting summary, though. Our trail is the shape of a lopsided hunchback with a small head and T-Rex arms. Sketch that image in your mind.

Before dinner, I shopped at Walmart. I bought PG Tips tea bags to take home; water; and a T-shirt and dress to try on. I wanted to test the clothes before deciding if worth buying more. A Walmart in your backyard was convenient.

We dined at the Olive Garden, where I ordered steak to end the trip. I shared two desserts. It was handy having people who liked desserts as much as me. We shared a chocolate cake and a cheesecake. I'm still not counting calories. My weight increased by three kilograms during this trip. It's easy to understand why.

Do you know an incredible thing about a storm chasing tour? With most participants male, the line for the men's toilet is longer than the women's toilet. We girls always had to wait for the boys to finish. Such a refreshing change. We highlighted it every day. Now they know how we feel.

June

1st June (2019) Norman, OK, USA

For breakfast, I enjoyed the smaller buffet at the Golden Corral next door, in an attempt to not overeat.

We headed out in groups to the National Weather Museum. I found it interesting learning about the cloud types and formations. But if it looks pretty, I like it. Don't ask me what it's called.

They included information on various tornadoes from the history books, and displayed cars flipped, rotated, and spat out of tornadoes. There's safety information for what to do when a tornado warning is issued–a basement is the ideal option. Or an internal room with no windows.

There's a green screen to practise presenting the weather on television. I won't be applying for a job anytime soon. The footage of my attempt is on someone else's camera, thus I've not seen it since.

I had a photo taken with a picture cutout turning you into Dorothy with her *Wizard of Oz* friends. Dorothy is famous around these parts.

We visited the museum as no storms to chase. However, a storm brewed while we were there. We ended up outside for a last hurrah of Mother Nature's prowess. With howling winds, the skies turned grey. The wind increased in strength, requiring stamina to stand still.

For a new guy who'd arrived early for the following tour, this became his first chase. He ran inside as the wind picked up while we stayed, watching to see what might happen. When he noticed we'd remained, he returned. We had no intention of missing our last chance for a storm. He had a lot to learn.

After testing my clothing purchases from yesterday, I returned to Walmart for more. I bought two additional dresses and T-shirts, a pair of sandals, laundry pods, dryer sheets, four boxes of Cookie Dough Bites and the largest ziplock bags I've ever seen.

I bought the dresses for use as respectable pyjamas. I am comfortable yet appropriately dressed to answer the door.

The white, stretchy T-shirts were perfect for my "plane clothes" outfit–an ankle length, flowing black-and-white-striped skirt with a white T-shirt. The skirt has lasted for years, only requiring an elastic refit after the COVID hiatus. White T-shirts don't last long. The more in my wardrobe, the better. The length must be appropriate to complement the skirt, though. That's why I purchased one yesterday to test it with the skirt before buying additional ones.

You can't imagine the options in the ziplock bag section unless you see them in person. I have seen amazing ones over the years that American travellers have brought with them, and they're just not available in Australia. I bought giant versions, including ones with standalone bottoms. Americans will laugh, but our options in Australia are pitiful compared to what they take for granted.

The hotel carpet remained too dirty to walk on with bare feet. I rectified the situation by placing towels on the floor at jumping distances. I hate wearing shoes inside.

We ate our final tour dinner at BJ's Restaurant and Brewhouse. I had pork chops with sweet potato fries and asparagus, followed by a hot fudge brownie.

2nd June (2019) Las Vegas, Nevada (NV), USA

Departure transfers started at 3:00 am. We left in groups with similar flight times. I left the hotel with the midday group for a 4:28 pm flight.

We hung around together in the food court, where I indulged in Cinnabon. People left as their flights boarded. I'd qualified for Qantas Gold Status earlier than expected, with the confirmation coming through during the tour. However, I stayed with this motley crew, who I was going to miss, rather than experience the airport lounge.

One of the Europeans pulled out a massive bag of coins with plans to leave it on the table. He'd been hoarding the coins he received as change throughout all his American trips, never using them as payment. He'd pay with a note and take change at every transaction. That revelation dumbfounded me.

I love counting coins so asked to count his collection. He agreed, and I spread them over the table, sorting them into denominations. I convinced him to take some quarters and others grabbed the remaining quarters. No one wanted the pennies. I can't remember how much it added up to, but I had a lot of fun playing. We spelled the word "FREE" using forty-two pennies. I formed eighty-five pennies, piled in towers of five, into a heart shape.

I'd booked a first-class flight to Los Angeles so didn't notice any changes because of my new One World Sapphire status. However, once at Los Angeles, I had a second flight, on a separate economy-class ticket, to Las Vegas. My status allowed me to check in at the first-class desk.

With American Airlines, you pay $10 for checked bags during check in. I presented my boarding pass, showing my One World Sapphire status, and handed over my bag. I held my credit card ready to use as payment. But she did not ask for payment. I watched her put an orange priority sticker on my bag and wondered if she did it by mistake because I'm checking in at the first-class counter without realising I held an economy ticket. I let her do her thing and waited.

"Enjoy your flight," she said, indicating the process had ended.

"Ok. Thanks."

Confused, I turned to walk away, clutching my credit card.

She'd forgotten to take payment.

Surely she'd call me back any moment.

But nothing happened. I made it to the escalator leading to security without being stopped.

Free luggage? I thought I'd got away with doing something wrong.

Once through security, I found the lounge. The sign displayed the blue sapphire logo on the door. I sheepishly presented my boarding pass, and she let me in. It's exciting when it's new. To be honest, it remained exciting right till the pandemic halted my travels. If I retain my status, it will excite me all over again.

Utilising the lounge's free Wi-Fi, I searched for privileges of One World Sapphire status. It stated free baggage on American Airlines. So she hadn't forgotten payment. I had three further visits to America in 2019. With no bag charges and free food and drink in the lounge, my status saved me at least US$100.

My bag arrived on the baggage carousel as one of the first thanks to the orange sticker. I arrived in Las Vegas at 9:15 pm after gaining two hours, so 11:15 pm, to my body clock.

I caught a SuperShuttle from the airport to my second favourite Las Vegas hotel, Caesars Palace. I had a two-night stay booked. The extensive check-in line snaked around and around. I waited ninety minutes before reaching the desk.

"You're not staying with us."

I glared at him. "Yes, I am."

"You have been upgraded to the Nobu. They have their own check-in desk."

"You mean I have to line up again? Why didn't anyone tell me?" The thought of having to start again sent me over the edge. It's 2:00 am.

"They never have a line."

To this day, I can't believe I stood in line for no reason.

The Nobu Hotel, a hotel inside a hotel, had no line. Check in took two minutes. The room was an upgrade. But the style was not what I wanted–elegant, modern Japanese. Nice, but you don't come to Vegas for nice. You come to Vegas for vulgarity and ridiculousness, hence choosing Caesars Palace for its over the top glitz with an ancient Roman flair. I laughed at my oversized bathroom sinks, in which you could bath a toddler, and went to bed.

3rd June (2019) Las Vegas, NV, USA

Waking in Vegas is a delicious thought. I ate at Caesars' breakfast buffet, named Bacchanal, for my morning indulgence. As early, I paid the Morning Fare, rather than the Brunch fee, saving a few dollars. My diary never goes into enough detail about what I ate. But I remember taking my time, enjoying long cups of tea and multiple trips to the food stands. And needing to be rolled out.

I wandered through to The Forum Shops and luxuriated in my surrounds. I must ride the circular escalators. It's hard to hide the pleasure I get from this simple ride. I hope no one notices I'm riding for fun rather than to get somewhere.

I had one free day to indulge in my favourite things and relax. After walking down part of Las Vegas Boulevard, I returned to my room to enjoy the air conditioning.

After a Vegas breakfast buffet, you don't need to eat again till dinner. I ate Panda Express from the food court eating my favourite American Chinese dish, orange chicken with rice and vegetables. I eat it whenever I'm in America.

By this time, it was dark enough to appreciate night-time Vegas. I continued further down Las Vegas Boulevard to the magnificent Venetian Hotel. This is my favourite hotel in Vegas, but tomorrow's activities were taking place at Caesars, so no point staying anywhere else on this quick trip.

After wandering every inch of the Venetian complex, I headed to Bellagio's water fountains. I love the majesty of the water and the perfect timing with the music. It can take several attempts to find the optimal viewing angle. Ideally, you're in the front row as close to the centre as possible. I would never watch just the end and leave. Instead, I would relish the finale, secure a better position as people departed, and await the commencement of the next performance.

I love Vegas. I don't gamble or drink, but I love the atmosphere and the varied activities one can do and sights you can see. It's an adult Disneyland that never closes.

4th June (2019) Las Vegas, NV, USA

Registration started at 7:30 am for an 8:00 am start. I'll never get used to events starting early in America. No workshop starts at 8:00 am in Australia unless breakfast is included.

Today was a work related workshop. I could not believe my luck when the dates matched with my already booked trip. I was going to be a "Preemie for a Day". Or in Australian English, a premature, or prem, baby for a day. A medical equipment company made adult sized versions of baby equipment, and practitioners pretend to be babies to discover the world from a baby's perspective.

When I tell people about this, including nurses I work with, they say I'm raving mad. But it's a lot of fun and educational. You're pushed outside of your comfort zone, but the workshops are well organised. You will rethink how you handle babies after experiencing this. I'd love to replicate the ideas at work for the newly graduated nurses. It's such a unique learning opportunity.

For four hours I played with three other participants at being premature babies. I can say from personal experience it's easier to suck a bottle in the side-lying position than in the traditional cradle hold. Just saying. Those in the know will understand.

I ate lunch at Panda Express again, soaking up my last bit of Vegas. I had a 4:00 pm flight to Los Angeles and a 10:40 pm flight to Australia.

There was no charge for my baggage. And I gained access to the lounges at Las Vegas and Los Angeles. What a difference an International Lounge makes on your long haul flight.

In the Los Angeles lounge, I sat to the side feeling like a fraud. The bathrooms were nearby, and the food wasn't far. I sat in a single seat with a view of the main concourse. I enjoyed the gentle tranquillity, far from the usual airport hustle and bustle.

Having no line for food was a treat. The airport food court area is woefully small. The ordering lines are long with inadequate staff. Then you experience long wait times for food delivery as the pre-prepared food runs out. KFC ran out of chicken once. I've learnt to go for the more expensive choices as quicker service. Then you can't find a table. I once sat on the floor to eat. So the lounge is bliss.

I ate free food and drink in my single swivel chair, watching episodes of the television show *Unreal* on my iPad with noise cancelling headphones. Travel doesn't get any better.

5th June (1996) Copenhagen, Denmark

It was an early summer's day. Susanne and I met at Bellevue Strand, strand being Danish for beach. Denmark is full of coastline and beaches, but the ones in

Copenhagen suburbs can be narrow. Bellevue is the widest beach in the area and had access to public transport, shops and bathrooms.

We spent the day relaxing, reading, talking and writing letters. It was snail-mail era, so we were always hand writing letters to someone somewhere in the world.

We had an idea to write letters to ourselves—our future selves. We each wrote our dreams and desires for the next ten years. With our names on the fronts, we sealed the envelopes and swapped them. I got Susanne's letter, and she got mine.

We planned to meet in ten years at Susanne's favourite holiday location of Fuerteventura, in the Canary Islands. With my plan to travel everywhere at least once, it was a perfect place to have a reason to visit, given I'm not a beach holiday person.

> We wrote our letters to each other and swapped them for our meeting in 2005 in Fuerteventura. It's exciting. I hope we will really do it.

I'm uncertain why ten years meant 2005, but that's what was inscribed on the envelope in Susanne's handwriting:

> Not to be opened until 2005 in Fuerteventura.

6th June (2018) Sacred Valley, Peru

I booked a tour with a hotel pick-up. When getting late, I became nervous they'd forgotten me, but I was the last pick-up. I should have expected this as I mentioned it in my travel bible under the hotel information section. I research well, but sometimes I forget to read what I wrote.

We headed to the Sacred Valley for a half-day tour. It was lower elevation than Cusco, which helped stave off the altitude inducing "I can't be bothereds". I continued to drink often but only reached 2.7 litres. Not enough in altitude.

The obligatory shop came first. They gave an informative talk on alpaca wool and the dyes used to colour it. We conversed with their alpacas and llamas. I prefer alpacas with their gentler faces.

The complex had an extravagant guinea pig house. Guinea pigs are a food source in Peru. The ones here led a lavish life prior to being devoured–a mud brick mansion of the most intricate design, complete with towers, balconies, and a straw strewn garden. Do happy guinea pigs taste better? I couldn't bring myself to eat any guinea pig while in Peru.

We paused at a scenic overlook, where I engaged in conversation with some of the younger travellers. Throughout the years, I've gained valuable knowledge from the older generation, and I now imparted that wisdom to the younger generation. Travel hacks, I guess you could call them. A practical topic of conversation as we looked across the valley surrounded by mountains.

The next stop was Moray, with its terraces built like amphitheatres. They carved out twenty levels, each layer having its own micro-climate. It has been suggested that the Incas were conducting experiments with various climates to determine the optimal elevations of different crops. An agricultural laboratory, if you will. It is devoid of crops now, but has left a unique feature in the landscape.

We finished with a highlight at the Salinas Salt Pans. These pans have been used since Incan times. Saltwater from a hot spring is diverted into salt pans or baths downstream, creating the scene before us. Kind of like a striking patch-work factory with a view. Each pan a different shade of brown or white. You wander around the edges, trying not to fall in.

The salt mines were amazing. They took my breath away when I got a first glimpse from the bus while driving there. I had no idea there were so many. It just kept going. Was fun to wander around and through them.

I had the afternoon free to relax. I needed downtime after the busyness of the first tour. Today was day twenty of this trip, with another twelve days of adventures ahead.

Before heading to my room, I bought a five-litre bottle of water from the corner shop. I'd hate to run out, given the altitude factor.

I had an early dinner at the hotel restaurant—alpaca burger.

7th June (2018) Cusco, Peru

Without a hotel pick-up, I walked down the hill into town. I could not locate the departure point, so asked advice from another tour company. They also did not know, but rang the company to ask where I needed to meet them, and gave me directions to the correct spot. I thought I was going to miss the tour.

Once on the bus, we stopped multiple times making pick-ups. My hotel was in the opposite direction of travel for today's destinations. We encountered issues with blocked off roads. A rolling strike was moving through Peru around the price of gas. On the first tour, it looked as if we'd miss Machu Picchu because of the blockages. We stayed ahead thanks to notifications of the roads to be closed and changing our itinerary accordingly.

None of today's sites were big in scale, or what I expected, but worth doing. We visited Tipon, Pikillaqta and Andahuaylillas.

Tipon showed Incan water management and irrigation systems. I can appreciate all water systems even when not ancient Roman. Water flowed through man made waterfalls, and the site had Incan stone steps to walk on, which made me smile.

Pikillaqta is a pre-Incan site, making it the oldest I visited. It required more imagination than the previous sites being more ruinous and spread out.

The town of Andahuaylillas contained an unassuming church from the outside but Peru's Sistine Chapel on the inside, surrounded by a magnificent mountain vista.

We returned to Cusco in time to see the end of the Corpus Christi Parade of Saints through the Plaza de Armas. This is when the saints leave the cathedral to return to their parish churches. We saw the saints arriving at the cathedral on my first tour, but couldn't stop to watch. Today I stayed to witness the spectacle.

They parade decorated statues depicting ten patron saints and five patron Virgin Marys around Cusco's main square. The statues sit on wooden frames, supported by the shoulders of twenty or thirty men. It's an excruciating task, as evidenced by the strained expressions on their faces. Bands and devoutly religious crowds follow. Some statues travel eleven kilometres to their parish church. I found the statues eery to be honest, but was an interesting cultural experience.

Hoping to have sufficient clean clothes for the rest of my journey, I completed a load of laundry. I ordered room service for dinner—lomo saltado, a Peruvian beef stir-fry–and packed my bags.

I drank 3.3 litres. A wonderful effort.

I started my doxycycline, an anti-malarial, to prepare for the Amazon.

8th June (2018) Titicaca Train, Peru

Today I travelled 350 km from Cusco to Puno on a ten-and-a-half-hour luxury train called the *Titicaca Train*, previously called the *Andean Explorer*. The current *Andean Explorer* is a sumptuous overnight touring train out of my budget.

I caught a taxi to the train station where I recognised a family of four from the *Hiram Bingham* train a few days earlier. Also, the Japanese girls who did not want to share a booth with me. We're all doing the same tourist trail. The family, from somewhere in Europe, had a guide with them taking care of their luggage and the check-in process. They sat while the formalities were taken care of for them. That level of service isn't cheap. I bet they wondered how I could afford to be here. My trip costs might surprise them. I received a nod of recognition.

The boarding experience had less fanfare than on the *Hiram Bingham*, including no champagne being served, but music played in the background.

I had the cutest single table and chair. I appreciated that they specifically designed it for one rather than being a two-seater table adjusted for a solo occupant. There was no vacant seat to gaze upon, making it the perfect arrangement for a single traveller.

Every group had their own space. They configured the carriage to match the day's passengers. Couples sat opposite each other or beside each other, and groups of fours sat around tables. I was the only single.

The chairs were classic wingback armchairs, offering comfort and style superior to the bench seating found on the *Hiram Bingham* train. Tables were elegantly set with a menu, flowers, seasonings, and a lamp, all placed atop a linen tablecloth. With each chair and table perfectly positioned by a window, the train exuded opulent old-world charm.

There was a glitch when I booked online undercharging me from what I expected to pay, and been happy to pay. They issued me a ticket, so I left it. I was curious, though. I asked my neighbours, a retired American couple, what they paid. They confirmed what I thought. I got my ticket for half price. No idea why.

I adored being at the rear of the train in the open carriage, observing the train tracks. Since I was the first to venture there, I had the space to myself. Our journey followed a stream with trees growing alongside, leading to the meadows at the foot of the mountains. As we ascended to higher altitudes, the trees gave way, revealing a landscape blanketed with grass and snow-capped mountains.

As people began exploring and arriving at the observation car, the entertainment began–pan flute music and dancing in colourful outfits. I returned to my seat and watched the scenery in comfort and quiet solitude.

The train stops in the middle of nowhere at La Raya at an altitude of 4338 metres, or 14,232 feet. There is a market and a church. Costumed locals with llamas and alpacas of various ages pose for photos. We stopped here on my first tour, so I observed the bustling activities from afar and captured pictures of the train against the mountainous scenery.

The passenger opposite me was a retired nurse. She had brought a pulse oximeter with her to monitor her oxygen levels. My curiosity made me ask if I could try it. With the pulse oximeter on my finger, I reached 75-85%. I did not feel any different from normal. No one said I was looking pale or blue. Levels should be 95-100%. I have since bought my own pulse oximeter, and it will be on the packing list whenever I'll be at high altitude.

Lunch comprised three courses: entrée being soup with cheese, crackers and oil; for main I chose the beef tenderloin wrapped in bacon; and finished with a chocolate dessert in strawberry sauce. A surreal experience having fine dining at my table for one with a forever changing backdrop. The chairs were comfortable for sitting throughout the day but not designed for short me to eat at.

There was a Pisco sour tasting in the bar car, but I remained in my seat. I'd had more Pisco sours than I care to remember. I don't like any alcohol, so nothing to do with the individual drink.

Afternoon tea with sandwiches and cakes was served. The day kept getting better. This was not a train for reading books. Time flew as we gazed out the window and ate.

I was soaking up every bit of the experience until we hit the town of Juliaca.

> And it just seemed so poor and hopeless that I started to feel guilty. I am so lucky to have been born in a good country where I've had options and opportunities. They can only imagine what we take for granted.

> Honestly, I think I liked it more than the *Hiram Bingham* [to Machu Picchu] but glad I've done both. I could have kept going and going, but it did have to end.

On arrival in Puno, I shared a taxi with the American couple, as booked at the same hotel. I paid nothing, as only cost 5 soles each, or US$5 in total. I wouldn't have taken any money either if I'd paid first. It's too little to quibble over.

I did not need dinner after afternoon tea on the train. So I didn't leave the hotel.

Puno's altitude was 3830 metres–600 metres higher than Cusco and 500 metres lower than our highest point on the journey. It is best to sleep at a lower altitude than the highest you reached during the day. Being sick was a real risk. I'd experienced this with travellers on my last tour with two of the group hospitalised.

I drank around 3.5 litres.

9th June (2018) Lima, Peru

I slept well thanks to the combination of melatonin and not having an early start. I arranged an airport shuttle through the hotel for my 1:00 pm flight.

The journey to the airport, which should have taken forty minutes, ended up lasting an hour and a half because of multiple stops. I was anxious, but everyone was on the same flight.

I could use the preferential line to check in with One World Ruby, or Qantas Silver Status. It was nice avoiding the long line, seeing as we all arrived at once. I had not expected to get special treatment as a Silver Qantas member. I thought the perks started with Qantas Gold. An unexpected treat.

I bought lunch on the plane—a chicken sandwich. Always best to eat when you can, as who knows what will happen later?

My next tour included an airport transfer, so met on arrival. He was not a pleasant man, so I did not tip him. He looked disappointed, but hey, next time be nicer.

Today was day one of a nine-day G Adventures tour called "Amazon Riverboat Adventure In Depth". Group tours often have meetings on the first night. This was a weird meeting, but it finished with people wanting to have dinner.

It's disappointing when there is no official dinner on the first night. The itineraries always mention dinner, but they rarely happen. Sometimes the meetings don't even happen. There's nothing worse than waiting to eat till the dinner after the meeting, and there isn't one. I've learnt that lesson the hard way.

I did not pay the single supplement, thus had a roommate for the night.

10th June (2018) Amazon River, Peru

I got little sleep in part because of sharing with a snorer. Thankfully, we weren't sharing for the rest of the trip. But why change today? She didn't pay the single supplement; however, she was allocated a room to herself from now on. How?

Why? Maybe because she's a snorer? Who knows? I have heard if you're paired with a snorer and it affects your sleep, thus your ability to enjoy your holiday, you can complain and get your own room in compensation. I have never tried it, and I doubt I would.

We left at 7:00 am to catch a flight to Iquitos to meet our boat. I have never utilised the same airport so much on the one trip. Lima's Jorge Chavez International Airport is familiar, with today my fourth visit.

Guess who also showed up at the airport? The European family. One boy pointed at me and smiled. We have the same itinerary. I'm sure they'll be on the expensive Amazon boat I found when researching. It looked fantastic, but only a four-day tour, not like G Adventures' nine-day tour.

I had a window seat for a change, with sensational views over the Andes. The window seat was worth it on this three-hour flight. I took photos of the Peru I was used to. By the end of the flight, the bare mountain tops gave way to thousands of trees. Tropical rainforest trees.

I didn't buy food on the plane, as meals are now included. I love included food. We know how weird my travel diet can be.

The temperature rose in Iquitos, as did the insects. It was time for bug spray. The heavens opened and rain beat down on us. It turned into one of those travelling moments I will never forget.

> Getting onto the big boat by a little boat was an interesting experience. They gave us big (smelly) green ponchos. I had my backpack on my front underneath so I could barely see anything over this big green lump in front of me with a wet bottom and rain pelting down while on a boat in the Amazon River—memorable.

I recall sitting there smiling as the rain hit my face thinking, I should savour this moment and remember it forever. It's a moment you only get once. I'm glad I only experienced it once. I tried focusing on the unique situation rather than my soaked underwear and the resulting discomfort.

Vivian and I found our room, changed clothes, unpacked, and settled in. At first, the boat disappointed me. It appeared more rustic than the photos online, but the cabin was nice enough. Importantly, it had air conditioning.

We each had space to unpack rather than live out of our suitcases. I stashed my backpack under the cupboard while not in use. This had later repercussions, but I was blissfully ignorant of what would later transpire.

The wood clad cabin had two arched windows looking to the external corridor and the Amazon River beyond. Blinds provided privacy. A mirror hung on the door. Four shelves sat under one window with a bed opposite. A tiny desk and chair sat under the second window. The other bed had a draw, shelves and hanging space. The private small bathroom housed a shower, toilet and basin.

We shared the hanging space. I used the shelves beside my bed and Vivian used the four shelves, and the bed opposite, as her space.

Our cabin was on the entry level, with the kitchen at the front and the engine room towards the rear. On the next level, there were cabins along with the dining room. Each level had four cabins on both sides.

The boat had three levels above the water. Half the top level was open to the elements but covered by a roof with oscillating fans. There were cushioned seats; table and chairs; and a bar. The other half of this level housed an air-conditioned lounge with extra comfy sofas along full-length windows.

Our first activity was lunch in the dining room. A grand room with floor-to-ceiling windows; tables with linen tablecloths and folded napkins.

We had an information talk about the boat, the trip and so forth. They informed us there were no malaria-carrying mosquitoes in this area. I had expected to need anti-malarial medications, having commenced them a couple of days ago as per medical instructions. The entire crew was adamant they weren't required. Some passengers continued their choice of medications. My chosen anti-malarial was an antibiotic, and the less antibiotic use we have, the better, so I stopped taking mine.

They also informed us because the cabins are wood, not to spray deet containing insect repellent inside them. Deet ruins the wood. We had to apply it outside in the external corridors.

In the afternoon, we had our first skiff ride. Since we didn't have a routine or know what to bring, it took us time to get organised. Vivian and I boarded last, which became a theme.

We spread out over the two skiffs, one accessible from each side of the boat, and headed into the Pacaya Samira National Reserve—our home for the next few days.

There are birds everywhere, but I couldn't tell you what species. A bird watcher's paradise, though. We saw toucans which I can name thanks to their signature beaks. The one we saw had a red and yellow belly.

We also found tiny yellow frogs amongst the green reeds. How the guide spotted them, I will never know. Their bright colour would help, but their size makes them easy to miss.

We headed back to the boat for dinner.

11th June (2018) Amazon River, Peru

We had skiff rides in the morning and afternoon. I changed clothes multiple times to match the activity and weather. I wore cutoff trousers to cover legs when around insects but they could become shorts when hot. Between skiff rides, and when hanging out on the boat for lunch or moving down the river, I preferred wearing a skirt to aid relaxing given the heat and humidity.

Our first sighting of the day was an iguana climbing in the trees. He almost blended in to his surroundings. I expected iguanas on the ground rather than high in the treetops.

Sloths were on my wish list, so ecstatic to have a sloth in front of me. He looked soft and fluffy, sporting an orange and white patch on his back with a black line running through it. His long claws stood out. The tree was devoid of vegetation, allowing the sloth to blend in as it stretched out its arms and legs in slow motion. And they are slow. He took forever to reach up to the branch he wanted to pull down. They must have loads of patience.

We noticed a commotion happening in one village and it seemed they were handling an anaconda. We went closer. They were about to release the snake into the wild after rescuing it from their fishing net. We arrived in time for a photo opportunity. The villagers wrangled the snake around each of our necks. There's nothing like having a thick, long, heavy snake around your neck. The villager held the snake's mouth firmly shut. I felt safe as I smiled at the camera.

We continued our exploration to an area of the river known for its lily pads. They were huge. I've never seen lily pads from a boat before. We saw a variety called Victoria Regia. They can grow to three metres in diameter. We cruised along the edges of these large, round green plants.

Later we had a second sloth sighting curled up like a koala in a tree. This one had different markings being white on his back and legs, with grey areas. We couldn't see his claws. He was awake but not moving.

The skiff cruised fast, making our way back. The water reeds along the banks danced and bobbed in our wake. I loved watching the movement as we passed.

12th June (2018) Amazon River, Peru

An outstanding day on the Amazon River with multiple highlights.

We started at a butterfly sanctuary, discovering every stage of their transformation and hung out in their temperature controlled environment. The keepers tie banana pieces to plants for food. Seeing the array of coloured wings fluttering around never loses its charm. But I was fascinated by the butterflies whose wing markings resembled eyes. This is a safety feature to make predators assume it's a bigger animal.

We continued walking round the village that started the sanctuary and found a baby sloth in their congregation. One of the group got to hold her, which made me jealous. Their little faces are so cute.

One child had a pygmy marmoset monkey as a pet. The smallest monkey species in the world fits into the palm of your hand. Their enormous eyes glare at you. They are cute because of their size, but have mean faces.

We crossed paths, well wakes, with a luxury boat I had seen during my planning for this trip. I'm guessing it's the one the European family caught. We saw no one to wave to. The boat is the same design, having three levels with the open-air lounge and two levels of cabins. The cabins, though, had floor-to-ceiling windows with curtains. I'm guessing they could spray insect repellent in their rooms.

We happened upon a woodpecker with a bright red tuft on its head. We heard him before we saw him pecking away. I enjoyed watching this juvenile going about his business. Australia doesn't have woodpeckers because their beaks cannot penetrate our hard trees, making this a first encounter.

It was a pet, but we saw one macaw. A flash of colour appeared as he flew around the village. Blues and yellows with a teeny piece of green on his head.

We pulled onto the bank when the guide sighted a pygmy marmoset monkey playing in the tree. How did the guide spot this tiny creature? He kept his back to us most of the time, so we moved on.

Our next sighting was a capuchin monkey, almost doing yoga poses in the trees to reach food. We watched him go about his day. These are the cheeky monkeys depicted in the *Night at the Museum* movie. After seeing them in the wild, you can understand where they got the character's personality from.

The cuteness factor rose when we came across three squirrel monkeys huddling in a tree-trunk hole. One monkey appeared to be lying upside down on the other's back.

We cruised past an eco lodge accessible only by water. The accommodation appeared rustic, but they did have electricity. It came from a raft floating on the river, holding around thirty solar panels. I loved the idea. The dense rainforest canopy permits minimal sunlight to filter through, and the river's edge lacks a bank. Creating extra space using a raft is brilliant. They can also float it to point in the sun's direction as the sun moves throughout the day. I admired the practical ingenuity.

We watched a magical sunset from the skiffs, with the water turning pink with the light and the clouds' reflections. We stopped to bask in the serenity. A splendid end to an animal-sighting-filled day.

13th June (2018) Amazon River, Peru

Frequent application of sunscreen and insect repellent had become tiresome, as had the necessity of donning clothing that shielded every inch of skin from the sun and bugs. The heat, humidity, and stickiness were unbearable. I showered three times a day.

> I must stop going to hot countries and doing this to myself. I forgot my electric fan and spray bottle, silly me. I focused on the cold part

of the trip. Never mind. I'm surviving but I think I will look into the air-conditioned jackets again as the main difficulty was USB power but now you can get great power packs that I might be able to use as power!!! How cool—literally—would that be?

Air-conditioned jackets are real things. I want one.

The cabins are air-conditioned but don't cool down enough. We set the thermostat in our room at 21 degrees, but the room never cools below 24 degrees—too hot for sleeping. I was struggling.

I changed multiple times, taking off clothes full of sweat, but I didn't have enough clothes to be changing so often. Washing clothes wasn't simple. The chief difficulty was drying the clothes in the humid conditions.

We visited a town called Nauta, having a tour by bicycle taxis. We ended at a pond full of turtles. We watched as they exited the water, clambering over one another to occupy the same log. Not sure why?

When back on the boat, the rooftop area became too hot, so I hung out in the air-conditioned lounge reading. Insects covered the windows like your car grille on a country drive. It ruined the view a bit. But my surroundings were elegant, and I stretched out in air-conditioned bliss.

I often had the room to myself, as the others preferred the bar. Everyone had a bar tab but me. Drinking water was included and non-alcoholic drinks, as in daily juice specials with meals, were also included. So why would I need anything else?

I went early to lunch, to snag a good table. Some sat at an angle because of the boat's tilt. This meant your glass or plates would slip down, or we short people would struggle to reach the table and cut our food. They set tables for four, but one in the middle of the curved windows sat five. We were five single girls who tried to get a table together. Whoever arrived first saved a seat for the rest.

After lunch, we ventured on land into the rainforest. The temperature drops when between the trees, a welcome reprieve. Our visit started with a shaman audience. She said she received positive energy from our group. It was interesting gaining an understanding of the different medicines produced from the rainforest plants. Though, a pygmy marmoset monkey playing on a tree behind the shaman often distracted me.

We ventured further into the rainforest on foot, looking for local animals. We found a tarantula, but the guide warned everyone, and I walked in the opposite direction without even a peek. If I didn't see it, then it wasn't there. That's how I tolerated it. I hate spiders and want nothing to do with them. I figure if I leave them alone, they will leave me alone.

Even in the Amazon jungle, you exit via the gift shop. I came away with two souvenirs. One is a sloth figurine crafted from balsa, now hanging and swinging on my study's door handle. The other was a dolphin made from porcupine tree wood. Is that a genuine type of wood? It sits on display in a dust requiring position, but I love it.

I know what to look for when bringing wood into Australia. I declare everything. The sloth passed, as did the dolphin's wood type. But I overlooked the dolphin's eyes, which may have been seeds. I was devastated as prided myself on getting it right. The customs lady tried to pry them out so I could take it home, but they didn't budge. After a previous disappointment I did not want repeated, I paid my money to have it fumigated. The price had changed from per piece to a flat rate. What used to cost $40 now cost $100. The dolphin turned into an expensive souvenir.

14th June (2018) Amazon River, Peru

We skipped breakfast in the dining room, heading out for a picnic instead with pink dolphins swimming around us. You looked for circles on the water's surface, followed the movement and hoped a dolphin appeared. They would just break the surface, giving you a flash, and gone. But they are definitely pink. They are born grey and become pink over time, particularly the males. It's speculated to be scar tissue from fighting rather than from their diet, as with pink flamingoes.

Breakfast came wrapped in a large leaf containing boiled eggs, a roll, a sandwich, a cake, fruit and biscuits. A dining room breakfast would have been tastier, but no complaints about our view.

June is high-water season, causing trees to be submerged in water that would not otherwise be during the low-water season. I enjoyed the eery spookiness of the swamp-like trees in the water and cruising under their overhanging branches. During low-water season, the tour includes land walks where our skiffs cruised.

At one point, our guide pulled over, saying he'd spotted something. We struggled to find what he'd seen. It looked like a tree, but was covered in bats. The bats were so well camouflaged they looked like natural knots in the trunk. If motionless, you struggled to see them. I had to zoom in to extreme lengths on my photos before I realised they were there. Nature is clever.

By this point, my insect bites had become unbearable, covering my legs. I never left the room without immediately putting on insect repellent and lathered it on multiple times during the day, but the bites increased.

Deet, the active ingredient in insect repellent, is not healthy to leave on your skin. It's recommended you wash it off before bed. Every night I washed off the combined sunscreen and insect repellent mix, then applied anti-itch cream on each bite. I have photos of my legs covered with red dots with white dried lotion over the bites and surrounding skin.

Because we couldn't spray repellent in the cabin, the insects thrived. Squashed bugs covered our sheets. Despite our efforts to control the insect population, they kept getting in. We'd be killing them as going to bed. One full mosquito I killed with a clap splattered blood reaching my face. Gross. Every morning, Vivian and I would wake with fresh bites. I had more than anyone else.

Will be Googling how to do effective bug spraying when have internet and before going anywhere like this again.

15th June (2018) Amazon River, Peru

We went piranha fishing this morning. I caught nothing. I partook in piranha feeding. The meat we used as bait would disappear off my hook the moment it entered the water. The guide caught one, and he showed us its teeth–vicious. When their mouth is wide open, it looks like an enormous tongue inside, but do fish have tongues? Their skin is shiny. Their eyes bulge. Not pretty creatures. More colourful than I expected, with a flash of orange or red on their underside.

At the end of the day, we stopped for a surprise sundowner, including champagne. We tied the skiffs together and toasted our last night on the river. The clouds rolled in, dulling the sunset but a nice way to bid farewell to our skiff adventures.

I ate well on this trip. All meals came with multiple choices and we pointed at what we wanted added to our plate, almost buffet style. There were plenty of vegetables, including beetroot which is nice for us Australians, but often considered weird by other nationalities. Being Peru, we ate potatoes of varying varieties, plus rice and meat or fish. Dinners started with soup, which I sometimes skipped. And dessert followed, which I also sometimes skipped.

I took hot chocolate powder to dinners to enjoy a hot drink while the others had coffees. The dining room contained a boiling water tap I could access.

With the trip ending, I captured many photos of life on the boat, after realising I hadn't taken many. I attempted to preserve the memories, wishing I had taken more photos throughout the trip. Writing these stories has changed my photo habits. I might become annoying on my future tours. Apologies in advance.

I also documented my insect bite situation, and it is not pretty—red polka dots covered my white legs. And they itched. Not pleasant.

16th June (2018) Iquitos to Lima, Peru

Breakfast this morning, our last on the boat, had the expected bacon, eggs and toast. As I mentioned yesterday about plenty of vegetables being offered, breakfast was no exception. I had a side of broccoli, cauliflower and sugar snap peas with my bacon and eggs.

After breakfast, we left the boat heading into town. We visited The Dallas World Aquarium Amazon Rescue Centre. Here, we found creatures behind bars. They are rescue animals who otherwise might have died, but I don't enjoy seeing animals through fences. I enjoyed watching the sloths doing acrobatic moves, though. They moved faster than the ones in the wild.

I loved the baby turtles. The sight of dozens of turtles attempting to climb onto ledges from the water captivated me. They weren't always successful, often flipping onto their backs. I stood there for ages, watching their struggle.

Unbeknownst to me, my camera was recording. It's pointed towards the ground, but the conversation while watching the turtles is hilarious. The macaws are providing the soundtrack, adding to the atmosphere. It's me with one tour mate. Here's a transcript:

"Does he have a broken leg or something too? Is he dead? Oh, there he goes... Oh oh oh oh. OHHHHH. Nearly did it." [We both laugh.] "So close, mate. What does he have to do just lie there till someone rescues him?... Oh, oh oh oh ooooh. Interesting sort of neck movement there... If you were in the wild, you'd have to learn to do it yourself. Why do they climb on top of each other?"

"I don't know, but they are so funny."

I love mistake recordings.

Groups of turtles have a few different names, but bale is the main one. A bale of baby turtles, black apart from yellow polka dots on their heads, are so cute.

From here, we flew to Lima.

I ate dessert for our last trip dinner, picarones—deep fried doughnuts made of pumpkin and sweet potato. YUMMM. Five rings of deliciousness arrived on a thick wooden skewer. A jug of syrup on the side. A perfect last meal in Peru.

They delegated the hotel rooms differently yet again, which made no sense. We tried to fix it based on departure times but one person flat out refused, suddenly wanting nothing to do with us. She mentioned not feeling well before shutting the door on us. Fine. We left her alone. Nice knowing you.

17th June (2018) Flying home from Lima, Peru

I returned to sleep after my roommate left at stupid-o'clock. My flight was early enough, being at 8:00 am. I had a 5:00 am pick-up and my roommate was 3:00 am. Way too early unless you have been up overnight. My sixth and last visit to Lima's airport.

I arrived in Santiago, Chile, by lunchtime with a two-hour layover. Followed by a fourteen hour flight to Sydney. I flew via Auckland on the way. You don't notice a quick hop on the way over, but stopping at Sydney coming home is tortuous. As is transferring from International to Domestic terminals when exhausted. Direct flights are better.

18th June (2005) Warrnambool, VIC, Australia

It has been over a year since I drove my Toyota Arkana from Perth to Melbourne. Not much has changed except she now has a name–Lottie. The seats remain in place, which is handy when you organise a group getaway. Only one car is needed to transport everyone.

We had six in the back, the best navigator up front, and me driving. Off we drove for a trip through the Otways, to Warrnambool for the weekend.

It's more fun with everyone in the same vehicle, rather than a car convoy, which we have done in the past. We piled the luggage in the back row area. Music played via the cassette deck in the front as we drove down the highway.

We take the road leading to the Otway Fly, but we don't enter. I can't remember why. We made the best of the situation, having a picnic lunch at their tables. It was freezing, and we rugged up, hats and all.

After a recent video camera purchase, I have footage of us first in Lottie driving and of freezing our butts off outside of the Otway Fly. I'm grateful the camera documented the day. I watched it before writing this after not seeing it for years. My lips curled into a smile and my body warmed from the inside out. Such wonderful memories.

I remember driving on the narrow curving roads in the Otway region and being nervous, wondering whether I had the skills to manoeuvre Lottie. Could I make the curves without tipping us into the surrounding trees and valleys? The drawback of having one car was no backup vehicle if an accident occurred. We made it through the rainforest and onto less precarious roads, fully intact. Phew. I wonder if my friends could tell I was nervous. I don't believe I voiced my fears.

We made it to Warrnambool, parking at the house we'd rented. It overlooked the water with large glass windows, allowing sweeping views of the coastline. Living here would be a dream.

We unpacked and divvied up beds and bedrooms. The cook amongst us whipped up a feast while we enjoyed each other's company. We ate well whenever together.

One activity on the agenda was "the operation." I had a splinter in my hand requiring extraction. I had removed most of it, but it snapped at the last second, leaving a tiny slither under the skin. The pretend nurse in the group opens the first-aid box and asks if the patient is ready. An actual nurse was not involved, and I was yet to become a nurse. Thank goodness for the pretend nurse.

The video camera captured the procedure, with me making varying faces as a friend digs into my hand with a needle-like instrument. Meanwhile, dinner is being cooked in the background. Others have the weekend newspapers spread out on the living room couch. Domestic bliss with the girls.

With the splinter out and a bandaid protecting the site, we folded newspapers away, and dinner with dessert devoured. Then the games began. My favourite game was Cranium–the game for your whole brain, according to the box. Trivial

Pursuit, Pictionary, charades and word games rolled into one. What's not to love? My friends appreciated games, but were unenthusiastic about Cranium. I never understood why. We played though, and I have it on video; the frustration, the elation, the misunderstanding, the laughs.

The amount of footage taken over this weekend surprised me. I feature in the footage. So it was not me directing. I guess being a new toy, everyone wanted to play with it.

We would enjoy whale watching the next day, despite being early in the season, and Lottie would get us home safely by the end of the weekend. No regrets in buying Lottie.

19th June (2022) Wilson's Promontory National Park, VIC, Australia

I woke early at 3:15 am, after coming off night shifts, turning the lights on an hour later. I was unimpressed with the hotel room, but the bed had been comfortable and I'd slept well. Being early, I drank two cups of tea in bed with the electric blanket on, reading and finishing my book. I also consumed breakfast in bed, being cereal, a banana and two cheese slices.

The shower grossed me out, so I washed in the sink, standing on towels so not barefoot on the tiles. I packed and checked out. I prefer to not stay in cheap motels anymore.

I stopped in Leongatha, to add to my food supplies. My shop included fresh milk for tea; more snacks; a fresh salad to be eaten today; and bread for toast. This further increased my large amount of stocks. I prepared for every imaginable situation, including buying food consumable without the need for electricity in case of a blackout. I was in disaster preparedness mode.

I also bought a Boston Bun and a Chive and Garlic Twisted Delight from Baker's Delight.

It wasn't a long drive to my destination of Wilson's Promontory, or the Prom, so I had sightseeing planned before making it to my accommodation in Tidal River, the Prom's official accommodation area.

I love driving through the countryside, enjoying the open land and the trees. At one point, the tree canopy stretched over the road, forming a tree tunnel.

I reached the Prom's National Park gates around 11:00 am, but had another 30 km to Tidal River. First stop was the Wildlife Walk where emus greeted me, but I wasn't sure how it worked as appeared to be an open field. I photographed an emu and continued on. I'd read the Wildlife Walk was better in the late afternoon or early morning for animal spotting. Also, my bladder needed the toilet as soon as possible.

With empty roads, I took my time enjoying the surroundings. The trees cleared to a view of the water and oh, my, goodness; it was jaw-dropping. I pulled over to look and capture on film.

My first planned stop was Whisky Bay, which had a toilet at its carpark. Or so I thought. With the toilet marked closed, I would have to hold on.

It was a 425 m walk from the carpark to Whisky Bay itself. The path starts off as gravel, becoming a wooden boardwalk covered in chicken wire to reduce potential slipperiness. I took a slight detour to the lookout before continuing down. You walk over a hill, then greeted by the ocean. Superb. I only met one other visitor leaving as I arrived on the beach. Convenient timing. There's something extra special about staggering vistas when you have them to yourself without annoying distractions or noises.

Talk about unspoilt landscapes. The sandy path opens to a wide beach with crashing waves ahead of you and rocks with orange hues to explore to your left. Spectacular. I headed straight to the rocks, finding a water outlet I'd have to cross first. Deeper than it looked from a distance, I ventured downstream in search of a narrow section to traverse. I had to leap and hope I didn't sink. I made it across and appreciated wandering through the rocks looking for secret exits and entrances and watching the waves crashing in closer and closer.

The tide was coming in and I didn't want to get stuck on the wrong side of the water. I walked back to the original crossing to find the water had increased. I wasn't brave enough to follow footprints in the sand from a previous visitor at the widest, most direct route.

A path led to my next stop, but I drove, considering I needed the bathroom. The toilet at Picnic Bay Carpark was open. A good old drop toilet. It's the spiders worrying me at these wooden shed facilities. I didn't close the door and tried not to look at anything. If I don't know what's there, it can't scare me. It worked. I survived the toilet.

Again, the path takes you to a lookout point and to the beach. High on a hill, I overlooked Whisky Bay to my right and Picnic Bay to my left. I had this serene view of the expansive ocean to myself. The water was shades of blue and green, with rocky islands in the distance. The winter sun shining away. Wilson's Prom had already blown me away. I skipped the stairs, saving my legs, happy with what I'd seen from the viewpoint. You don't need a beach to appreciate the ocean.

I caught up with the crowds at my next stop at Squeaky Beach. I was not happy with people and cars everywhere. A line formed where you crossed water by walking on rocks one person at a time. I didn't try to make the sand squeak given the surrounding crowd. Others tried without success. If I'd had it to myself, I might have played around. I didn't linger here.

Checking in early meant my allocated cabin had just finished being cleaned, to the point the floors were wet. But I didn't mind.

The one carpark serviced all the cabins, thus a walk from the car to the front door. I had so many items for "in case", it took me five loaded trips to transfer everything. On my last run, I saw others putting everything into a trolley I'd seen beside the path, completing their unpacking with one trip. Why didn't I think of that? I saw the trolley but assumed it belonged to the cleaners. Thus, not for me. I'll know for next time.

The cabin wasn't what I had expected; a big tent with walls. None of the walls reached the ceiling, posing a heating challenge. I'd brought my electric rug so that would keep me warm with targeted heat.

I loved the living area with the deck looking out into a forest of trees. The photos of this section made me choose a "cabin" over a "unit".

I made myself at home, filling the entire kitchen bench with food and drink. Seeing it spread out assured and surprised me. I'd never starve with or without power. I plugged my heated rug in and curled up on the couch with a hot chocolate within an hour of arriving. My day was done. Wildlife spotting from the warmth and comfort of my couch, the only activity left.

Upon the initial sighting, I mistook a plant near my deck for an echidna. Without the option of un-seeing it, the plant remained an "echidna" for the rest of my stay. Funny how it never moved. With animal skat everywhere, I was on the lookout as dusk came. But alas, the only spotting being my resident echidna.

I sat reading on the couch under the heated rug until I began falling asleep around 6:00 pm. I stayed awake until 8:30 pm when I took melatonin and hopped into bed.

I walked 8181 steps throughout the day. I was two weeks into a broken toe on my left foot, which had been suffering on the uneven sand and paths, and my old broken right ankle also did not appreciate uneven ground. Without a "safe" side, I had to tread carefully and not overdo it.

20th June (2022) Wilson's Promontory National Park, VIC, Australia

I slept well, stirring at 4:30 am then dosing until 7:30 am. I drank tea under the electric rug, planning the rest of my stay with the maps and information I received at check in.

My first wildlife spotting came through the kitchen window where a swamp wallaby ate breakfast. It was exciting seeing animals from the comfort of your own place, but I had to remain calm to not scare it.

I settled on walking to Mount Bishop this morning, getting there by 10:20 am. The sign said "3.7 km/1.5 hr". I utilised the toilet facilities before commencing the walk to ensure I'd make it. I left the door of the metal shack around the drop toilet open. The carpark contained one other car and no people in view.

You start on a gravel path with glimpses of water through the trees, then dirt and rock underfoot as the water disappears. My toe and ankle did not appreciate the rocks, but I forged ahead. The Australian bush surrounded me and the sun found gaps to shine through, giving the tree trunks orange glowing highlights. Australian eucalyptus trees are exceptional with their multiple coloured trunks. There were ferns and mushrooms in a fascinating variety of shapes and colours to explore.

The path steadily climbs, and the trees become sparse, opening up the view. You walk out on a single rock with uninterrupted views of the surrounding hills. I thought I'd reached the end and stood there for a few minutes breathing in the scenery when I remembered the end has ocean views. I noticed a pathway continuing on to my right.

Then, bam, I'm faced with the ocean as far as the horizon. I can't believe I almost missed the end. It was marvellous. It was here I found the rocky island resembling E.T., as in the movie *E.T.,* lying down. I was thrilled to discover it, as I did not know what to expect. I only knew it existed because the people checking in before me mentioned it. The ranger said it was still there, but an internet search revealed no information, let alone a photo. But it does look like E.T. lying down with his tummy sticking out of the water. I'm glad I overheard their conversation and discovered E.T.

I had the walk to myself apart from one slow walking couple ahead of me after around halfway. I hung back to increase the distance between us to continue the impression of solitude, only to catch up with them because they sat on the ground at a junction point. It annoyed me I'd wasted time giving them a bigger lead, which they squandered. They were weird, to be honest. I walked past them, thinking I'd rather be in front, anyway. They stood straight away, confirming they'd been waiting for me, but why not wait another few minutes rather than walking behind me?

They tried to stay back and eventually disappeared. At the summit, I heard them walking behind me. I turned to see, but they'd already retreated. I was glad they didn't ruin my summit experience. They could wait at the boulder. I planned to remain in this peaceful, serene atmosphere with no concern about those who might be waiting for me. Standing on the farthest ledge I was comfortable with, I soaked in the view and the sun's rays.

I stayed at the summit for twelve minutes, never seeing the couple. I assumed they'd be sitting on the boulder enjoying the mountain views, but no. Their car remained in the carpark, but I never saw them again. Where did they go? I was concerned they'd fallen over the edge. But I would have heard screaming. I'll never know what happened to them. If their intention was to have the summit to themselves by hiding and waiting, they made a mistake because I encountered two groups ascending on my descent.

Out of the two groups, only one said hello. The other acted like I was invisible. I believe the fewer people on a trail, the more you should acknowledge anyone you see. Is it really that difficult to greet someone with a simple "hello" or acknowledge their presence with a nod? I was not happy.

It took me an hour and a quarter to reach the summit, and fifty-six minutes to walk down. I did it in 12,050 steps.

The temperature was a steady eleven degrees, making it cold to start, requiring gloves to keep my hands warm. On reaching the top, I removed the gloves and cardigan.

I ate pasta salad for lunch at my cabin under the heated rug. And at 2:15 pm, I ventured out for another walk to Pillar Point, a suggested location to watch sunset. The start is over the iconic Tidal River Footbridge which everyone photographs. It is a picturesque spot. I took more than one photo of the bridge and its surrounds.

They signposted Pillar Point as a "1.8 km/45 min trail". The terrain differed from this morning–more open with salt hardy scraggly plants. Norman Beach is to your left. This walk contained more mud patches and rock scrambling compared to Mount Bishop, which wasn't ideal, but I managed the uphill walk.

When I reached the summit, in thirty-six minutes, I found three people sat atop the giant boulder. I don't know how they climbed up. There was no path I was willing to take. I found a spot on a smaller boulder to appreciate the view. Despite a tree sort of in the way, the view was worth seeing. Though not as good as Mount Bishop's view.

There were more people on this walk. One group was the one who ignored me earlier today. But this time I received a sign of acknowledgement showing improvement.

Back on the bridge, I met two older ladies, seasoned walkers of the area, and we chatted. They were doing small walks on this trip after knee and hip replacements. I was jealous of the three wombats they had seen. They said wombats are everywhere through the campground at dusk. That's the problem with being tucked under a heated blanket by dusk—you miss the wombats.

I did an extra walk based on the ladies' wombat sighting recommendations. And I'm glad I did. No wombats, but astonishing scenery! It was the Loo Erm

Walk, a water boardwalk with reflections of the trees in the water. Wilson's Prom is breathtaking and continued to blow my mind. The short but sweet walk ended at my cabin.

I tucked myself under the electric rug with a hot chocolate by 4:00 pm, followed by dinner. I cooked pesto pasta and watched pre-downloaded television shows on my iPad, remaining under the heated rug until bedtime at 9:40 pm. My rug was the best thing I packed.

My afternoon walks added up to 8,292 steps for a day total of 20,342 steps. Not bad for someone with a broken toe and a dodgy ankle. My legs were tired.

21st June (1997) London, England, United Kingdom (UK)

I had waited a long time for tonight. I would often buy theatre tickets last minute getting the cheap seats. Not tonight. I bought tickets the day after release and waited. Jerry Lewis live on stage in the musical *Damn Yankees*. I wanted to be as close as possible.

My memory has always said I sat in row B. My ticket stub says row G. Whether it was B or G, it's close enough to feel a part of the action.

I grew up watching Jerry Lewis and Dean Martin black and white movies on Saturday afternoons. I loved them, but Jerry was my favourite, watching all his movies without Dean. My favourite is *Rock-a-Bye Baby* when his character has to look after newborn triplets on his own. I have this on video and DVD.

What I did not understand was Jerry was playing a character in those movies. He did not use his natural voice.

I remember the anticipation building in the audience, waiting for Jerry to appear. He walks onto the stage and the audience bursts into applause. Jerry waits for the clapping to die down. He speaks, and disappointment sets in. That's not Jerry Lewis' voice. I want my Saturday-afternoon-movie Jerry Lewis.

The show continued, and it became our lucky day. One actor forgot his lines leading to silence on the stage. Talk about an awkward pause, but it became the highlight of the night. To break the awkward silence, Jerry put on his Saturday afternoon voice and a roar of laughter erupted with a thunderous applause. I wasn't the only one wanting to hear that voice. I don't remember what he said, but he said it in the voice I desperately wanted to hear, thus elated.

I can't hum any of the songs, or explain the storyline, but I saw, and heard, Jerry Lewis live.

22nd June (1996) Copenhagen, Denmark

Our international crew of six headed out for a night at Tivoli in central Copenhagen. We had two girls from Germany, one being Susanne as in the beach letter writing Susanne; a girl from Holland, also Suzanne (or Dutch Suzanne); an Irish girl, Annette; Carrie from America; and myself from Australia. We paid our entrance fee and entered a world of fairytales and lights; a whimsical atmosphere with something to delight at every turn.

With names such as Wild Swans and Viking Ship, how can you not imagine you've journeyed back in time? The Gondola is a must. As is the Ferris wheel giving you an overview of Tivoli itself and outside the walls into Copenhagen. Of course, there are bumper cars and the carousel.

If you only do one ride, it has to be the roller coaster, Rutschebanen. It is one of the world's oldest wooden roller coasters built in 1914. Our Scenic Railway in Luna Park, Melbourne, was built two years earlier in 1912. The Danish train has a brakeman, similar to ours. However, they have a seat for the journey, in contrast to ours, who stands throughout the ride.

We played arcade style games and ate junk food as the colourful lights twinkled around us. Spend an evening at Tivoli if you are ever in Copenhagen.

This night holds joyous memories for me, evidenced by a group photo taken that remains displayed in my lounge room to this day.

23rd June (1993) London, England, UK

Today is a prequel for the 4th of February, 2015, in Heidelberg, Germany, about the Elizabeth Gate. I hinted at a reason for the interest. Today is the date from which the interest stems.

I caught a bus to Hampton Court Palace, but one day I'll arrive at the palace as intended, by boat. The River Thames was the highway of the day when they built the palace. For now, the bus was cheaper.

On the tour of the palace apartments, I lingered longer than the group in one room. They'd moved on, leaving me alone in the vast room with parquet floor and floor-to-ceiling wood panelling. I was enjoying my sumptuous surroundings, and I turned around slowly, facing my back to the windows. Here before my eyes, above a white marble fireplace, was a portrait of me! I was stunned, shocked, bewildered.

Who could this woman from the past be?

She looked like me.

Could be me.

I asked a museum employee if she knew who the woman in the portrait was. She found a book in a secret cupboard in the door frame, and informed me it was Elizabeth, Queen of Bohemia. My excitement was palpable.

Elizabeth Stuart was the youngest daughter of King James I, who had been King James VI of Scotland. Elizabeth married the Elector of Palatine and lived in Heidelberg Castle, where her husband built the Elizabeth Gate for her birthday in 1615.

This is where family history stories collide. The Heap family told stories about being German aristocracy, which fit the Heidelberg story. In my grandmother's Stewart family, there were rumours of links to the Scottish Royals. So here is a daughter of the King of Scotland, marrying into German royalty, who looks like me. Talk about fuelling my imagination.

I will never forget that moment of turning around in the expansive empty room, and coming face to face with myself. How many things had to align to create that moment? It had to mean something.

After more research, I discovered the current English Royal Family descends from Elizabeth's youngest daughter, Sophia of Hanover, who became the most direct Protestant heir to the throne in 1701. Sophia's ancestors began the run of King Georges, with her son becoming King George I of England in 1714. I looked into Elizabeth's thirteen children, finding no connection to my ancestors.

I continued my interest in Elizabeth for years to come, reading books on her and her children. She became the Queen of Bohemia in 1619, leaving Heidelberg Castle behind and moving to Prague. Here she gained her nickname of "The Winter Queen", after her brief reign. She spent most of her life in exile, begging royal relatives around the world to help her afford to live. Her life was not what you'd imagine given once a queen, and the daughter of a king.

The story from this day also enhanced my trip to Prague and its castle in 1995. No regrets over indulging my interest in this woman who may, or may not, look like me.

24th June (2022) Melbourne, VIC, Australia

In my head I'd booked myself to leave for Tasmania today, but in an oopsy I booked for tomorrow instead. Oh well. It gave me a day to get everything sorted.

I watched YouTube videos of people travelling on the Spirit of Tasmania. I was nervous about driving on and off the ferry, so I made sure I knew the ins and outs to increase my confidence. One of these videos reminded me of what you can and can't take into Tasmania. I knew fruit wasn't allowed, but I did not know they could open your boot inspecting for plant and soil-based debris.

After being in Wilson's Prom, the car had leaves in every nook and cranny. I would have to wash the car. I started an internet search on car washes in the area, settling on one nearby with good ratings and price.

First, I emptied the car, finding a fascinating collection of trash and treasure in my boot. Out of sight, out of mind. It was thrown away or put somewhere safe for my return. The boot looked large when empty.

I headed to the self-serve car wash with apprehension as only my second ever time. After watching more YouTube videos, I felt armed with enough insider information to achieve a good job. I vacuumed inside and hand cleaned soil and leaf build up wishing I had extra paper towels. Then headed for the trickier hoses and high pressured functions. I followed the recommended soap and rinse routine, making it in the allotted time. I swiped my credit card, hoping I would not pay a fortune. Which I didn't. It cost $7.40.

Now I turned my attention to making the car ready for a two week driving holiday around Tasmania. I needed to buy a few things, including my first ever phone holder. I thought that might be useful for when using the navigation system. With so many options, I spent ages picking one and even longer deciding where to place it in the car. I'd hoped to use it to take photos and videos of picturesque scenery along the way, but that proved too difficult. I thought I could do videos of me talking while driving, which also proved too difficult. Fran is not tech friendly.

I experimented with plastic storage containers in the boot and settled on two large ones fitting perfectly length-wise and allowed width-wise space to house extra bits and pieces. I would complete the packing tomorrow.

25th June (2022) Spirit of Tasmania, Australia

The excitement was building. Finally, I was going to Tasmania, and doing so via the Spirit of Tasmania overnight ferry.

I spent the day packing, filling the car boot. Two plastic containers housed the bulk of the supplies. One housed winter clothes and weather protection. I had everything from snow boots to waterproof pants, and multiple options for gloves and winter layering. I imagined freezing and snowing.

The second container housed food and kitchen supplies. Again, I had food requiring no cooking and food needing cooking, along with the paraphernalia for each scenario. I had food storage containers; UHT milk; tinned fruit and vegetables; tomato sauce; cereal; cutlery; crockery; tea towels; paper towels; toilet paper; you name it. I was prepared for anything.

I also carried water supplies in two ten-litre cartons; plus another five litres in smaller bottles; and three packs of soft drink cans to mix it up. I would not be thirsty if I broke down.

In the backseat I had my main bag with clothes and toiletries; a range of loose coats and fleeces; a doona; pillow; my heated rug; and more food and water supplies in smaller bags. In the front seat, I had an overnight bag packed for the ferry and my handbag.

The ferry departed at 7:30 pm with check in commencing at 5:00 pm. I wanted to arrive early and joined the check-in line by 5:15 pm. Signs said no filming or photos allowed, so wondered how people got the videos I watched yesterday. I'd planned to take photos, but because of the signs, only snapped a couple of sneaky ones.

Driving on proved easy. The inspection process was simple to what I'd expected as well. They took a cursory look in the boot for fruit, which I stated I had none. I went a bit overboard with cleaning the car, but there's nothing wrong with a clean car.

Boarding was meant to start at 6:00 pm, but I arrived at my cabin at 5:50 pm. The process was quick and done with a glorious sunset in the background.

They allocated me cabin 7006 on deck 7. My deluxe cabin was grander than I expected. The room included a complimentary bottle of wine. Shame I don't drink. With the window blinds drawn, it took me awhile to discover I was at the front of the boat. It had grown dark, so I couldn't see much. The windows were filthy, so no point taking photos, anyway. I left to check out the boat.

> Love the vibe of the ferry. I feel like I might like cruising after all.
> Was exciting exploring and adventuring around inside and outside.

I purchased my Tasmania National Parks pass at the tourist desk. For $80, my car and I had unlimited access to the National Parks for three months. I believe you save money if you are visiting three or more parks.

For dinner, I chose the buffet, with my favourite pork being the roast of the day. I started with quinoa salad followed by carrots, corn, broccoli and cauliflower. Only then noticing the roast vegetables ahead. I piled on roast carrot, pumpkin and two baked potatoes. I asked someone behind me for the butter packets I had passed. Baked potatoes need butter. I requested roast pork from the server and helped myself to a pile of crackling. I was in heaven. With a soft drink, I paid $27.50. I decided I would have the same on the return journey.

Our pre-departure information had said to wear a face mask, which I did. It had since changed to mask recommended. Most people weren't wearing them, but I kept mine on when outside my cabin. People were looking at me.

On returning to the cabin, I started preparing to avoid seasickness. I'd brought ginger tablets and wrist bands. I didn't know what to expect, throwing everything at it just in case. A last minute Google search ensured I had the bands in the correct place. They were tight, but I guess that's how you hit the trigger point. They announced expected swells of two to four metres, which sounded a lot, creating apprehension.

I hoped to be asleep before the swells. I took the ginger tablets and was in bed by 9:30 pm.

26th June (2022) Stanley, Tasmania (TAS), Australia

My first night sleeping on the open ocean. It was rather weird. I hadn't considered the position of my bed, but it was perpendicular to the front of the boat. I expected waves to move the boat from side to side. In this position, I experienced my head being lower than my legs, alternating with the sensation I might slip out from the bottom of the bed. Strange. I hate being tucked in, but it may have been useful in these circumstances.

Whenever I'd come into a light sleep, I'd experience this sensation and have a moment where I'd be scared I'd start feeling nauseas but I never did. I also never actually slid out of the bed. That scenario had never occurred to me. Did that save me from being seasick? Did the ginger and wrist bands save me from being seasick? We'll never know, but I survived crossing the Tasman Sea.

I set an alarm for 5:30 am, but the boat's announcement at 5:45 am would have woken me and been enough time to be ready. I read in bed, waiting for the disembarkation call.

I looked out the window, seeing the same view I saw before bed. I was skeptical we'd gone anywhere and expected to hear an announcement saying we were in Port Melbourne. But no, it was Devonport, which became clear as the sun rose. I must do it during the day next time to see the ocean views.

You embark based on your car deck. Decks one, two and five are called first. A few minutes later, my deck number six was called. I had my reminder ticket of where I parked, six port blue, so easy to find. You drove forwards to leave, had a short drive with no checks, and you're on your own.

I drove round to the area opposite the docks to get photos of the ferry with a yellow, orange and lilac sunrise as a backdrop. It was 7:10 am. I stayed watching until the colours disappeared, then headed to the shops.

I saw familiar faces from the ferry at the supermarket buying fresh produce. I bought apples, bananas and tomatoes; small packets of UHT milks; two salads being potato and pasta; and biscuits in Mint Slice and Chocolate Digestives. It was only 7:30 am.

My first sight didn't open until 9:00 am. I didn't buy breakfast on the boat, and the internet had been spotty, so headed to McDonald's for food, Wi-Fi, and to linger without question.

I downloaded directions to my next two destinations but also hand wrote them in case. They gave me hot water and milk to make my cup of tea. It's different at McDonald's though, because you get the milk and water already mixed, which looks weird, then I add my tea bag.

I drove to the Don River Railway. My receipt is timed 9:02 am. Go me! I wasn't even the first. What a wonderful place to start my holiday. I headed straight for the signal box. Heaven. After viewing photos of the signal box online, I knew I had to visit.

There were over thirty hand signal controls lined up, and I smiled from ear to ear. I took tonnes of photos and played with everything. You could press buttons and hear bell signals for different circumstances and learn how to decipher the bell calls. I was loving the information and clicked away. It's all inspiring details to file away for a future book. I had it to myself so lingered goofily as long as I wanted.

I explored the old engines on display in the yard. The work shed housed a carriage converted for Edward, Prince of Wales' visit in 1920. I'd love my own train carriage with separate lounge rooms and bedrooms, bathrooms and dining rooms. How wonderful would that be? They also had models of how engines worked, which I played with helping me understand the train's inner workings.

It was freezing, well, nine degrees. I needed to warm up, so visited the museum while waiting for my 10:00 am vintage train ride. The train was a mixture of carriages from varying decades connected to a diesel engine. I changed my seat a few times, trying to choose the best carriage without noisy children. Alas, more noisy children jumped on to my carriage as leaving.

The ride was thirty minutes, reversing the engine halfway. I tried to watch the coupling of the engine to the carriages, but a training conductor was in the way. I wanted to see, but he needed to learn to keep future visitors safe.

On my return, I asked if possible to play with the signal controls. He said they were locked, but number one may move and yes, I could play with it. He warned me to be careful, as not attached to the normal mechanical works.

I ran up to the signal box full of glee and, yes, I still had it to myself. From seeing videos online, I knew the signals can be heavy, so I put my bags in the corner and placed two hands on lever number one. I take the lock off and pull it towards me and it moves. It is heavy, but I keep pulling it toward me and I've turned into a Cheshire cat. I've moved a signal lever! The highlight of my day. I am so glad I asked the question.

I repeated the action for the camera as evidence I've done it and for later reference. The recording phone took one hand, making it extra heavy and tricky to manoeuvre. I managed, but there's no way if it had been fully functional. Such a gratifying way to finish my visit.

I had 130 km to Stanley. I found the driving easy and the roads good.

> I could tell not in Victoria, but not sure why. Maybe because new? So few miles done yet so far from home. The ferry doesn't add kilometres to your odometer. It's weird. Glad I filled up with petrol. All prices here are around the $2.17-$2.22 mark. It will end up being my highest paid yet. Not an ideal time to start doing all these road trips, but all good. It's nice to travel again. Adventures and freedom. If only I could do this all the time. So many places I wanted to stop but terrible at stopping/changing quickly so missed the parking places. They'll all be on my side as drive back tomorrow so can stop then.

I stopped at a town called Penguin. How could you not? Being a Sunday, there were people everywhere, so I didn't linger. I parked in a ten-minute zone and jumped out; said hello to the giant penguin made of fibre cement in 1975; walked to the water for a view; took a photo of a *Dr Who* Tardis, which doubles as a free book exchange; and got back in the car.

From here I drove along the coast road rather than the highway. It was stunning. All beach and water.

I made the outskirts of Stanley by 12:30 pm. My first stop was a viewpoint over The Nut. They had constructed a massive frame and built a designated spot for your phone to facilitate capturing a photo using the timer feature. I tried it seeing as by myself, and terrible at selfies. With the phone in the holder and the timer on, I ran to climb into the frame. I'm too old to climb and pose in ten seconds, meaning the first four attempts show me in the process of climbing. It's hilarious.

Then another car comes by. I ask them if they'd press the button for me while in position. At last, I captured a picture of myself in the frame with The Nut. She also took photos of me on her phone and AirDropped them to me. A selfie would have been less effort, but at least I tried and I think it's great the council set it up.

It remained cold, so sat in the car to eat lunch. I have a photo of a pasta salad on my dash with the windscreen wipers visible and The Nut in the distance.

The Nut is the remnant of an ancient volcanic plug resembling a flat-topped hill at the edge of a peninsula, giving the appearance of emerging from the ocean. It is the most famous sight in this area and one you can climb. A chairlift operates in the summer.

I visited The Historic Highfield Site. It is a home and farm built in the 1830s and formed part of the Van Diemen's Land Company. This company is the Australian version of The East India Company in India and The Hudson Bay Company in Canada. The house overlooks The Nut and the ocean. It was built by, and ran on, convict labour. You can explore the barns, stables, chapel and schoolroom.

Here I found a description of Australia's native trees. The English settlers and convicts alike weren't impressed. One convict described the trees as "ugly, with their bark always falling off." I had never thought of it that way, but it's true. The bark does peel off, but that exposes the multi coloured-ness underneath that I love. I have no problem with their falling off bark.

Moving on, I naughtily stopped in the middle of the road to take a photo of the magnificent line of Norfolk pines. And again at a road sign telling you to slow down for penguins. How many places around the world have road signs featuring penguins? I needed that photo.

I'd planned to climb The Nut, and could see the path, which appeared steep. Then the rain started, so I pulled the plug on climbing. I'll come back in season and ride the chairlift.

I arrived at the hotel at 2:45 pm to find my room's heater on. I appreciated walking in to a heated room after the cold. With a view of The Nut, I opened the blinds, made a hot chocolate and drank in the view while I planned my next day. Even though the rain stopped, I had no intention of stepping outside again.

My packing did not impress me.

> Not quite streamlined. Did two trips. Two shopping bags, big bag and overnight bag. With big bag being all clothes, I barely need it. Maybe a clothes box is better and take out what I need and only bring a small amount into the room each night. Information for next time, I guess.

I ate a packet mix of macaroni cheese for dinner, thanks to a guest microwave in the laundry. I mean, doesn't everyone have a microwave in the laundry?

7,163 steps.

27th June (2022) Launceston, TAS, Australia

By mistake I paid for a breakfast box, which I found in my room. I had breakfast supplies but nice to have something different, including toast which I didn't have. The box had two pieces of bread, a small pack of Cornflakes, an orange juice box, an apple, a muesli bar and milk in the fridge. I'm guessing few people utilise this service as my Cornflakes had an expiry date of today. I appreciated the milk with enough leftover for tea.

They provided butter, jam and Vegemite for the toast. I remember having my large Vegemite jar in my hand to pack, then putting it back in the cupboard, suspecting I wouldn't use it. Well, I would have used it. Those tiny packets of hotel Vegemite aren't enough for me. I had one piece of toast with Vegemite and one piece of toast with half Vegemite and half jam with no-man's-land between. Jam and Vegemite is not a thing.

I got up at 7:00 am and departed at 8:30 am. Belinda Carlisle joined me. I had a travel thermos of tea and drank it over two stops. The first stop was for the toilet at Little Pegs Beach State Reserve. At the second stop in Somerset an hour later, I drank my tea on the beach, chatting to a local dog walker who'd been to the dentist. Neither of us are fans of dentists, so we bonded. I couldn't get enough of the ocean views and seaside towns.

A railway line appeared to follow the coast. I investigated at Burnie, where it looked like a junction. It confirmed my suspicions about not being an active line. At various points, it disappeared behind trees. It would be magnificent if running. A tourist gold mine.

I needed to use the toilet again in Burnie, but it took me some time to locate one. While searching, I had to pay for parking, showing I was in a tourist area. I changed the CD while stopped, now crooning out Chicago as I drove.

A sign pointed to Lillico Beach Conservation Area and I pulled over. It turned out to be a free penguin watching location with boardwalks and penguin information. The penguins had their own mini boardwalks to help them up the hills to their burrows. Shame it's not penguin season. But out of season meant I could walk to the pebble beach. I loved the variety of colours and pictured my garden filled with stones from here.

I had planned a pub lunch at Beauty Point, but being down a ditch, I missed the turnoff and nowhere to turn around. I continued to my destination in the hope they had a cafe.

The Platypus House offered a chicken and cheese toasted sandwich which sounded perfect to a hungry me. I ate my toastie in a room where a documentary on platypuses played while waiting for my 1:00 pm pre-booked tour.

To my embarrassment, no one else had booked. New guides were undergoing training, so I had three staff with me. It felt weird. Anyway, I got to see platypuses playing and eating in the water making me happy. With water tanks, you can see how a platypus swims and moves more than if saw one in the wild barely breaking the water's surface. The guides said only one per cent of Australians have seen a platypus in the wild. They are elusive creatures. I liked how they floated to the top when ready to take a breath. They are so unique you can understand people not believing they were real when first discovered.

You also interact with echidnas. I did not know they had such soft, cute and gentle faces. Sweet faced but cheeky when food involved. Their spikes aren't as sharp as you would expect, either.

I drove to Launceston, stopping at Brady's Lookout for an expansive view over the Tamar River. Arriving at Cataract Gorge carpark at 3:00 pm, I started with the chairlift. I bought a return but should have got a one way. It moved slowly, allowing time to soak in the view. I did not appreciate the bumpy bits through the cable joins. I also did not enjoy the getting on and off process. You stand poised, ready to fall into it. When getting off, you jump and run to the side. I got hit both times getting off. It was not an elegant dismount.

The end of the chairlift was an excellent spot for seeing wallabies and quolls. The attendant fed them dried corn kernels, and they munched away. The sound of crunching in unison was intriguing. I hadn't expected wildlife in the city.

I did the Cataract Walk, embedded in the cliff face and stretching the length of the gorge to the main road. The walk took less than forty minutes. An easy, wondrous walk in the city's heart.

Taking the chair lift down, I walked to the Alexandra Suspension Bridge. I had it to myself until the very end. I bounced my way across gleefully and managed photos without people.

By 5:00 pm, I headed to my treat night in an upmarket hotel paying with vouchers. I arrived during sunset and the view from outside my room was exceptional. The sky was orange and red as it reflected in the River Tamar.

The hotel was in a converted silo. My room contained round walls. I upgraded to guarantee the curved walls, allowing me to see I was in an old silo. I loved it. You know I'm easily pleased. Even the bathroom had curved walls.

The massive room became a problem when I wanted to watch television; the television being too small for the distance from the bed. I watched shows downloaded on my iPad instead.

> Tried something different with packing as a fancy hotel and didn't want to do multiple trips or look like a packing mule with my Woolies reusable bags. So took the day bag from the boat and handbag to start and checked in. Then decided what I needed and went back to the car and put all the bits and pieces in one Woolies bag and walked back in with that. I can take it all at once in the morning. It's strange and stressful trying to pick out bits and pieces. What if I get it wrong?

> I decided on room service dinner so no dinner needs but wanted a hot chocolate so brought a mug and chocolate tin. Couldn't find information on breakfast, so bought up one portion of cereal in a Tupperware container and mini milks by two for hot chocolate and cereal. There was 300 ml of full cream milk in the fridge so perfect for tea—so brought tea making stuff. One litre of water in case, cutlery container, new trousers and top and underwear for tomorrow. I changed my cardigan to brown and shoes to sneakers. And a Sprite.

I did not have the packing situation under control.

I looked forward to room service dinner, only to be disappointed. I received an ugly burger and chips delivered on a plain black tray. No fancy presentation, no cute tomato sauce bottle. I wasn't sure if it was specific to Australia, since most of my room service experience was from Europe and America; or a pandemic thing; or something else. All I know is it didn't feel special. The food filled me up, so a satisfactory end in theory.

I did 9,135 steps.

28th June (2022) Scamander, TAS, Australia

I was in bed from 10:30 pm to 7:30 am, but stayed in bed for breakfast and tea. I'd been excited to find a 300 ml bottle of full cream milk in the room fridge. It expired today. I boiled the kettle, opened the milk, smelt the milk which seemed fine, but it curdled as hit the hot water.

I drank two-thirds of it and didn't make another.

I can't remember what it looked like, but it sounds disgusting. How did I drink any of it? That's how much I love my tea, if I'll drink it with curdled milk.

This trip was about being outdoors, so had no planned activities in Launceston itself. I was heading to the east coast. I filled the car with petrol and made additions to my food supplies. My hand written instructions included:

Coles on left—buy cheesecake and dip. Right petrol.

I found Baker's Delight at the same shopping complex buying a chocolate croissant for tomorrow's breakfast, and a Twisted Delight, which ended up being my main sustenance throughout the day as could eat it while driving.

Google Maps directed me, but I'd planned my route, preferring apps only as a backup. We disagreed about the best route prompting me to write:

> I made the Google Map's voice take me the way I wanted to go. Eventually, she acquiesced.

Those voices can be stubborn.

I paid $2.15 per litre for petrol. I wanted to start the day with full tanks before heading into country areas.

No cars followed me until near the end of the day. I love having the road to myself with no pressure to drive a certain way. It's easier to enjoy the scenery and slow down on the curvy bits. I love driving, but I can be a nervous driver. That makes me a cautious driver, though. I don't understand why people speed around curves on cliff edges. An accident would mean the end of my trip and the end of who knows what else. It's not worth the risk.

I booked a hotel in Scamander with stops at Eddystone Lighthouse and The Gardens on the way. I played on Google Maps, finding a few interesting mini sights and worked out my route based on their locations.

My first stop was at The Sideling Lookout with a carpark, toilet block, and a viewing platform over the valley below, and no one else around. I had a snack while there being an apple, yoghurt and orange juice.

Thirty-minutes later, I stopped in Scottsdale, at the Big Thumbs Up. It's what it sounds like, a giant hand giving the thumbs up sign. It's a bit worse for wear, but I couldn't resist stopping for a look.

The next rest stop, Derby, had a modern amenities block for campers. It would have been easy and cheap to camp along the way. I imagined having a roof top tent on the car. I love the idea. This site had a creek running alongside, making it a relaxing place to hang out. The town itself was quaint, and I wish I'd stopped. It is a known mountain bike area with shops on theme, and local trails. I will have to return, hire a bike, and ride through the Derby Tunnel. I'll have to re-learn to ride a bike first, though. A small hurdle.

I turned onto a B road to reach my next planned stop at the Little Blue Lake. Exquisite. I was in awe. It transported me to Switzerland, and I had it to myself. The small view point didn't show what I'd seen online. The road further in was a pock marked dirt road full of muddy puddles. I didn't want to drive down it. I parked at the first section, walking further along the road to investigate, and it was spectacular.

No official paths, but plenty of unofficial ones to wander until I'd seen the lake from every angle. I kept exploring and getting as close to the edge as I dared until I found the perfect spot to see the entire lake, thus the full effect of its blueness. It's a turquoise blue caused by the white clay, exposed from mining, reflecting the blue sky.

The mining practices resulted in acidic water, thus no swimming or drinking. Such a shame. Swimming in the middle of that colour would be enthralling. I found a spot to sit and drink in the view while eating Twisted Delight for lunch. It would be a charming place to build a cottage. I could look at it forever.

As leaving, three cars, not travelling together, arrived in the first carpark. They too had the initial confusion, but one four-wheel-drive (4WD) car continued down the dirt track. A second car attempted the road but encountered the first car returning, leading to a standoff. The third car contained a family unfolding a pram. I suggested they continue down the path as even though it seemed like nowhere to go, it was worth proceeding. I hoped those first two cars didn't drive away without exploring. Such a shame if they did.

I continued along the B road until my next turnoff, a C road. I saw my first road sign picturing a wombat and another with a kangaroo meeting a car. It said: "Wildlife Dusk to Dawn". I hoped not to drive between those hours.

This is when the dirt roads started appearing and the scenery became stark. Open and flat, with dead trees sitting against a backdrop of a greying, moody sky. Eerie and ethereal, a bit of a change.

The next road sign pictured a Tasmanian devil. Tassie has the best road signs. Poor devil, though, with the word "endangered" under it. And again a reminder to "Slow Down, Watch Out, Dusk to Dawn."

At this stage, I entered the Mount William National Park. Signs explained a National Parks Pass was required. Lucky I'd pre-purchased one, as no place to buy one here, but also no one checking.

I survived the rough roads, making it to Eddystone Point Lighthouse to find two other cars. Thankfully, I had not encountered them on the road, since impossible to remain within your lane. I drove the path of least resistance, avoiding potholes, puddles, and slippery areas, requiring zigzagging across the road. The fear of my wheel getting trapped or breaking as I unwittingly drove over a concealed hole loomed over me throughout. But my little car made it in one piece.

It seemed the cars had just arrived, despite not seeing them on the road. One was a Toyota Corolla hatch like mine, which I appreciated as I'd thought I'd been stupid to drive my car here. Parking proved difficult, with at least three quarters of the carpark being turned into a paddling pool by recent rain.

Each group walked in different directions as I pulled in. I saw the directions they took and chose a third option to escape them. It worked. I didn't see them for the rest of my visit.

The third direction led to a metal drop toilet. It was freezing and dark with the door closed. I kept my eyes shut, getting out as fast as I could.

The path continued over a hill. I could see the lighthouse behind me and the beach in front. The winding sandy path vanished as I traversed it, making it impossible to see what lay ahead or where I'd been.

I walked through green salt shrubs, then came the brown rocks with splashes of orange next to the blue-grey of the ocean and a white-grey moody sky. Outstanding! The wind blowing, the shrubs swaying. Heaven.

The water's edge had become turquoise. Waves crashed on the beach. Not a single soul other than me. The dirt road saga was worth it. I'd arrived at Gulch Point at Larc Beach, a ten-minute walk from the toilet.

I then walked towards the lighthouse. I passed a few old stone houses which looked like rental accommodation. What a wonderful place to stay for peace, quiet and views.

They built the stone lighthouse in 1889. A staircase led to a locked entrance. I peeked inside to find an intricately designed wrought-iron staircase. Climbing that staircase would have been smile inducing.

The panorama from the lighthouse extended across the water, and more orange-hued rocks. I spent an hour in the area. Then back on the dirt roads. As leaving, the family from the Little Blue Lake arrived. I found it incredible they had the same bizarre itinerary as me, but wondered how an hour behind. Maybe they had a sit down lunch somewhere. Curious, I wanted to know if everyone found the rest of the lake area. They replied saying everyone continued on and I drove off, hoping they wouldn't catch up with me.

I skipped a planned museum stop to arrive at The Gardens at sunset. I timed it perfectly for the best angle of the sun on the orange rocks. It was magnificent.

I stopped along the way at a beach because I couldn't resist the name. Cosy Corner South was divine–emerald water, brown rocks with orange spots, white sand and a darkening moody sky. The colours complimenting each other.

I continued to the The Gardens' carpark, to discover a circuit trail with a lookout. I could see orange rocks ahead and the clouds began dissipating. The information sign explained the white sands originated from the high quartz content of the granite boulders and the orange was lichen.

I continued round the circuit as the beaming sun broke through the clouds, lighting the orange rocks with spectacular results. Perfect timing. The orange sparkled, and the colour reflected in the shimmering water. Enchanting. This was the highest concentration of orange boulders I'd seen, and I loved it. I had chosen here for that reason. I'm thankful my research suggested being here for sunset.

The clouds lingered, imitating a theatrical performance, with the sun entering and exiting in sync with the clouds' motions. Nature's spotlight. Captivating. It is wonderful without the sun, but that extra dimension was worth it.

I had a selfie practice trying to see if my hair matched the orange rocks. The rocks are more orange than my hair as my colour fades, but I love these rocks.

As leaving, a few cars arrived. They appeared to know each other. I commented how they had just missed the sunset, they just smirked. I wondered if they knew something I didn't. Until they arrived, I again had the landscape to myself.

Driving south, the sunset continued to colour the sky and reflected pink hues in the water. Stunning. I stopped twice to appreciate it as the pink deepened. For the first time, I experienced a driver on my tail, annoyed at my efforts to enjoy the sunset.

I arrived at my pre-booked hotel in Scamander at two minutes past five. Unbeknownst to me, check in closed at five. My paper work said 9:00 pm. I found a phone number to ring for assistance. The number reached a recorded message saying they were closed. I mumbled, "Well, that's useful. A number that goes to an answer machine."

At this point someone appeared saying, "The phone will ring through to the after hours manager if you stay on the line. We are open from nine to five."

"I guess I'm late. Can I check in?" We started on the wrong foot.

"Name," she snapped back.

I gave my name, and she disappeared into the back office, then appeared out from behind the desk and headed to a lockbox outside. She put in a code and found an envelope with my name. I'm not sure how I was supposed to know about the coded lockbox. I checked my e-mails, and I never received one with instructions, so I believe they mishandled it. Another customer was accessing the box as we approached. How did he know what to do?

The whole encounter put a sour note in my mouth about the venue, making me no longer interested in frequenting the restaurant as planned for dinner. I wanted nothing to do with them. I had dip and crackers in bed, followed by cheesecake and biscuits. And planned a pre 9:00 am departure.

I covered 285 km. My thoughts on the driving:

> I went as slow as I liked up hills and around bends and stopped for road sign photos. I was not expecting the dirt roads though on C routes. Some bits were slippery. They were shiny patches, query ice or just wet. I had two hands on the wheel, holding tightly and making sure I didn't break on the skiddy bits. I felt like I was in the middle of nowhere.

Various incarnations of Jewel accompanied me over the day.
6,711 steps taken.

29th June (2022) Freycinet National Park, TAS, Australia

At 8:45 am I departed, accompanied by Sophie B Hawkins. I stopped at Four Mile Creek in a semi-official pull out. The road ran along the water. No sandy beach, just a small amount of vegetation, rocks, then water. The sun was making its way to the sky, leaving a distinct reflective pathway. It shone pure white. Not a hint of colour.

My next stop came fifteen minutes later, at a sandy beach. I stopped often to appreciate the gorgeous scenery. Following a sign into Lagoons Beach Conservation Area, I discovered a free campground. There were toilets, permission for dogs, and up to a twenty-eight-day stay. I continued planning a camping trip in my head.

Soon after 10:00 am I arrived in Bicheno where I filled the car at $2.15 per litre. Bicheno had walking trails I planned on taking. The first being the Whale Trail. The whole coastline was whale watching territory and it would be fantastic if I saw one. Off I marched with excited anticipation. To my delight, the walk contained sections traversing orange boulders, but no whales.

I drove to the second walk, beginning at the Bicheno Blowhole. People were playing at the blowhole's edge, so I did the walk. No one else was walking. The trail followed the coastline under tree canopies. Then opened out to ocean views and orange rocks. I explored quiet coves away from the noise of the blowhole visitors.

It took fifteen minutes each way, and the blowhole remained crowded. A lady sat with binoculars focused out to sea and I asked her if she'd seen any whales. One had been spotted in a town further north, so she was expecting a sighting. That clinched it for me. I returned to the car, put together a menagerie of leftovers to form an early lunch, retrieved my binoculars and headed back to one of the quiet coves for a private whale watching session.

It was twelve degrees, so wore a few layers to ward off the cold and sat leaning against a boulder, staring out to sea with my binoculars while finishing the dip and the Twisted Delight. I had brought my stellar African wildlife spotting binoculars, but no whales. I gave up on the overcrowded blowhole, continuing to my final destination of the day.

Freycinet National Park is the home of the famous Wineglass Bay and my home for the night. It was too early to check in, so headed straight to the Wineglass Bay Lookout walk. The walk to the bay itself contained one thousand steps down and up again, so I cut it off my list with a broken toe.

There were visitors everywhere. I joined the crowds heading up the hill. We walked through typical Australian bush with trees brandishing multicoloured trunks and wacky directions of growth. You'd get vistas of the sea, then turn a corner, disappearing into the bush. I stopped for breath catching, and photo taking. Uphill the whole way. Then came the steps. I met many people struggling, but everyone encouraged each other.

We made it to the lookout with Wineglass Bay spread before us. It is glorious. But I couldn't understand the connection with a wineglass. Someone had a better imagination than me. I later discovered the name has nothing to do with the shape, as I had expected. It refers to the colour the bay turned during whale slaughtering. I wish I didn't know that. I don't recall the information panels explaining that.

It took thirty-five minutes to reach the lookout. The same on the way down. Down is often quicker, but I struggled with my broken toe and old ankle injury. My ankle flairs up the more I use it. My left foot normally picked up the slack, but the broken toe removed that option. Breaking my toe two weeks before a walking holiday was the worst timing. I had to be careful, take purposeful steps, and go slow.

I'd pull over to let people pass. One couple asked if I was okay. I explained the toe and ankle issue and they offered to walk with me if I wanted. I appreciated the offer but said I would be okay, just slow. In the end, they stopped multiple times to take photos, meaning we spent most of the walk together, anyway. We chatted away, only parting when I veered left for the bathrooms and they went right to their car.

I did a few of the shorter walks nearby in Honeymoon Bay, being similar in shape to Wineglass Bay but smaller and less pristine. I had it to myself, though, which made it special. Sleepy Bay came next with a twenty-minute return walk to rocks for scrambling. The best view occurred in the first couple of minutes, the turquoise water meeting orange rocks.

The highlight of the walks was Cape Tourville, featuring a magnificent dark wood boardwalk meandering the cliff's edge, overlooking the vast Tasman Sea. Nothing in sight for a thousand kilometres until reaching New Zealand.

My diary on today's driving:

Some idiots on the road today driving down the middle of narrow roads, too fast on park roads, early in the day up my arse, almost making me crash. One point up the hill to the lighthouse, I thought the car didn't have enough momentum and was about to roll back down the hill. I should have had it serviced before coming. I'm worried it won't make it through the trip.

Oh dear. I didn't roll down the hill, thank goodness, and no accidents, but only thanks to my cautious driving.

I'd booked at a hotel inside the park, and received an unsolicited upgrade. The upgrade blew the staff member away. He said it was unheard of. I had no idea at this point. I'd booked the cheapest option and received an upgrade to the most expensive option, averaging $629 per night with a two-night minimum. What?

I'd been assigned a Pavillion which came with room service; free mini bar with wine and whisky; and hand delivered chocolates. He explained all this, but I couldn't comprehend what was coming. I found the carpark allocated to my room number and walked in to check it out.

Oh.

My.

Goodness.

On opening the solid front door, a glass passageway with a view of the water greeted me. To my right, I could see the bedroom, decorated in wood and black accents. The grey sheer curtains masking the view.

I realised this was something monumental, and I needed to capture it on video. I stepped outside to start again. Opening the door, I checked out the glass entrance area again, then opened the bedroom curtains to reveal the deck and water views. I opened the opposite door, expecting a bathroom. To my right, a sink sat beside a floor-to-ceiling window, showcasing a stupendous view. The shower also enjoyed this picturesque view. To the left, a hidden toilet.

The corridor continued opening to a lounge area with floor-to-ceiling windows, couches, rugs, light boxes, mini bar, snack bar and television. I had a lavish apartment. I was in complete shock, but glad I arrived early enough to enjoy it.

I unpacked the car and made myself a hot chocolate to enjoy on the deck. I layered up for the freezing temperature and had a second hot chocolate to help warm my hands and heat me from the inside. Once the sun started setting, I was not leaving. It surpassed all the previous sunsets. Watching from my private deck overlooking the water added to the atmosphere. The colours were in the burnt orange to red variations standing out in contrast to the black of my pavilion and water reflections.

At its peak, I heard knocking on the door. My hand delivered chocolates. I apologised if I had kept him waiting, saying I was on the deck watching the sunset. He stated he'd seen bits and pieces of it walking over. I invited him to the deck to watch, which he accepted. It was too exquisite not to share.

We started talking, and I admitted I received a free upgrade. He was in disbelief too. It obviously didn't happen often. I wonder how it happened to me? I imagined perhaps they'd found my website and hoping for a positive review, picturing this as my new lifestyle. However, reality suggested that was unlikely.

I opted for room service for dinner, allowing me to stay in the pavilion. Upon check in, they informed me breakfast could be delivered to my room, however, a more extensive breakfast selection would be available at the restaurant. No way I was leaving this phenomenal haven of opulence until one minute before check out.

I arrived at my room at 3:45 pm after driving 115 km and walking 16,174 steps. Dinner comprised a pulled pork burger with sweet potato fries and a sparkling raspberry lemonade from my free mini bar. I ate the free chocolates while watching two free movies; *Off The Rails,* which was funny; and *Miss Willoughby and the Bookshop*, which differed from my expectations.

I attempted to stargaze, but the clouds had rolled in.

30th June (2022) Swansea, TAS, Australia

I woke to find ants had discovered last night's plate. It never occurred to me ants would discover it. I did a spot of cleaning before making my morning tea.

I dressed in the hotel dressing gown and luxuriated in my surroundings. The sun shone through the windows as I drank my cup of the tea on the chaise. I took a photo using the timer setting; ten seconds being enough to pose relaxed on the couch.

My breakfast box arrived in a wooden crate comprising carafes of orange juice and milk; two pieces of toast; a bowl of cereal; two pieces of fruit; and a cheese and charcuterie plate. With too much food for one sitting, I took the leftovers with me.

I reluctantly packed the car, checking out right at 10:00 am. I warned the woman at reception about the lurking ants, suggesting she should send someone sooner rather than later to pick up the room service dishes. She seemed surprised but appreciative I'd let her know.

I headed to the Friendly Beaches where I found parking tricky, with multiple areas marked as camping sites. Eventually, I found a day carpark with bathrooms and parked there.

I strolled along the beach for more than an hour, soaking in the refreshing breeze and the soothing waves, and experiencing the tranquillity being near the water brings. People came and went, but the beach was expansive enough to share. No one stayed as long as me.

As leaving, one chilled wallaby sat with his tail between his legs leaning on it. I didn't know that was possible. I learnt kangaroos can't do it, only wallabies. My car didn't bother him, even when stopped opposite him to get a photo. He was too busy sunning himself to care about me. A couple of shier wallabies hid nearby.

I had a short commute to my next stop. The original plan had me heading to the Maria Island ferry, but it closes for one week a year for maintenance, and they chose this week. They had not announced the dates when doing my initial planning. I tried to book a second night at Freycinet but had sold out. I doubt the upgrade would have occurred if I'd booked two nights. Staying in the vicinity would allow more time at Freycinet should I need it. I didn't need it, creating a welcomed quiet day.

I arrived in nearby Swansea by 1:00 pm where I walked the Loontitetermair-relehoiner. Don't ask me about pronunciation. It's the local First Nations name. The walk has views over Great Oyster Bay with the Freycinet National Park in the distance. A delightful walk on the water's edge and over orange boulders. I basked in the sun while filling in time.

Such a perfect place to stay. They allocated me the end cabin, meaning I only had neighbours on one side. I closed the blinds, and they disappeared. I sat on the balcony overlooking the beach with a hot chocolate, heading inside under the heated rug as it grew colder.

I finished a book while eating the Anzac cookies I appropriated from my free mini bar before leaving the pavilion. Delicious. I needed a quiet day. My ankle needed rest. Perfect timing for an afternoon on the couch reading.

I ate the breakfast leftovers as lunch and a microwave macaroni cheese packet for dinner.

Being a slow day, I only walked 7,084 steps.

July

1st July (2022) Port Arthur, TAS, Australia

I had another lazy morning not leaving until check out at 10:00 am.
An eager cleaner arrived at 9:00 am whilst in my pyjamas having a cup of tea. Oops. The milk for my tea came from yesterday's breakfast, after surviving a few hours in a thermos. The upgrade kept on giving.

I found the croissant I'd bought and forgotten to eat a few days ago. I utilised the microwave to revive it back to edibility.

As I drove along the A3, I observed individuals pulling over in a roadside carpark by some sort of structure. Go me, I turned round and drove back to investigate. That's huge for me, turning round. I was proud of myself.

I discovered the Spiky Bridge built by convicts in the mid-nineteenth century. The parapet stones sat upright for an unknown reason, giving the impression of having spikes. A cute little roadside detour. The area housed a bigger walk taking in other convict era ruins, but I would have to save that for another visit.

Today was a weird day driving-wise and not because Bryan Adams accompanied me. I hadn't expected the abundance of dirt roads. Why are they on the map? It was my fault for wanting to follow the coast as often as possible. The views were spectacular. I wanted to find a realestate agent and buy a house.

A pit stop at Mayfield Beach produced the best bark falling off a eucalyptus tree yet. The sun spotlighted the branches, sporting shades of greens, browns, and yellows in swirling patterns. It was beautiful.

I drove the wonderfully named Pirates Bay Drive. Here you reach the Tasman National Park Lookout. Continuing on, you reached the Tessellated Pavement on Pirates Bay Beach. I loved this. Nature creates stunning landscapes without even trying. The precision grid pattern appears man made, but no, just Mother Nature decorating. I enjoyed walking across it, but the tide was rising. The waves crashed in, spreading out between the patterned cracks, making them slippery.

Further along, I arrived at the Officers' Quarters Museum, housed in an 1832 building constructed to accommodate officers. The compact museum provided valuable insights into the experiences of the prisoners, the officers and the officers' families. Exposed ceilings and walls unveiled the shifting positions of windows and doors throughout the years, as well as numerous layers of wallpapers reflecting various trends across the centuries.

A brief stroll from the Museum leads you to a canine sculpture on what they called the "dog line". They tethered ferocious dogs along the line to notify guards of convicts attempting to flee.

I visited a blowhole near Doo Town. You had to be patient, but I witnessed the blow. Other sites at this location included the Fossil Bay Lookout, and the Devils Kitchen and Tasman Arch formations, with Tasman Arch being the best.

> So many dirt roads today. One had a single entry over cattle grates and said "End 60 Zone". Then it became four wheel drive only so had to find an alternative. Amazing water views though. Some people's views from their houses AMAZING! Very jealous. Doo Town okay, but not exactly great. Devils Kitchen is not good. Couldn't really see.

Back on the A9, I drove to the Maingon Bay Lookout, hoping to visit Remarkable Cave. Google Maps told me my destination would be closed by my arrival. I wasn't sure what that meant seeing as an outdoor feature. Would I find a gate closing off the carpark? I continued on regardless, to find the site empty but open.

I jumped out, glimpsing the sunset before realising I needed to get to the cave before the light faded.

> Google said Maingon Lookout closed, but open, and sort of saw sunset and Remarkable Cave was in low tide, so could see it. Loved it. Big spray while water rolling in through the cave and then one splash almost getting me, then the movement of the rocks, the sound as the water was dragged back out to sea before the next wave. All to myself most of the time.

I stood for twenty minutes watching the dance between the rocks and the water, discovering a pattern. Knowing when a colossal blow was coming allowed me to stand back, so I didn't get wet. The power was intoxicating. The sound of rocks scraping against each other as the water receded was captivating. If I'd listened to Google Maps, I would've missed out.

My hotel in Port Arthur was closed. A note on the door explained restaurant and reception closed while undergoing renovations. This confused me as I had a booking. I rang the phone number given, but no one answered. I wandered around trying to find something or someone, but nothing. Another car pulled up, looked for the restaurant, then drove away. I needed somewhere to stay the night. Why did no one contact me?

Eventually, I spoke to the owner, who explained the hotel rooms remained in use. A key safe sat near each door. She gave me my room number and its code. To check out, I'd return the key to the safe and drive away.

I cooked two minute noodles in the microwave for dinner, then rushed off to a Ghost Tour at Port Arthur beginning at 7:00 pm. I turned the electric blanket on, but it hadn't warmed before leaving.

Port Arthur was the site of Australia's worst mass shooting in 1996. It led to strict gun controls, meaning it was the last mass shooting. I visited the site for the convict and early Australian history. Yes, this was a shameful part of Australia's history in how we treated the prisoners and the traditional landowners, but ignoring it won't change anything.

I liked the idea of starting in the dark, learning its secrets, then revealing itself in daylight. For selfish reasons, I volunteered to be a lantern holder—to see where I was going. They nominated me to bring up the rear of the group, which suited me, as I could linger longer everywhere we ventured.

The hauntingly beautifully lit church was the highlight, as was the open starry sky. I couldn't take my eyes off either of them. I'd be happy to pay again to experience the lit buildings and stars. Every time we stopped, I turned the lantern off and craned my neck to the sky. Magnificent. Millions and millions of twinkling stars with the full Milky Way. The longest ever shooting star sped across the entire sky. And yes, satellites were spotted.

An increase in step count taking 11,349.

2nd July (2022) Port Arthur Historical Site, TAS, Australia

I woke unrefreshed from a terrible night's sleep. I was so cold I turned on a second heater and added clothing layers in a fleece and socks. The electric blanket never warmed. Later, I watched the sunrise from bed with a cup of tea.

I arrived at the Port Arthur Historical Site at 8:52 am, but the sign said open at 9:00 am. The website stated 8:00 am. Other people arrived also expecting it to be open.

Being too cold to wait outside, I sat in the car for another ten minutes. I entered first and checked out the museum while waiting for my included introductory tour at 9:30 am.

You receive a playing card with an identity of a real inhabitant of the site. I received the ten of clubs. In the museum, you find out more information on your alter ego; John Thomas, aged 39 from Liverpool, England, sentenced to seven years' transportation to Australia for stealing a tablecloth and spoons in 1829. They sent John to Port Arthur after escaping his convict gang and attempted to stow away on a ship. He continued to get in trouble throughout his time at Port Arthur.

For the introductory tour, my brilliant guide was Tammy. She has four ancestors connected to Port Arthur, two on each side of the law, adding an extra layer to her storytelling.

Once let loose, I was determined to experience everything. The map had sites marked 1-33. However, the sites weren't in order. For example: 1 sat between 3 and 4; and 9 was between 10 and 11 to the back, and 3 and 2 to the front. That makes it hard to feel you've seen each site. I found a couple of back entrances before the front entrances and so forth. With back tracking and side-stepping, I visited each numbered site.

I enjoyed the Commandant's House. Having it to myself allowed me to do strange activities such as following the call bell system wire from the servant areas to the reception rooms. Inner workings are fascinating to me. It's unusual to visualise the full line connecting the button to the bell.

Ruined buildings are always fun. Your imagination can go wild. The internal floors of one ruin had long since fallen away. They placed beds on the second level, as though floating, giving you a sense of how it looked without recreating the space with modern construction.

The semaphore signals used to send messages intrigued me. Watch out for them to feature in a future novel.

I attempted to walk the Convict Water Supply Trail while eating lunch, being a pre-bought ham and cheese baguette from the site's cafe. The trail appeared to go forever, and unclear if I had to retrace my steps. Fearing I would run out of time, I turned around. Later, I discovered you came out the other side without walking back. I'll know for next time.

I continued to the asylum and separate prison. Both heartbreaking but important to explore to understand the conditions and treatment of the site's inhabitants. It's hard to imagine what it would have been like. How could they believe these conditions would lead to reform?

The church ruins were disappointing in the daylight. I did not linger.

In the memorial garden, I sat contemplating the terrible massacre that occurred there, paying my respects.

I was a frozen popsicle by now. It never warmed up enough to remove my hat or gloves. I headed to the cafe to buy a large hot chocolate to warm up.

I pre-booked a tour of the Isle of the Dead at 3:00 pm but received no instructions on how to join the tour. Every visitor had a boat cruise around the site and islands included in their entry fee. It ran every half hour. I figured out you catch the 3:00 pm boat tour and they announce when you get off to join the tour. The guide meets you once you are off the boat and on the island. I didn't appreciate the boat ride, as nervous I'd miss the tour.

A short but excellent tour, thus worth the angst. It wasn't what I expected, but being run by Tammy from the introductory tour, it was riveting. The Isle of the Dead is Port Arthur's cemetery. The convicts buried here only had headstones if their family paid for one. Their section is a mass of unmarked graves. The other half has gravestones and stories to match. With Tammy's interest in family history, she'd researched a few of the graves giving incredible real life details. The tour was genealogy from start to finish.

I left just before closing, heading to Hobart for the night. Another spectacular Tasmanian sunset followed me on the drive, changing from orange to pink, to lilac, to mauve, to purple. Stunning.

It was dark by the time I arrived as roadworks added detours. I turned the heater and the bed's electric blanket on and ordered room service dinner before unpacking the car. I arrived at 6:14 pm with roast pork delivered at 6:32 pm. Perfect.

I drove 102.8 km and walked 16,083 steps.

3rd July (2005) Seymour, VIC, Australia

Lottie, the Toyota Arkana, had undergone a transformation and now resembled a camper van. No permanent changes; everything was removable or returnable.

I lived in an apartment with one low undercover carpark. I had an everyday car in my Toyota Corolla, and my flatmate had her car. Lottie had to park on the street. An annoyed neighbour reported her as abandoned, and I had to explain to the council she was parked outside the premises at which she was registered.

"I can see that now," came the response.

They should have figured that out before sending a letter saying they would tow Lottie unless I removed her. Lottie received permission to stay.

Lottie was not an everyday driving car, so she didn't move often. When I did drive her, there was only one place to park her in the street, so I always parked there, making it seem she never moved. It was a short dead-end street with well-established trees. Lottie did not fit underneath most of the trees. And if I did not have her facing towards the exit, and everyone in the street was home, there was no way I could turn Lottie around. I'm sorry, but I refuse to reverse out onto a main road.

It was a substantial job to remove all but the rear row of seats. I lay on the road, underneath Lottie to undo the bolts. The seats now lived on my balcony under a tarp. I did this myself apart from one bolt I could not reach. My wonderful mechanic let me bring Lottie in before opening, where they put her on the hoist and used their pneumatic tools to undo the bolt in five seconds. Each bolt I unscrewed took much longer. I wished I'd ask for their assistance earlier. There was no charge. They were excited to see Lottie after hearing about her.

With the seats removed, the space in the back was amazing. It felt luxurious and oozed potential. I kept it simple to start with. Bubble bathmats covered the worn carpet. They were perfect. Easy to wash if dirty, and replace if ripped or too dirty to save. I carried a spare in case required.

The back row of seats now looked like a couch in a lounge room, but I used it as a base for a bed. By that I mean, I built up the space next to the seats to widen it even more than I did when driving Lottie home from Perth. There was no mattress from memory, but must have been old doonas and cushions, etcetera, to make it soft and even. Whatever I did, it was solid enough to sleep on. I have photos of the empty space but none of the interior set up.

Plastic drawers in stacks of threes were held in place by lashing straps and bungee cords. This formed my wardrobe.

Lottie came with a built in fridge stand. I did not have a fridge at this stage, but this formed my kitchen area with a portable gas stove and a stock of gas canisters. There was storage for cooking items, plates and cutlery. A well-stocked home on wheels.

I had a goodbye brunch with friends and now it was time to leave. Another 3000 km to drive, to Far North Queensland. I was nervous and excited. I had memories of Lottie and me driving across the Nullarbor. This time, I was more prepared. I was travelling in style and comfort. I had first-aid kits and tool kits; bungee cords and cable ties. What could go wrong?

Less than two hours later, it was over. The gear stick shook and stopped working. A sign for a services area appeared, and I exited the freeway. I had to decelerate without working through the gears. I eased off the pedals and navigated away from people and structures, making my way to the truck parking section. Somehow I limped the car along. I did not make it into a parking bay, straddling three. Lottie just stopped.

I jumped out, seeing I'd left a trail of fluid. Was it gearbox fluid? Could it be a quick fix? Plug the hole, fill her up and off I go?

I had RACV Roadside Assist, the highest cover available. The extended benefits kick in when over 100 km from home. My trip odometer read 101 km. I couldn't believe that.

I rang the RACV. They contacted a mechanic in Seymour, a few minutes further down the road. And I waited.

The tears flowed. I rang a friend in Cairns. She answered the call with such gusto that my tears lessened. Within a couple of minutes, I was giggling away.

The giggles confused her. "It sounds serious."

"It is, but if I don't laugh, I'm going to cry."

"Well, you continue to giggle away then."

Chatting helped pass the time.

> The trip is off. Gearbox gone. Lottie will be towed away. So much is going through my mind right now. Even thought of driving my little car up. Or get Lottie trucked up to Cairns and then get work done up there. [My Flatmate's] on her way to pick me up, but what about Lottie? Maybe I should stay in Seymour and sort it out. Though Melbourne would be easier, but how will I get her back up to Cairns? Oh, there's too much to think about. I don't know what to do... I feel my dream slipping away.

All my money will be gone once Lottie fixed. So what do I do? I trusted Lottie and she let me down… I've left all my jobs, spent my money… HELP!! What do I do to fix this?

[My friend from Cairns] just called. She gave me the right idea. I can get two tows and unlimited kilometres. [She researched my RACV benefits.] I wonder if I can get it towed to Cairns? Then I fly up to meet it? I can get a name of a gearbox specialist and get it taken straight to them. I need to pack, I think.

The mechanic loaded Lottie on the truck, and I went with them to Seymour. We talked about Cairns being my destination. The mechanic was excited by the prospect of RACV paying him to tow Lottie to Cairns and drive home again. Apparently, I could also have gone for the ride. The easiest road trip ever. I'd be a passenger and have my car at the end.

On this Sunday afternoon, two friends who had no plans received a call informing them of my situation and enquiring if they wanted to go on a road trip. It was great when three of my friends met me at the carpark. They gave me hugs and drove me home via the Seymour mechanic. Much better than RACV's offer of a taxi voucher and a night at a nearby hotel. I felt such a failure.

In the end, RACV agreed to cover the cost of getting Lottie to Cairns. Best insurance ever. It was going to cost around $1500. They informed me that was within my entitlements. The highest level of roadside assistance entitled me to $1650 worth of benefits a year. I paid around $150 for the year's membership. That's value for money.

I did not take up RACV's offer. Lottie stayed in Seymour, and I paid the mechanic to fix her gearbox there. I stayed in Melbourne while waiting.

4th July (2022) Hobart, TAS, Australia

I ordered breakfast requesting an 8:30 am delivery. By 8:00 am when getting into the shower, I heard a knock. I thought breakfast was early, so exited the shower. It was the next room's breakfast arriving, just sounding like my door. I recommenced my shower and assumed the next knock was breakfast, but no one was there. It was next door again. I knew they'd had breakfast.

"I think that's for me."

The server realised she'd knocked on the wrong door and gave me the tray.

I ate at the table with a view over the Derwent River while the sun shone into my room and a flock of ducks waddled along.

ABBA and I headed down the road at 9:45 am. It was a relocation day with mini road-side adventures planned. First stop was a bathroom break at 10:30 am at Hamilton. This was a council campsite with showers, toilet and laundry facilities by the Clyde River. I was noting the places you could camp for future use.

I stopped at the Tungatinah Power Station and read the information signs. It was the largest hydroelectric power station in Australia when built in the 1950s. The water pipes down the hills were massive.

Around midday, I discovered the monument marking the geographical centre of Tasmania. The sun was in the perfect spot to capture a photo of my shadow waving with the monument. That's easier than a selfie. I also snapped photos of excellent wombat poo specimens.

Thirty-minutes later, I entered Lake St Clair National Park. Along the entrance road, I took photos of road signs with echidnas and wombats to add to the collection. This was supposed to be a quick side stop. Google Maps didn't mention a visitor centre, boardwalks, and a lodge. I was getting up-and-down looks from serious walkers readying themselves for multi-day hikes. I'd planned a five-minute stop and was wearing a dress.

I walked to two viewpoints of the deepest freshwater lake in Australia and hopped back in the car.

My next stop was the Franklin-Gordon Wild Rivers National Park for a short walk to Frenchmans Gap suspension bridge. It was a simple walk on gravel paths that turned into boardwalks and over bridges to get to the goal. I had it to myself, which was convenient, as only one person was allowed on the bridge at a time. It is single step width and swings easily. A pleasant stream runs underneath you. I went across a few times taking videos and testing the swing capacity.

I had taken an umbrella on the walk but could not hold it, and my camera, and steady myself on the bridge. At one point, the umbrella was lying on the walkway and I was concerned it would fall into the stream, but it couldn't have, as no gaps in the railings. It was a fun cheeky side stop on the drive. People were arriving as I was leaving. I was glad I'd had it to myself.

Within half an hour, I was at the Nelson Falls Track. This is one of Tasmania's 60 Great Short Walks. You wander through rainforest on boardwalks for ten minutes, then greeted by a waterfall. It is narrow at the top and widens as it reaches the ground. Waterfalls are better in winter with increased water.

I discovered my next stop thanks to Google Maps–ruins of the Old Royal Hotel. It was difficult to find a place to pull over and I may have parked on private land. I later realised there was a street on the other side of the building off the highway.

It would have been a beautiful building in its day. It is now a burnt-out shell of a Victorian era hotel. I would have loved to explore the inside, but it is privately owned and considered unsafe, so I admired it from the outside only.

It rained on and off throughout the day as I climbed in altitude. By the time I got to the Iron Blow Lookout, the fog was so intense the view had disappeared, only white mist could be seen. I wondered if I was foolish to be driving in these conditions, but there was nowhere to turn around, so I continued. It makes for an eery atmosphere which is wonderful to experience, so no disappointment. Not the view I was expecting, but interesting all the same. I was glad to see one car coming down as I neared the top. I felt better knowing I wasn't the only silly one driving the foggy hill.

I snapped a photo at the metal Queenstown sign. The cutouts spelling Queenstown stood out more with the fog in the background. I thought it might look different when next passing.

I arrived in Strahan at 4:45 pm. It had been a long drive and scary the last couple of hours with the fog and winding roads. There weren't many cars which helped, and no dirt roads which I was grateful for.

I arrived early enough to enjoy a hot chocolate on my hotel balcony watching sunset over the water of Long Bay. Subtle colours in the clouds reflected in the water. Very peaceful.

I headed out early for dinner to discover everyone else had the same idea, creating an hour-and-a-half wait for a table by 6:00 pm. Being on my own, they offered me a bench across from the bar. It was still a wait for the food, but the steak and scrumptious garlic potatoes were worth it. I rolled myself home.

I drove 296 km and walked 6,758 steps.

5th July (2022) Strahan, TAS, Australia

I was so excited for today. It was the first activity I booked with the rest of the trip planned around today (and tomorrow). I arrived early for my train ride to take photos and see the engine turned. I watched the engine cross the turntable, but it didn't stop, instead continuing in reverse throughout the morning. Disappointing, but I knew other opportunities would arise.

While planning this trip, I watched a YouTube video a passenger made of their day on this train and by coincidence they allocated me the same seat. I knew it was a good seat. It was a double rather than a table for four and you faced out the back of the train, thus the best views possible.

I thought I'd have the double seat to myself but COVID restrictions had ended, so I had a seat mate. We got along fine. He probably found me annoying getting up and down out to the balcony, but he never commented.

I paid for the first-class carriage, which included food. We started off with a glass of champagne. Even though a non-drinker, I will accept free bubbly on a train. I should have gone for the orange juice option, but I finished the glass.

And we were off. Exciting! And food came. Our canape was "House baked dark rye crostini, citrus crème fraîche, radish, and Macquarie Harbour cold smoked salmon finished with Avruga caviar". There was not a lot for me to like, but I ate it and was edible.

The scenery changed as we trundled along the water, a small farm and onto rainforest. I was the first to head out on the balcony and I could have spent the entire journey there. I loved the fresh air and the uninterrupted view. There was a four person limit, meaning I reluctantly had to let others have a turn.

Before long, we were in the middle of nowhere with no signs of civilisation apart from the train and its tracks.

An hour into the trip, scones with cream and blackberry jam were served. Oh, I haven't mentioned the availability of unlimited hot chocolates. A slight shame we were last to be served our scones, as arrived at a station while eating. Knowing we would stop here on the return journey, we enjoyed our food and drinks before alighting.

We'd arrived at Lower Landing Station, where we could access the Teepookana State Forest. I left the walk for the return journey. I used the bathroom facilities, as there are none on the train, and took photos of railway workings. There will be trains involved in my future books, you can be sure of that.

With the train continuing, I utilised the balcony as often as the other travellers would allow. It became a running theme every time I came inside to let someone out, a bridge would come along. I love bridges and viaducts and so forth and I missed them over and over. The whole carriage was aware of the bridge situation by the end of the trip. I said many times, "It's not a bridge day." I have loads of photos of bits of bridges. All part of the adventure.

We arrived at our turnaround point, Dubbil Barril, at midday. I snuck a peek at the second class carriage while empty. With no tables, there were more seats. Snacks and drinks were available for purchase, as no food was included. The carriage itself was gorgeous, but first class, called the Wilderness carriage, was better.

They didn't utilise the turntable, but I spoke to the train conductor who gave me hints on where to stand for my journey tomorrow where she guaranteed me they'd turn the engine around.

I partook in the walk so I could save tomorrow for the turntable. The walkways meandered through rainforest and under trestle bridges. When taking a photo of a trestle bridge, someone remarked how I finally got a bridge shot. We spotted a pademelon in the brush. Very cute and inquisitive. I did not know what one was until this trip. The moss-covered trees and ground fascinated me and I loved the otherworldly look it created.

Back on the train, lunch awaited us. We had "caramelised sweet potato and Dutch carrot soup finished with basil pesto and micro herbs with ciabatta roll, Tasmanian Bush Dust and olive oil". Yum. It wasn't easy eating soup on a swaying train, but I enjoyed every mouthful. I was unsure about the Tasmanian dust, as under the impression it might be spicy, but it was delicious and no kick materialised during or after.

On the return journey, we had the locomotive in front of us. Gone was our panoramic view, but it was interesting seeing the engine driver and watching the couplings. I had no idea the plates of each carriage did not have to touch to be connected. When carriages come together, they match up the plates, but there are other connectors, meaning the plates don't remain touching. I spent more time on the balcony and noted the plates were twenty or more centimetres apart at times. That boggled my mind.

I was disappointed at missing the Iron Bridge on the outward journey, so determined not to miss it a second time. I had the balcony to myself and I stuck the camera out of the glass protection just enough to get a better angle, but no further than the widest part of the train, and I got my photo of THE bridge of the trip, the Iron Bridge, with the locomotive in the frame. Then switched to video as we crossed over. I couldn't have asked for more.

The Iron Bridge was built in 1899 and the only original bridge remaining. It was bought pre-built and shipped from London. It is the line's oldest, yet requires the least amount of maintenance. Our ancestors knew how to build things to last.

Once inside, I discovered a Christmas in July surprise of a mince pie and a Christmas cracker. I hadn't expected that.

The final touch was a pepperberry and gin chocolate truffle made exclusively for the train. It looked stunning. Being gold coloured, the chocolate glowed in the sun. It was almost too pretty to eat, but I ate it, and my seat companions too.

Then we rode into the station, adventure over. I was happy I'd booked the trip and worth the extra money to experience the included food. I was already looking forward to doing a similar ride the following day.

It was early afternoon and after sitting most of the day, I stretched my legs by seeing a waterfall near the station. Hogarth Falls was another of Tasmania's Great Short Walks—a forty-minute-return jaunt.

The boardwalk had a strip of fake grass in the middle. A novelty I appreciated. The falls were full, with white streaks cascading down the rock face. It was a good way to stretch my legs before driving to my next destination.

With yesterday's fog gone, I saw the scenery I'd missed. It was spectacular. I couldn't believe what the fog had hidden. I was so pleased to see it this time. Mountains, treetops and blue sky. Gorgeous.

I found the roads frightening today as Amiel and I drove round the winding roads. The cars from the other direction were not courteous, straddling both lanes around corners. It was terrifying seeing them coming at you. They didn't slow down. All I could do was slow down myself and be hyper vigilant.

I spent the night in Queenstown at the famous historic Empire Hotel. It was an old school Australian pub style hotel which you can't beat in a country town. It's famous for its National Trust listed staircase. They shipped Tasmanian Blackwood to England for carving, then it returned for installation. It has a multitude of angles with more than one entrance and multiple exits. I took the wrong exit every time and had to walk the long way round to my room's corridor. It was fun.

I attempted an early dinner downstairs in the pub, only to be thwarted by every person in town already seated. I ordered at the bar, got my table marker but couldn't find a table. The server was trying to work out what to do. There was another room she could open but hesitant to take that option.

One rowdy local made an offer, "If you're on your own, luv, you can join us."

The server ignored him finding another option. A table set for eight was split with a couple at each end. The server moved one of the extra middle seats, creating space on either side, allowing me to sit between the two couples. I was embarrassed. One couple looked at me like I was an alien, and how dare I sit at their table. The other couple were work colleagues, happy to have company. We chatted away throughout our meals, turning it into a lovely night.

They were a social worker and a lawyer from Launceston, specialising in elder abuse. I didn't know that was a speciality in its own right thus intrigued. They were each onto second careers, so add me being a nurse wanting to be a writer, and the conversation flowed. The lawyer asked me a pertinent question given that I want to write but yet published. He hit the issue on the head, asking, "Is it hard to call yourself a writer?"

When I'd earlier said, "I want to be a writer," a lump formed in my throat saying "writer" which would have created a pause in my speech. I answered his question by saying, "I'm sure you heard the hesitation in my voice when I was saying it." No one had asked that before, but I appreciated the insight.

During the conversation, I learnt the restaurant was busy because a movie crew was in town. I wonder who and what. I also learnt in the current weather it was best not to drive early in the morning. You were better off waiting for the ice to melt or be broken by the trucks. Good to know. I had been worrying about the drive to Cradle Mountain and the potential for snow and ice on the roads. Knowledge is power. I had no plans for morning drives, so it was sounding safe.

I had turned my bed's electric blanket on before heading to dinner, making it warm on my return. I love how it's the cheaper hotels, rather than the fancy ones, with electric blankets.

Only 42 km today and 8,730 steps.

6th July (2012) Nairobi, Kenya

The day started early, with a 2:40 am departure on an Emirates Airlines flight to Dubai, followed by a two-hour layover before arriving at 7:05 pm at Jomo Kenyatta International Airport, in Nairobi, twenty-four hours later. The date remained the 6th of July.

I exchanged money at the airport to pay for my taxi to the hotel, $30. I had brought American dollars cash as it is preferred by African countries over the Australian dollar. At this time, the American and Australian dollar were almost on par. 1000 Kenyan shillings (KSh) equalled US$12 and AUS$11.65. It is unusual to be so close but helps in understanding the true costs. You get used to dealing with exchange rates against the American dollar and forget the Australian cost is higher.

I booked an extra night at the departure hotel, with the tour starting the following evening. I had tonight and tomorrow day on my own.

I arrived at an upmarket hotel feeling out of place. 2012 was during my semi-penny-pinching phase of travel spending. I would not normally stay in a place such as The Fairview Hotel, but I lapped up the colonial-style building with its grand wooden staircase.

Once you made it through the hotel entrance boom gate, manned by armed guards, you entered a mini oasis away from the real Africa.

7th July (2012) Nairobi, Kenya

They hosted a buffet breakfast in a bright yellow semi-conservatory with a glass roof and a tropical garden running through the centre.

I arranged a taxi to take me to three locations on my must do list not included on the group tour.

First stop was the Sheldrick Elephant Orphanage. Such cuteness in enormous packages. The tiniest babies are hip height covered with red and blue blankets to keep them warm. They have wrinkly skin on their trunks, legs and body, but their ears are smooth. They arrived in a single file line with their individual handlers.

We watched them feeding. Wheelbarrows delivered the giant feeding bottles, holding litres rather than millilitres. I desperately wanted to bottle feed an elephant, but the opportunity never arose. I snapped loads of photos.

Next, at the Giraffe Centre, you walk along an elevated platform to even the playing field with the tall giraffes. You can hand feed them, which gives you a glimpse of their long tongues.

Last stop was Karen Blixen's house. Karen is the real-life person, and author, of *Out of Africa*. Meryl Streep played Karen in the 1985 film based on the book. I lived down the road from Karen Blixen's Danish house. So I had to visit her

African home. She'd built a stone house with a sprawling verandah to help keep the house cool in the African heat, surrounded by gardens.

My "Gorilla, Lakes and Game Parks" tour with the company Africa-In-Focus, had a welcome meeting this evening in the Lobby Bar. We sat on stools around a high bar that was a leap for short me. We met Brett, our tour guide, Will, our driver, and Ebron, our cook. The truck held a maximum of sixteen passengers, but we were ten. Three couples and four singles from America, Canada, UK and me from Australia. We did the usual business tasks of paying into the kitty, checking insurance documents, and discussing our morning departure and the rest of the trip.

Spending:
Taxi   6000 KSh
Elephant Centre   500 KSh
Giraffe Centre   700 KSh
Karen Blixen's   800 KSh
Bottle of water   300 KSh
Dinner at hotel   1250 KSh
Souvenir girafe   300 KSh.

8th July (2012) Kemba Camp, Kenya

Today was day one of fourteen. It started with the hotel's buffet breakfast, but today I ate with some of my fellow travellers.

Then we met Malaika. That is our big blue truck's name. It is NOT a bus. NEVER call it a bus. It is a truck. I scoured the internet for pictures, zooming in, looking at every detail. I wanted the truck to have every item and convenience I would have included had I prepared the vehicle myself. After all, I have read and studied Tom Sheppard's *Vehicle-dependent Expedition Guide* from front to back.

This trip was reconnaissance; spending two weeks with Africa-In-Focus on their trucks, and another two weeks with a different company, Acacia, to test their vehicle. I would choose the best company for a more extensive tour in two years. For me, it was all about the vehicle. I have experienced firsthand how the vehicle can influence your trip, as in Lucy from the 1998 Africa trip.

I can't remember how I became last on board, but I was. With the trip not full, we had enough seats for single travellers to have a double each. Being last, the only remaining double was the lefthand front seat. A couple from Canada had the righthand front seats.

The seating was comfortable coach style with reclinable seats and moveable arm rests. Windows ran the full length of both sides. In the front sat a television screen and two windows looking over the cab. There was no access to the cab, apart from a talking hole. The front windows couldn't be lower, or they'd look into the cab. They were too high for short me. But they let the sun through, heating the front seats more than the others. Only the side windows opened. Open windows allow air in, but most airflow goes to the back. The front seat was the worst place for temperature challenged me.

Leg space was like a commercial coach when looking at floor space. But each set of seats had their own foot lockers. This increased the distance between seats, or to the front wall. The front seat had less space, so being short helped there. I could sit with my legs stretched out in front. The tallest of the group, next to me, was too tall to stretch out his legs. But he was tall enough to see out the front windows. It was more spacious than Lucy the Land Rover, Lottie the Arkana, and any other tour truck I'd seen online.

This company did storage well. Each double seat had the full width foot locker with plenty of room for your daytime travelling comforts. Mine contained my day pack with water, reading materials, camera equipment, change of shoes and so on. A second lockable space sat inside designed for valuables, such as passports and cash. For your main luggage, there was an outside locker for each double seat.

We eased in to the trip with a three-hour drive to our campsite, Kembu Camp. While Ebron, our cook, set up lunch, we had a how-to-put-up-your-tent demonstration. The tents are larger than I expected, allowing plenty of space for two people and their belongings. And extra roomy for one with full standing height. The single travellers had their own tents. Each night, we helped each other until everyone's tents were set up.

After dinner, lightning appeared, providing an opportunity for our first photography lesson. The "in-focus" part of the tour company's name refers to photography. The tour guides are trained photographers and part of their job is to teach people how to use their cameras and take better photos in various settings. Tonight we discussed how to take photos of lightning. With only a point-and-shoot camera, I didn't partake in the lesson.

I brought two cameras as useful to have a spare if one breaks, and I wanted a camera with a bigger zoom. I loved my little point-and-shoot camera, which took quality photos and videos, and had a panoramic setting. My new, lower-quality camera featured the longest single-lens zoom available at the time without costing a fortune.

9th July (2012) Nakuru National Park, Kenya

We had an early start, but no tents to pack up because staying a second night. At 6:00 am we drove the short distance to Nakuru National Park, where we transferred into two smaller safari vehicles. Issues delayed our departure, but the local mischievous baboons provided entertainment while waiting. They rummaged through the rubbish with one finding a lollipop. There he sat, lollipop in hand, tongue out, licking away.

Our driver, Michael, was excellent at making sure we got the best wildlife sightings. After entering the gates, we drove along muddy roads framed by tall grass and birds atop the branches of scraggly trees and acacia trees in the distance.

We immediately spotted animals. Water buffalo first in varying states of mud coverings. One buffalo's head, from ear tips, to nose, to neck, was caked in mud, but clean everywhere else. What did he do, dip his head in the mud? The buffalo is one of the African Big Five ticked off.

More baboons, including the teeniest of the tiniest baby baboon you could imagine, were next. So small the branches camouflaged him while playing.

When we arrived at the famous flamingoes lake, only a small group remained. One name for a group of flamingoes is a flamboyance. I knew prior to the trip Nakuru was no longer the flamingo playground it had once been, but I'd hoped. There were some in the distance. I managed one blurry photo of a small flamboyance of flamingoes. Lake Nakuru's rising water levels were driving their departure. By 2013, there were none. They thought it to be permanent, but in 2020, the flamingoes returned.

Pelicans dominated the lake's edge instead. They were far away with swamp like conditions between the road and the bank, but thanks to my trusty zoom lens, I got great close ups of the pelicans.

We found the rhino known for hanging out near here. He grazed in the grass with hitch hiking birds on his back. That make's number two of the Big Five ticked off.

We saw the majestic Rothschild giraffes eating. It's a unique experience seeing them in their natural habitat as opposed to the Giraffe Centre in Nairobi. Their long, slender necks can reach the top branches the other animals can't. Their gangly legs and knobbly knees gave them a comedic edge.

Everyone is excited by pumbas. That's not what they are called, but that's what everyone calls them thanks to the *Lion King* movie's popularity. They are warthogs. But pumbas sounds better. They are one of my favourites. So ugly they're cute.

Rock hyraxes are sweet little bundles found playing in rocky areas. Imagine mixing a quokka and a guinea pig, and you have an inkling of what they look like. They dart between rocks, eating grass as they go.

In the distance, we saw a second rhino almost engulfed in birds whilst sitting. This rhino was a well known old fella with a predictable nap location.

Spotting zebras brings on smiles. Each zebra's stripes are unique, and they entertain you with their donkey like antics. It's obligatory to take animal butt photos on safari which we did of the zebras. Of course, a true "zebra-crossing" photo is a must. As in real zebras walking across a road. I only got one zebra crossing today. You need at least three in a row.

I wasn't expecting to see a leopard tortoise. This is one of the African Small Five list of animals. Not everyone knows there are two lists for animal sightings in Africa—the Big Five and the Small Five. We now had one ticked off from the Small Five list.

When we spotted a leopard, three cars jostled for the best position. The leopard appeared unfazed by the antics. He acted as if we weren't there. He strolled through the grass, a few centimetres taller than him, occasionally stopping to smell the flowers. His dark rounded spots stood out against the pale green straight grass. He stopped for a pee, and we moved on. Number three ticked off the list.

Excited chatter came over the radio, and our driver changed course. A lion had been spotted. We found him asleep in a tree. He had flopped himself over a solid branch, four limbs and tail dangling over the sides. He blended in well. Peaceful and relaxed. Not a care in the world for the sleepy kitty four metres above the ground.

Then the adventure level turned up a notch. They had spotted another lion in a tree. This tree had more vegetation, allowing animals to hide. Again, three trucks competed for a location. We didn't have a clear view through the foliage. Michael drove on to find a turning place to aid in positioning. He needed to drive off the road to achieve this. We almost got stuck, but Michael manoeuvred the vehicle out safely. Back at the tree at our new viewpoint, a second lion was visible.

Michael wanted to further improve our vantage point, driving off the road again, aiming to get closer to the second lion. Cameras are clicking furiously. The lioness wakes and is now watching our vehicle come towards her. The car slips and slides, taking us closer to the lioness.

In the back we are so enamoured by our view we're not noticing what's happening in the driver's seat. Michael realises he needs to get out. He puts the car in reverse and floors the accelerator. We in the back don't understand why he is taking away our brilliant view. We are yelling, "Stop."

The front seat passenger screams, "Go!"

We are about to become bogged underneath a lion who is staring at us.

The situation finally dawns on us and we stop taking photos and start willing the tyres to find grip. Michael gets us back on the road and we cheer with the unexpected adrenaline rushing through us. Number four ticked off the list.

Not all sightings are that exhilarating. We also saw waterbuck, impala, gazelle and eland.

Not being a bird watcher, I'll be inept at informing you about the many birds we saw. I know we saw lots of Egyptian ibises with long bright yellow beaks, heads red becoming white, orangey legs, and black tips on their wings.

Late in the afternoon, we had a break at the lodge. I enjoyed having a drink in the shade overlooking the pool and the national park. You looked over acacia forests with open grassland dotted between and the lake in the distance. I loved the acacia trees. A true symbol of Africa. A brilliant place to stay. Throw in a cabana and a palm tree and, bliss. I paid 150 Kenyan shillings (KSh) for a Sprite.

Michael did a brilliant job leading to a bountiful tip from us happy safari goers. I gave him 500 KSh.

Back at camp, we had a delicious roast lamb with vegetables for dinner, followed by an early night. Everyone was in bed by 9:30 pm. We ticked off four of the Big Five on our first safari.

10th July (2012) Eldoret, Kenya

It was a rainy day for transferring to our next camp in Eldoret. We crossed the equator, but the rain stopped people from hopping out for a photo. We would have other opportunities on our travels, so not deemed necessary.

Our camp site was part of a bigger complex with varying levels of accommodation, but we were the only group during our stay. You reached a communal bar/restaurant area by walking through a tunnel. Best entrance ever. At the end of the tunnel, you emerged into a cavernous area decked out in wood furnishing brandishing multiple areas in which to sit and enjoy. Streams ran through with bridges to cross and skylights let in light.

The rest of the day was free, with everyone hanging out here. You had drinks from the bar, conversations with our fellow travellers, and Brett helping people get to know their individual cameras, including me this time.

I booked this trip, deciding I would never find a house to buy, so might as well spend my money travelling. A week after I booked, I found my perfect house. I subsequently bought said house with the settlement less than two weeks after arriving home. I had to disappear to do house buying jobs.

Luckily, I had a Kindle e-reader. When I bought the Kindle, they were experimenting with internet capabilities, with my model being one of the first to have access and a built-in keyboard. It supposedly came with free and unlimited internet. Did that include Africa? I did what I needed to do and decided I would accept any consequences.

I never received a bill for any internet usage, and at times, my Kindle was the only device in our group getting a signal. I was impressed and grateful. There's nothing like organising an Australian house loan from a tent in Africa.

I spent 590 KSh on snacks, and another 50 KSh on a drink at our campsite's bar.

11th July (2012) Eldoret, Kenya

Today, our plans went awry. Not sure where the fault lay. Maybe a miscommunication between the tour company and the local tour operator? Or incompetent local guides? The itinerary offered a two-hour walk through forests to a waterfall. Sounds idyllic.

We were unaware of the two-hour drive to the start of the walk when they crammed us into a minivan. It was midday before we began walking. The hottest part of the day.

We planned for a two-hour forest walk, but walked open green hills. Where was the shaded forest? We walked through corn fields where I pictured scenes from the movie *Field of Dreams*. We passed stunning giant sunflowers bigger than our heads and scrambled over rocks and through streams.

We climbed in elevation. Some of us struggled with the altitude's extra strain. The rain from yesterday had given way to the blistering sun beating down. Covered in sweat, we were running out of water. Two hours had long since passed.

We'd started walking together, but now split into three groups. The fastest in front; myself and two others in the middle; and those who had given up.

The local guides were lost, asking for directions at a village. It was clear we weren't in the right location. We eventually came to a point where we saw the waterfall. Tall, skinny and not spectacular in any sense. We could walk to the waterfall, or sit and wait. I waited.

I had been shading myself with a thin waterproof rain jacket. I packed it in case of rain. It was not designed to keep one cool. It provided shelter to my skin from the sun's burning rays but exasperated the heat. Temperature, dehydration and elevation is not an ideal combination.

We found the van and crammed in for the return journey, exhausted. A storm brewed in the afternoon, so we hid in our tents, recuperating.

Ebron cooked fish for dinner, which I don't eat. He felt bad, but I was happy with bigger portions of rice and vegetables. From tonight onwards, if we had fish, Ebron made an extra dish just for me.

I collected the laundry I'd put in yesterday paying 200 KSh. A drink at the bar after dinner cost 50 KSh.

12th July (2012) Jinja, Uganda

Today we drove 250 km into Uganda. We had pre-bought our visas as instructed, creating a hitch-free border crossing.

Over the border, we stopped at an exchange to get Ugandan schillings (USh). I changed American dollars so if I mention costs it's referring to American dollars rather than Australian. 4880 USh equalled $2. For easy conversions I rounded it to 5000 USh being $2. But we didn't spend any money today. A bar tab was started at our campsite, Adrift Overland Camp, to be paid on the 14th of July.

Our campsite overlooks the White Nile River, a continuation of Egypt's Nile River. South of Khartoum in Sudan, it becomes known as the White Nile. There is also the Blue Nile in Ethiopia.

The camp ground hosts overlanders, and runs adrenaline activities including bungee jumping and whitewater rafting.

On arrival, we needed to set up fast to stake our claim before other groups arrived. We'd been informed an Intrepid group would arrive any minute with twenty or more young people onboard.

I discovered a couple of new tour companies here. One called Africa Travel Company, which appeared to cater to an older age group. Another was Drifters, an accommodated tour. This means they stay in campgrounds with non-camping options for sleeping. So no tents to put up. A tempting concept.

Most places we stayed had upgrade options, as in paying extra, to stay in a room. One of our passengers had already done this. This was his second tour, so he knew the drill. I don't think I knew we'd have that option prior to coming. But useful information for the longer trip.

13th July (2012) Jinja, Uganda

Whitewater rafting was on my to do list. I don't recall the term Bucket List being in common use in 2012. I associated the Nile River with Egypt, so I revelled in the novelty of being able to say I've whitewater rafted on the Nile. The Zambezi River, in Zambia, was the usual choice amongst African adventurers.

Our tour guide Brett joined as part of his birthday festivities. Prior to rafting, he did bungee jumping. He'd chosen adrenaline rushes for his celebrations.

Pretending to be a good redhead, I'd packed knee length board shorts and a rashie (a T-shirt style swim top). These items together formed the perfect outfit for rafting. I was the only one decked out in full swimwear. Most people wore shorts and T-shirts.

The eight of us, had our own boat. They decided our seats based on weight and height. The tallest guys in front, Keith and Will; the smallest girls in back, Val and myself; the second row, Brett and Julie; and the third row, Garrett and Karen.

We'd start slow. With a full day booked, we'd have four rapids before lunch and four afterwards, ranging from class three to five.

A couple of fun small rapids to start. I wasn't confident I knew what to do. I listen to instructions, but always forget them a few minutes later when I'm required to follow through on them. Being a strong swimmer, ending up in the water didn't worry me, just the falling out part if rocks nearby.

On the third rapid, our boat flipped, throwing everyone in the water. We suspect the raft leader can do this whenever he wants and does so for his amusement. At this point, I didn't care. I enjoyed being thrown into the water. I wanted more.

As we approached our fourth set of rapids, we discussed how to tackle it, being a class 5. I believe we could paddle around it if the group wanted to avoid the higher class rapid. They announced a high probability of falling out of the raft. I clarified if a rocky area, no, so we agreed to go for it.

This is how I remember it. We entered the rapid. It became rough and people started falling out. Something hits my face. Pow. Ow. I close my eyes for a second and when I reopen them, I can see water washing around me. I swayed with the swirling water without conscious control of my thoughts or actions. I hear, "Grab her," and someone grabs my arm. The water disappears, but the swaying in circles continues. I'm off with the water fairies.

Only four of the group remained in the boat, not including the raft leader; Keith from the front row, Julie from the second row, Garrett from the third row, and I from the back remained. We sat on the lefthand side. Garrett managed a full somersault from the third row to behind me. The rest floated around somewhere in the river.

Julie recognised I was not compos mentis and yelled, "Grab her!" Garrett grabbed me from behind. Our raft leader returned first, and we headed down the river to find the others.

Next came Val, an ENT surgeon. Julie put her to work, checking me out the moment she returned. In doctor mode, she checked my eye socket, tested how many fingers I counted and if I could follow her finger as she moved it from side to side. She concluded there were no broken bones, and having improved by this point, I passed the consciousness tests.

It was becoming obvious I'd come out of this adventure with a shiny left eye souvenir. At least it's a souvenir you don't have to dust.

I haven't mentioned this yet, but it was Friday the thirteenth. A stupid date to take risks. I honestly believe if I had not, by pure miracle, stayed in the boat, I could have died. I was out of it. If I'd been face down in the water, this story would have ended differently.

I elected to end my day at lunch. A headache from hell was brewing without access to any pain medication. I'd be scared and vote to avoid the rapids, which wouldn't be fair to the others. There was no point ruining the rest of their day.

With everyone gone, I sat alone, feeling miserable and full of self pity, wondering how my face looked. I had nothing with which to distract myself.

We bought the official photo package and split the cost. This is when we began to figure out what happened. It appeared Garrett kicked me during his somersault. We jokingly blamed Garrett. Then we decided an oar hit me, but unsure if mine or Garrett's.

The photos show the raft vertical, with my section submerged. As it flattens, the right side gets dunked. You can see everyone on the left except me. I must have slid across after Val slid forward. Once flat, Will is in the water, Brett is nowhere to be seen, Karen's head is in the water with her bottom in the air, Val is falling overboard from the second row and Garrett is starting to fling backwards. Keith and Julie, the only two in their original positions, are holding on for dear life.

I have a pained look on my face with my left eye closed. The end of my oar is sitting on my left shoulder with my arm twisted over it. Garrett and his oar are nowhere near me. It appears to be my oar that hit me. I think the swirling water I remember occurred when the right side of the boat became dunked while the raft tried to right itself. Our raft leader was nowhere in sight.

The next photo has me almost wiped out as covered by waves. Only Karen's feet are visible and Val is disappearing under the water. Garrett is next to me with his oar in his lap rather than near my face.

Then my oar moves down to my chest and Garrett's momentum has his legs moving in an upward direction. His legs get higher and he loses grip of his oar. We are practically touching hands while his oar moves up to my head and my oar down his arm. I'm contorting my face in agony. Garrett is smiling away, having the time of his life. Our raft leader is beside the boat. Keith and Julie remain in place, the others not even a toe in sight.

The last photo shows our raft leader climbing back in with Val next to him. Garrett's holding onto my arm and Keith has a worried look on his face in my direction.

The photos are amazing to have. They explain what happened. Kudos to the photographers. It's a day I will never forget. I got to tick two items off my Bucket List: whitewater rafting; and a black eye.

We made it back to camp in time for a yummy dinner of pork chops, and I called it an early night. My eye shined away.

The black eye, I mean rafting, cost US$125. I did laundry costing 20,000 USh.

14th July (2019) Warrnambool, VIC to Adelaide, SA, Australia

I was in bed by 6:30 pm after coming off night shift the previous night. Awake by 2:00 am, I got up at 3:00 am. I had breakfast, cups of tea, a shower, and packed to leave, departing at 5:30 am.

I stopped at a service station as one of my tyres looked flat-ish. When paying for petrol, I asked for tyre advice. I played dumb as had been a while since I'd put air in my tyres. He told me a general psi required saying if he wasn't alone he'd do it for me.

A man coming home from a night out drinking bought greasy hangover food from the service station. He offered to help me in exchange for a ride home. I needed the help but was reluctant to give a ride to a stranger. I held his fried dim sims as he checked the tyres. Only one needed air.

Then crunch time. He kept insisting he was a nice guy, and I'd be safe with him. Isn't that what a serial killer would say? He said he just wanted to sleep as soon as possible. I agreed and off we drove. Within five minutes, he said, "Pull over here. This is close enough." With no cars around, I stopped on the road. He hopped out, saying, "Thank you," and it was done. I was alive.

I utilised back roads to the Western Highway. It was pitch black for the first couple of hours. I stuffed up the route early on, making my planned route on Google Maps obsolete. With gaps in internet reception, my phone could not re-route. I sat at a four-way intersection, unsure of which way to drive. Everyone was asleep being a Sunday morning. I had to guess a direction and hope for the best. I went round in circles before finding my way.

Minor country roads rarely have marked road signs. And some are too small to be on the map. I stupidly trusted technology without a backup. To be fair, even if I had written directions, it's not guaranteed I would taken the correct roads given the lack of signage. I drove dirt tracks I'm not sure were roads. Was I on someone's farm by mistake? No street lights. No house lights. Only the car's headlights.

Dawn arriving brought relief and light. I found the highway and drove 600 km to Adelaide. I gained half an hour when crossing the South Australian border, which I appreciated.

A midday arrival gave me an hour before heading to the theatre. I wanted to see *The Book of Mormon* musical again but missed the Melbourne performances. I could have seen it during visits to London and New York, but the ticket prices were too expensive for a second viewing. So I turned it into a weekend road trip, buying tickets for the Adelaide run.

Warrnambool had been a detour but I love its craggy cliff walks, where you experience choppy water with grey, moody skies as a backdrop. I had a facial, manicure, and pedicure at the hotel spa. A relaxing long weekend to celebrate the end of six weeks of night shift. I split the driving, seeing as tiredness levels would be an unknown factor.

I'd made it to Adelaide, and a brilliant hotel apartment. It is convenient having a full kitchen, lounge area, and a bedroom. I imagined myself living in the one-bedroom apartment and planned the extra storage I would need to assess whether I could live in the apartment full-time.

I'd chosen this hotel for the apartments and the location. The theatre was within walking distance. No more driving or finding parking at the theatre. I enjoyed the exercise and fresh air after driving for seven hours.

I stayed awake throughout the show and made it back to my apartment with ease. I enjoyed the musical for a second time and was glad of my decision to travel to Adelaide via Warrnambool.

6:30 pm became bedtime, sleeping soundly until midnight, then on and off until 3:00 am. Once ready, I drove home to Melbourne. A short but sweet weekend away.

15th July (2012) Kampala, Uganda

We departed Jinja heading towards the Ugandan capital, Kampala. On our way, we visited Ngamba Island, a chimpanzee sanctuary with around forty residents. They were rescued from varying fates; from loss of habitat, to farming, and poachers.

On the boat to the island, we crossed the equator from the northern hemisphere to the southern hemisphere, but no sign marked the occasion.

The island is around 100 acres and the chimpanzees have free rein in 95 acres. Five acres have been given over to a visitor centre and human occupation. This area is fenced off by an electrical fence so the chimpanzees can't access it.

Four times a day, the rangers feed the chimpanzees and visitors can watch. They throw tomatoes, carrots, bananas and pineapple slices over the fence. The staff try to spread the food out, but it doesn't always land where they hoped. The chimps scavenge and hoard whatever they find. Some scampered into the bush to eat in private.

Occasionally, pieces would not make it over the fence. After being zapped by the electrified fence, the chimpanzees learnt to use a stick to entice the food onto their side. They understand a dry stick is better than a wet one. Smart.

As always, it's hard seeing them from behind a fence, but they have it pretty good here. It was brilliant watching them manoeuvre a carrot through the fence without being zapped.

We headed to camp, where an upgrade was suggested because of an early departure. I jumped at the chance paying 22,000 USh for a room.

Being in a city and near a local market, Ebron the cook gave everyone money to buy their own dinner. We walked together, seeing the hustle and bustle of an African market. Noise filled the air with motorbikes revving, dogs barking, kids laughing. It was reminiscent of my 1998 Africa trip, which I loved.

Will had recommended a meal involving an omelette and flatbread. Some of the group did not enjoy the experience and returned to the camp restaurant. I stuck with Will and tried his recommendation. Sally and I shared meat skewers as well. I had an iron stomach after my many African sojourns, so was not worried about after effects. And there were none.

During our drive in the morning, we stopped at a shop, spending 27,050 USh. My notes say "shopping". I do not know what I bought. I also spent 5000 USh for tea, and 2000 USh for a drink. My notes for this trip are useless.

16th July (2012) Lake Bunyonyi, Uganda

Leaving by 6:00 am, we stopped after an hour for breakfast at a crossing of the equator photo opportunity. We missed the first sign because of rain and the second had no sign. Finally, time for photographic evidence. Rather than one foot in north and one south, I took photos of myself with two feet on the equator.

We continued to drive throughout the day and used the onboard video. By vote we watched heart wrenching *The Constant Gardener,* followed by the comedic *The Gods Must Be Crazy*. They had to be African themed. I had never seen the latter movie and the click pop language of the tribe depicted fascinated me.

Eventually, we arrived at our destination of Lake Bunyonyi.

17th July (2003) In transit to Jamaica

Today's story started back on Saturday 28th June. I was a member of the Phoenix Netball Club, the precursor to the current Vixens Netball Club. I helped run the Cheer Squad and make the pre-match run through banners. This allowed me entry to the after match functions which players attended after their cool down routines. I got to know the players after being involved for a couple of years.

When Sharelle, as in netball legend Sharelle McMahon, greeted me with a hug and a kiss, I knew I was part of the netball family. We started chatting, and I confirmed I would not be travelling to the World Championships in Jamaica beginning on the 10th of July. The look on her face showed utter disappointment. And I have a witness.

"Oooh, but you're our good luck charm."

Oh, my god! She said it was because of me they win by one goal. I said, "Oh I'm so sorry. If it was anywhere else, I'd go."

We discussed who else might go, discovering no one was going. How could I not go now? If Australia lost, it would be my fault, and I was not willing to take that risk. So I started organising flights, accommodation, tickets to the games, and asked for time off from my two jobs.

Once people heard I may go, one of the club's committee members, Barry, said he'd join me. I believe his wife said he couldn't let me go alone. If I went, he had go, too. Whatever the motivation, it would be nice to have a companion.

My initial flight searches brought up figures over $4000. That's expensive now, but back in 2003, it was extortion. I scribbled my research in my regular diary, so I have the details. The different routes were fascinating. Some had flights via Japan, or London, or New York. I even researched trains and buses from Los Angeles (LA) to Miami as a way of decreasing costs.

> 1st July 3:35 pm. I'm in shock at the quote I got. I can't not go at about $2500. That's so cheap... I just can't believe I am taking this seriously. How amazing just to be able to fly to Jamaica at a week's notice. I love my life... What the hell? Why not go? I've got nothing to lose.

I can't believe I considered $2500 cheap. Everything's relative. After starting with $4000, $2500 was cheap.

> 3rd July 10:10 am. Well, I'm going. The LA to Kingston is booked and paid for, and the hotel reserved and I'm just waiting for Elisha at Bestflights to ring me back so I can book here to LA...

> 1:45 pm. I'm going. All booked and reserved. No stopping me now. I can't wait... So it's cost a little bit more but will be worth it

if all comes off. So flight and accommodation will be about $3500 and now only one night in LA which will be cheaper as well. I don't even have to leave the airport on the way. All the way through.

Actual cost from Melbourne to Los Angeles, $2833, and Los Angeles to Kingston, Jamaica, $805—totalling $3638 on flights alone.

To cut costs, I bought two milk-runs, meaning multiple stops to reach your destination. It was over twenty-eight hours to Los Angeles, double what it should take. My flight plan:

Melbourne to Sydney	8:30 am to 9:50 am	Qantas
Sydney to Taipei	11:30 am to 6:30 pm	China Airlines
Taipei to Los Angeles	10:40 pm to 8:05 pm	China Airlines

8:10 pm Taiwan time. I am so tired right now. My eyes are already blood shot and I've still got a 12 hour flight plus three more in another 9 hours! I don't know what goes through my head sometimes. You never remember these bits. All I'll remember is the time spent at the netball.

Wrong. I remember being thirsty and wandering around Taipei Airport, zombified, with the shop's shutters rolled down. You don't expect that. I had a four-hour layover with nothing to eat or drink.

10:30 pm. Los Angeles time. Can't believe it is still the 17th July. It's been a very long day! I'm a bit revived now, though. I did pretty well sleep-wise on the last flight. I slept on and off for 9 hours. Not bad. I didn't look at my watch the whole time, so not awake for long each time I woke. I've just had a lovely cup of tea. Free. I bought a bagel at Starbucks and asked for a cup of hot water and no problem. I want another one but feel weird asking just for hot water. They had chocolate brownies but could do without eating that. I'm sure I'll enjoy it, but I don't need it...

Can't wait for a shower! I stink, or at least feel like I do. I feel grotty. I had a full strip down in the bathroom here but put same clothes back on so it didn't really make me feel refreshed...

I need to brush my teeth and get another cup of tea, I think. My teeth are gross!

18th July (2003) In transit to Jamaica

Continuing my milk-run journey from Melbourne to Kingston, Jamaica, with a further three flights today. My American Airlines itinerary:

Los Angeles to Dallas	12:25 am to 5:20 am
Dallas to Miami	6:10 am to 9:51 am
Miami to Kingston	11:00 am to 11:47 am

7:30 am Miami Time. Flying is disgraceful these days. I can't even **buy** headsets today on this flight as they only had two to sell! Now they are out of blankets for someone up ahead. On a 3-hour flight from LA to Dallas, all we got was 2 drinks and a packet of pretzels. I was starving. Not even any tv screens. This flight has screens, but I don't think they'll be used. The movies on the long-haul flights are three years old; *X-Men* and *Down with Love*. And they are the same on both flights, in both directions. Unbelievable. Flying used to be a pleasure. Not so anymore. I hope it picks up in the future. It's not a way to attract customers. That's for sure. Though, every flight I have been on has been full or only a couple of seats free. They always make it sound like the planes are flying empty. What an epic journey, though. Up to flight 5. One more after this.

It was comforting to see my bag be loaded on this plane. I arrived at my window seat just in time to watch it go on the conveyor belt up into the cargo hold. So at least it's made it this far. I've been travelling for 37.5 hours straight. I think this will be my longest ever. In total, it will be 42 hours. Mind-boggling. But I'll survive it. I have so far and only 5 more hours to go.

In this entry, I'm referring to the changes after 9/11. I had no concept of individual seatback screens with thousands of movie and television options to choose from back then. I'd never heard of noise cancelling headphones, let alone know I would own a pair. Airport lounge access never crossed my mind. I thought travel standards had gone downhill, but over time they bounced back better. Now we have post-COVID changes.

I was nervous about arriving in Kingston. Flying is easy. After flying is when travelling gets complicated. I secretly hoped Barry would meet me at the airport.

Otherwise, how would we find each other? Of course, he wasn't at the airport, so I caught a taxi to my hotel.

To my delight, Barry met me at my hotel, arriving while I was waiting to check in. Perfect timing. We had lunch together and Barry insisted on paying. The weather was not as bad as I had been expecting, heat and humidity-wise, but Barry said it was the coolest day since he'd arrived. I hoped it would stay cool over the next few days.

The World Championships had reached the quarterfinals. I had tickets for the afternoon matches. Barry invited me to travel to the stadium with him. He was travelling on the Australian Team's bus, thus he introduced me to the entire Australian Netball Team. Annoyingly, he introduced me as Frances, but better than not being introduced. Sharelle knows me as Fran. The coach, Jill McIntosh, seemed to recognise me, which I loved. Sharelle was friendly, but cooler than I had expected when she first saw me. Maybe I should not have come. Sharelle said, "So you came after all."

"Yeah. You never know what I'll do."

Barry organised for me to catch the official team bus to and from the venue for every game, which was brilliant. It allowed me to become one of the support crew, helping to carry their gear and really be involved. Though, I felt like an imposter.

Empty stadium seats allowed Barry and me to sit together, despite our different ticketed seats. I assumed the stadium would be full for the grand final. Sharelle was being rested for later games, so not taking the court today. There had been some physical games in the competition highlighting the different styles of play from around the world. One poor Australian player had come off after being poked in both eyes and seeing double.

I was shy in the cheering department but I will pick up my game by the grand final. I didn't take any photos or take my Aussie flag to this match. It has "Go Sharelle" on it from the 2002 Commonwealth Games in Manchester. I have added "Go Aussies" for this competition. Ideally, I'd get the team to sign it, but

I'm very shy about such things. Strangers do it all the time. I'm not a stranger, but I'm not one of them. I'm something in the middle which can be hard to navigate.

I had room service for dinner costing US$13. We know I hate eating at restaurants by myself. I'm not sure what Barry and the team did, but the streets of Kingston weren't safe after dark.

19th July (2012) Ruhengeri, Rwanda

Ruhengeri in Rwanda, is a staging town for gorilla trekking. We stayed at a Catholic retreat with Julie and I sharing an upgrade to a bedroom. It was nice to sleep in a bed. We had two single beds, each with a mosquito net. Every day the nets were re-wound. Julie and I loved undoing them, watching as they untwirled.

Everyone except Sally and I went on their gorilla trek. Sally and I booked last, meaning the permits were exhausted. We'd head out tomorrow.

I had noticed a hairdresser in town and, with another two weeks in Africa, I wanted my hair braided. Washing your hair is always annoying when camping. I loved the idea of not having to worry about cold water showers or dirty hair.

I encountered language barriers when explaining what I wanted. They brought out large-scale books filled with pictures of varying braid styles. I had no clue what to pick. In the end, I pointed at a picture I thought was what I expected. They questioned my choice. I nodded and hopped into a chair.

I experienced a fascinating glimpse into local women's lives. Women and children came and went. I hadn't expected it to take so long. I hadn't expected hair extensions, but they came out and were added. Maybe it was specific to the picture I chose? I will never know. The salon could have been anywhere in the world. A safe place for women to meet and socialise. I believe I became a novelty as the word got out. People wanted to see the white woman getting African braids.

They had big tubs of a greasy/wax type substance which seemed to be required to aid brushing the women's hair. I saw it being used multiple times by the women in the salon and sold in tubs to women visiting the shop.

I received smiles and nods of acknowledgement from many women and children over my four-hour hair braiding marathon. Lucky I didn't leave it any later in the day. I expected it to take a while, but not four hours. A unique experience I am glad I had. It cost me 20,000 Rwandan francs or around US$33. That's so cheap compared to what it would cost back home.

I returned to camp with my new hair. Ebron was the first to see it. He made me spin round. I wasn't sure I'd done the right thing, but too late.

Not long after, the others returned from the gorillas wearing smiles and chatting in excited voices. They'd had a fantastic day. Sally and I were jealous of what they'd experienced, hoping we would have the same good fortune. We spent the rest of the day hearing gorilla stories and talking about my hair.

The braids became tighter and tighter. I felt a headache coming on and wandered if the braids were too tight. For a short time, I considered taking them out because I hated how tight my head felt. I tried to semi loosen the braids pulling them out of their tightness towards my scalp, but it didn't have any effect that first night. I trusted I'd get used to the sensation, and they'd loosen as the days went on. They remained in throughout the rest of this African trip.

20th July (2012) Ruhengeri, Rwanda

We left at 6:15 am heading for the Volcanoes National Park. With daily quotas, each group contained only ten people. Provided entertainment involved dancing to drums by traditionally clothed locals while we waited.

They assigned Sally and me to a group. As a group, we decided on the level of trek we wanted. We were a mix of ages. No one wanted too easy or too hard, so we chose a medium trek. They told us there was a gorilla group a twenty-minute walk away. Perfect.

I am embarrassed to admit I've lost both the T-shirt and the certificate I received, naming our gorilla group.

I began packing the house for a renovation that never happened in 2020 and brutally discarded items. The certificate may have been a victim of this cleanup. I didn't know I'd be writing this book.

The T-shirt may have been a victim of the hitchhikers I brought back from Peru in 2018. I threw out a lot of clothing in the aftermath. Or it may be in one of the quarantine boxes, as yet unopened. I may find it, but for now it is lost.

So I've lost the name of the gorilla family I visited. I may never remember. That's how life goes sometimes. A stark reminder of how you need to write better notes/diaries of your travels. You will not remember details.

Remember Gilligan's "three-hour tour"? Well, that was our twenty-minute trek. It became two hours of climbing through dense forest with the leader using a machete to cut out our route. It was torture. I was unprepared.

I had bought new shoes as had nothing appropriate. I had not worn them yet on the trip and silly me did not wear them in beforehand. Buying them on the cheap, they did not fit well. Not an issue if on flat ground, but we climbed up and down for two hours on uneven terrain. The shoes were too big, containing extra space in which my foot could move around, particularly my left foot, which has always been close to a shoe size smaller. I slipped and slid because of the damp conditions of the ground, but my feet would continue to slip forward inside my shoe. The strange motion, made me extra cautious and scared. I lagged behind.

Before we started, I'd been undecided whether I'd pay a porter to carry my bag during the hike. It cost US$20. When I heard it was only a twenty-minute walk, I thought it a waste of money given my penny-pinching ways. Big mistake.

I gave in after an hour, asking Sally if I could share her porter. What I had not considered was that the porter could assist you with a hand to hold when needed. Absolutely worth $20 given how our trek turned out. With my bag being carried by a porter, and the tour leader taking my hand to aid the trek, I was in front of the pack rather than bringing up the rear. I watched the leader wield the machete in the dense scrub to make our way. It was like being in the *Romancing the Stone* movie with Michael Douglas. He moved fast, dragging me along, my feet slipping. It was an awful sensation which appeared would never end. We also had the altitude factor to deal with.

One piece of advice I followed was to bring light gloves so you could extend your hand whenever necessary, touching anything without apprehension. Excellent advice. There were stinging nettles, and other dangerous plants in the forest. I appreciated the gloves.

The gorilla group went for a walk, moving from their original location, and continued to move. Hence why we moved. I guess it was too much to ask that they stay put for a couple of hours for our visit.

At last, we were rewarded—our first sighting being a silverback sitting with his back to us. You are meant to keep a distance of seven metres, but when one appears beside you on the track, you can't help but be closer. We tried to stay as far back as we could as we passed. The guides were concerned about this gorilla being on his own, deciding he might be dangerous. We didn't linger. Our gorilla group remained ahead.

As we got near our own group, they had spread out. We saw a teenage gorilla playing with a stick and his feet. His feet and hands were incredibly human like.

We saw mother gorillas and their babies moving through the underbrush. We saw a lot of bottoms and backs. A large male, but not fully grown, sat scratching. He looked directly at us. A substantial silverback walked by. Huge and solid. Humans would come off second best in a confrontation.

The trackers carry guns, hopefully to scare rather than kill the gorillas.

Their faces are incredible up close. They have furry brows over small eyes. Their nostrils form the biggest feature on their face. The lips are a dark slit shaped like our own. They appear gentle and serene. You see emotion in their eyes. They are like us. We watched as they ate the surrounding plants.

Light rain was falling, but no one cared when you had gorillas before you.

We found the babies and they are cute, cheeky, little fluff-balls. I loved watching them play and joke around. They had a patient father/grandfather watching over them. The babies did not know the seven-metre rule and would often come quite close, curious about us. When they got too close, the large silverback would give a loud "humph", and they would move away.

In contrast to the bigger gorillas, the babies' eyes were bright and large. Why do oversized eyes create cute? The babies were making themselves dizzy, twirling and swinging around in circles. They proudly showed off their enormous bellies. I have a stack of blurry photos showing their antics.

We have a maximum of an hour to spend in the gorillas presence and, of course, everyone wants photos with them. We took time to ensure everyone got a photo before the gorillas moved again.

The first photo of me is hilarious. The gorilla is in the distance and I'm in close up mode wearing my light Space Camp rain coat and gloves. There's a "I'm not sure about this" look on my face, creating multiple chins. I'm looking off to the side. Then there's my black eye and braided hair. I love it!

I look more relaxed and the gorilla looks closer in the following photo, though I have someone's pink top on the edge ruining it. The third photo has a baby trying to join the picture, making the fourth the best.

There are many photos with my eyes in varying states of closure, highlighting my black eye. One shows my left eye bruised and swollen from brow to cheek bone.

Once the adult female gorillas arrived, the silverback rolled onto his tummy to be groomed. Then it was snuggle time with grandpa.

The silverback suddenly moved, making a couple of our group leap out of the way. With our hour of interaction time over, we didn't follow.

During the encounter, the trek became a distant memory, but the horror of it returned when told it was time to leave. I assumed we had to trek back to where we had come. Not a pleasant thought. Luckily, we were less than twenty minutes from where we could scramble over the park's stone fence and walk through open fields to the staging area.

What an encounter. Do not miss the chance to do this if you can. It is worth whatever it takes to experience these gentle human like hairy giants. It is not a cheap adventure. I was lucky buying my trekking permit for US$500 just before the price rose to $750. They now cost $1500. Ugandan gorilla permits can be cheaper.

I gave US$10 to Sally for the porter, 5000 Rwandan francs (Rf) to the leader and later 2000 Rf to the driver. As always, we exited through the gift area where American dollars was the preferred currency. I bought the now lost T-shirt and baby wooden gorillas for $30 at one stall; and a set of three wooden gorillas doing the monkey "see no evil, hear no evil, speak no evil" poses, and wooden spoons as a practical souvenir for $18 from a different stall.

21st July (1996) Copenhagen, Denmark

I had a lovely day playing tourist in Copenhagen with three friends. Our explorations began with a visit to the Danish Parliament housed in Christiansborg Palace. The site has held a castle since Bishop Absalon built his stronghold in 1167 to guard against marauding pirates.

The current building is the third incarnation of a castle, and had extensive reconstruction in the early 1900s after a fire gutted the inside in 1884. The new foundation stone, hewn from Absalon's original foundations, contained the King's monogram, the date, and three words signifying the highest authorities: the Crown, the Legislature, and the Judiciary.

During the rebuilding in 1906, they excavated earlier buildings and roofed them over for preservation. The public can view twenty-two areas representing the site's first few hundred years of history. I'm embarrassed to say I have no recollection of my visit here. I have the ticket stub, brochures, a photo of the outside, and that's it. It sounds perfect for me, though. I'll have to go back. I believe I would appreciate it more now.

From here, we crossed the water and walked to Rosenborg Palace. If you approach from the King's Garden side, Rosenborg gives the appearance of being surrounded by a moat. But only has water on three sides. It's an impressive Dutch Renaissance style building with a copper patina roof, built in 1633 as a summer palace for King Christian IV.

In 1710, the building of Fredericksberg Castle relegated Rosenborg to a storage facility for varying royal collections. It has acted as a museum for the public since 1838. You wander through history in over twenty rooms with names such as Christian IV's Writing Closet, and Frederik V's Room "The Rose", as well as The Stone Passage, The Long Hall, and the Old Regalia Room.

We treated ourselves to afternoon tea at Hotel D'Angleterre. A stunning five-star hotel at the end of the pedestrian street, Strøget, and overlooking Kongens Nytorv square. Each of us had passed this building multiple times, dreaming of being worthy to enter. The best we could do was splash out on afternoon tea.

We felt posh and grown-up. Paying by Visa added extra sophistication. This was my first bank card with Visa access, debit rather than credit, but it made me feel special. This was the card that landed me in hot water in Israel and Egypt six months later. Afternoon tea cost 232 Danish Kroner for the four of us.

We ventured to Christiania, an area in Copenhagen separated as a "free town" or commune. A group of squatters moved in back in 1971. It was not under Danish law allowing drugs to be freely available. Cannabis was accessible at every turn, but particularly along Pusher Street. This dumbfounded one girl; her mouth agape in disbelief. Over the years, the drugs dwindled. With Christiania now being subject to Danish law, drugs are illegal. Back in the 1990s, though, the drug availability was in full swing. They had a strict no photo policy to enable anyone to participate in whatever they wanted, without the fear of proof existing of their activities. We only observed.

22nd July (2012) Nairobi, Kenya

I had left my Africa-In-Focus travelling companions and flown from Kigali to Nairobi, arriving at 9:00 pm last night. I had prepaid an extra night of accommodation at the tour's starting hotel, Hotel Boulevard for AUS$151, and prepaid $30 for an airport transfer.

The Acacia trip had an 8:00 am starting time, so made sense to stay overnight beforehand. Not everyone did that, despite their arrival time. One couple slept on the couch in reception rather than pay for a bed and nearly missed the trip. They'd flown directly from Europe, arriving overnight. No one knew they were joining us. I remember seeing them when bringing my luggage downstairs. It wasn't until past our departure time, and two people short, that someone woke them to ask if booked on the tour. They were, so now we could start.

I arrived after the meeting held last night so I had to pay my US$1110 local payment covering our excursions to Masai Mara ($420); Serengeti and Ngorongoro Crater ($440); and Zanzibar ($160); as well as food and camping fees kitty ($90). I paid AUS$1126 before leaving home.

How we started is fuzzy in the memory. I have flashes of the group standing with the truck in front of the hotel, but we didn't travel in the truck until day four. My guess is we placed our main luggage in the truck and took a smaller bag for our excursion into the Masai Mara. We had three minivans with pop top roofs for when game driving. Each van carried six passengers.

We stopped at a shop where I spent $5 on snacks and a large five-litre bottle of water. From here we drove to the Masai Mara National Park. We stopped at the gate, taking the obligatory front gate photo before driving through to our accommodation for the night. The campsite was permanent, with camp beds under giant canvases. We split into boys and girls for the non-couples and had big group tents for our two-night stay.

Our car broke down along the way and required African style roadside mechanics before it restarted.

No official safari, but sightings are possible whenever driving through the park. We saw impala and zebras.

Jess and I went to bed early, having booked a sunrise hot-air balloon ride.

23rd July (1999) Woodstock 99, Rome, New York (NY), USA

Four nannies working in New York and New Jersey hired a car and drove to the Woodstock 99 music festival. It was being held in the upstate New York town of Rome at the former Griffiss Air Force Base, 160 km from where the original Woodstock took place 30 years previously. Over 220,000 people attended. This made the town of Rome the third-biggest city in New York State for the weekend. A twelve-foot fence surrounded the site to avoid gate crashers.

We booked in May. The tickets cost US$150 plus a facility charge of $7, a convenience charge of $10 and a handling charge of $3, adding to $170; more than a week's wages! I wanted to go for the experience. I'd only been to a handful of live concerts, but I wasn't missing out on Woodstock.

The number of attendees created a traffic jam. With twenty or thirty kilometres to go, we came to a standstill. Everyone got out of their cars, talking and laughing. It took hours rather than minutes to clear.

After parking, we had a long walk to the newly formed tent city. Our first task was to figure out putting up our tent. We'd bought it for the festival costing US$15 each.

Woodstock had two main stages, four kilometres apart, and other smaller venues. We chose one stage and camped out there each day.

We did not make the start of the lineup, which began at 1:15 pm. We started with Jamiroquai playing from 2:45 to 3:45 pm. Someone, not me, drew face symbols on the program I have. They express our assessment of the performers. Jamiroquai gets a slanted mouth, so I'm assuming they didn't impress us.

The afternoon's assessments: Live, with two happy faces; Sheryl Crow with one smiley face; DMX with a sad face; The Offspring got two smiley faces, one with eyebrows; Korn received two frowns; and Bush a smiley face with eyebrows.

The Offspring became my favourite performance. I didn't know any of their music, but the crowd's atmosphere was electric and phenomenal. Everyone enjoyed the music, and the company having a good time. The band and their crew actively engaged with the crowd. Being day one, everyone behaved having good, clean fun.

Early in the set, people at the back started throwing their empty water bottles forwards and those of us in the middle would throw them towards the stage. Hundreds of bottles flew through the air. You had to look away from the stage to see if bottles were coming your way. One hit me on the head. If empty, it was fine and done in good natured fun. The band enjoyed it too. On the screen, you could see the bottles hurtling onto the stage and it being littered with bottles.

Photos from the first day show us wearing big smiles, clean and sunburnt free, in a green grass backdrop.

24th July (1999) Woodstock 99, Rome, NY, USA

The heat was becoming an issue. It hovered around 38 degrees every day with no shade. As usual, being a terrible redhead, I didn't pack a hat. I was not the only one. Sunburnt people were everywhere. I had inadvertently packed dark clothing, which isn't ideal in the sun. I bought a lighter coloured souvenir T-shirt. One size fits all, which of course fits no one. It lives in my pyjamas drawer.

Having enough water to drink became an issue with constant lines for the water fountains. To mitigate the wait, people broke the pipes allowing more people access to water, creating a mud bath which people played in.

The toilets had no running water. It was my first exposure to hand sanitiser, labelled as "waterless hand cleaner". I did not trust it, and my hands didn't feel clean after using it. I'd take my water and wash my hands with that instead.

There were not enough toilet facilities for the number of attendees and they soon became blocked and overflowed. The overflow looked like mud created by the water fountains, so people started playing in it, unaware they were covering themselves in human waste, not mud. I avoided all the mud types, thankfully.

People began running out of supplies, walking around with signs saying what they needed. Some mentioned food, water, or money, but others looked for drugs, either in general or specific, with their desires.

We camped out at the East Stage. The day started with Tragically Hip at midday. They got a diagonal smile as an assessment, but the faces end after their performance. The East Stage continued with Kid Rock, Wyclef Jean, the Counting Crows, Dave Matthews, Alanis Morrisette, and Limp Bizkit.

During Kid Rock's session, he told people to throw water bottles onto the stage. Which people did, but you can't force atmosphere into the crowd. It failed taking a turn, as idiots started throwing bottles containing liquid which hurt. I don't want to know what liquid they happily threw away. It's fun until people get hurt. They landed near us, but we didn't throw them forward this time. It was not the same as with The Offspring.

Alanis Morrisette created a relaxed vibe. The crowd spread out picnic style, with towels making good blankets, seeing as the showers were useless.

Transitioning to Limp Bizkit was jarring. We had been sitting comfortably, enjoying the chill, when a different crowd took over. The crowd numbers swelled, forcing us to stand. None of us knew the songs. We stood like strangers stranded in a sea of anger. The male centric, drug fuelled crowd, jumping, and pushing forward shouting, "kill, kill, kill", repeatedly was frightening. None of us liked the mood. The light moved from day to twilight to night, adding extra doom to the atmosphere. We ended the night here, skipping the last acts being Rage Against the Machine and Metallica.

Limp Bizkit sparked a riot in the crowd, but not near us. The organisers blamed the band overall for the crowd's deteriorating behaviour. Management instructed the band to ask the crowd to mellow out as people started getting hurt, but the lead singer only further incited the crowd's misbehaviour instead.

In contrast, the lead singer from The Offspring the previous day told the guys not to molest the crowd surfing girls during his performance, based on what he could see occurring in front of him. What a difference the performers can make.

By today, photos are showing redder faces and arms with messy hair. More attendees in the background are topless. Rubbish covers the fading grass.

25th July (1999) Woodstock 99, Rome, NY, USA

The last day of the festival. Today's East Stage line up included Al Green, Willie Nelson, Brian Setzer, Everest, Elvis Costello, Jewel, Creed and the Red Hot Chili Peppers.

I'm obligated to say Jewel was my favourite, seeing as I was an EDA, which stands for Every Day Angel, the name used by official Jewel fans. Car pools full of EDAs headed to Woodstock. I arranged for a friend, who was too late to join our car, a ride in one of those car pools, so she didn't miss out. I have never met an unfriendly EDA, so I knew she'd be looked after.

Being a fan, I had been looking forward to seeing Jewel's performance. I am pleased to say the audience was respectful, well behaved and loving, compared to earlier sets. Signage in the crowd read "Marry Me", and "I love you Jewel". Two of our group moved closer compared with our normal position of halfway back. I appreciated being in the thick of a respectful crowd. Being that close during some of yesterday's performances would have been frightening.

With the temperature remaining at the thirty-eight degrees celsius mark, we welcomed the light showers and reprieve from the sun's harsh rays when the clouds rolled in during Jewel's set. Jewel put her hat on, saying, "I don't mind the rain."

Three days of intense trampling and heat had turned the once green grass into barren dirt. Though the ground was barely visible through the debris. The field would take time to recover.

We left before the end of the festival, after Jewel's set. Work beckoned in the morning, and had a five-hour drive home. We left content with our weekend experience.

After we left, the promoters handed out candles leading to multiple fires breaking out during the Red Hot Chilli Peppers set. The crowd was out of control, needing the riot squad to contain them. Friends and families had seen footage on the news and were worried. We were blissfully unaware while driving home. Without mobile phones or internet access, we didn't discover what had happened until we woke the next morning. The festival became more notorious for the crowd behaviour than the performances or overall experience. That was a shame.

The final tally of horror included three deaths, twelve hundred medical tent visits, forty-four arrests, at least five rapes, and multiple other sexual assault reports. HBO revisited the controversial weekend in a 2021 documentary called *Woodstock 99: Peace, Love, and Rage*. It is worth watching. I can't believe I was there.

I am glad our group avoided the trouble and have memories of a music and entertainment filled weekend away in upstate New York. I'm sorry not everyone can say the same.

I have no recollections of what we ate, but we must have brought food with us. I found a note with "Woodstock Spending" written on the top. It mentions a $4 pizza, $4 ice cream, $4 frozen stuff (a slushie?), and two $4 drinks. Four was someone's favourite number. The souvenir T-shirt cost $20. Car hire cost $62 plus $10 in petrol. Whatever the total cost, the experience was priceless.

26th July (2012) Serengeti National Park, Tanzania

We started with a briefing from our Safari HQ tour guides, who'd take us to the Serengeti and Ngorongoro Crater for three days and two nights. We had four vehicles, including a kitchen supply car. The staff did the chores in this section, including putting up our tents.

There's a photo of me listening. I'm clasping the pillow I bought yesterday and in which I have tucked my small pillow into the pillowcase. It looks fat and lumpy the way I am holding it, but I am sure I appreciated it at bedtime. I see my refilled five-litre water bottle.

We split off into smaller groups. Ours ended up being four Europeans, a couple and two guys; and two Aussies in Jess and myself. We had a friendly group, and I enjoyed our little crew more than when in the wider group.

Duncan, our Acacia guide, sat in the front seat, the boys in the first row, Jess and I in the middle, and the couple in the back row. I turned towards the back often, talking to the Danish girl. She grew up in the Copenhagen suburb next to the one in which I lived back in 1995 to 1996. That gave us a topic to talk about and bond over, which I appreciated.

We had individual comfy seats with moveable armrests. Luxurious and spacious. The roof could be raised when we reached animal viewing locations. Large windows sat to the sides and the front. Long-wheel-based Toyota LandCruisers are perfect safari vehicles.

The weather turned as we drove. A cloudy mist descended, making for an eerily exceptional experience seeing the contorting tree branches silhouetted through the clouds. It created an apocalyptic-like scene, which I loved. I took many photos trying to capture the atmosphere. It frightened one of the group.

We ate our provided packed lunch in the car with the eery mist surrounding us. Later, the trees gave way to vast scenes of open plains.

We made it to the gate of Serengeti National Park with the obligatory photo taken. Our first animal sighting happened at the gate, being a blue legged gecko. Bird watchers, I apologise. There was a beautiful yellow bellied bird with blue chest and head. He was perched by pink cactus flowers, creating a delightful burst of colour. Ibises wondered around amongst the humans without a care in the world.

Soon after driving through the gate, the sightings escalated. A lone lioness walked. Her ears twitching. Could she hear a noise in the distance? She stopped for a drink, lapping water like a kitty cat at home. There are photos where I have lost her. I watched through the binoculars whilst clicking the camera. The lioness took a rest on the rocks after her drink, flicking her tail as her eyes grew heavy.

We moved on to see a single warthog with a droopy tail.

The trucks emerge on an elephant and her baby. It appears one vehicle is falling over, but is resting on a ridiculous angle in pursuit of a good view.

A giraffe stared us down, and the animals disappeared. But there is always something to see. An acacia tree would hold court, if nothing else. Or a sausage tree would make you smile. They are ridiculous looking trees. The fruit is poisonous if not prepared properly. They can be up to sixty-centimetres long in a sausage shape. Its real name is Kigelia africana.

One tree had an antelope skin hanging over the branches. Leopards do this sometimes. They drag their kill into the trees where other animals can't reach, so can eat in peace.

Another giraffe is tall enough to reach the bottom branches of an acacia tree.

The baboons preen and clean each other in the middle of the road.

Hippos now have half of their bodies out of the water. Do hippos even have legs? We haven't seen any.

We finished as we started with lions being our last sighting. Two were play-fighting in the grass. As we widened our gaze, we discovered a pride of ten lions snoozing the afternoon away. They camouflaged well with the grass. If a couple weren't sitting up, we'd have missed the rest. One is lying on his back with paws tucked in on his tummy. One further away, rolling round on his back, maybe trying to scratch an itch. Such an impressive sight to finish the day.

We made it to the camp where the supply vehicle had set up our tents and started getting dinner ready. There is no perimeter fence, meaning animals can come and go as they please. For safety, cooking takes place in a gated kitchen and eating in a separate dining room structure. The humans are behind cages here. No food should be kept anywhere else and you should try not to leave your tent during the night in case you encounter an animal along the way.

At dinner, we sat at one long table. The fantastic kitchen crew had laid table cloths with placemats on top. There is a group photo. With inadequate lighting and the length of the table, you can't see me. I'm sure the others didn't mind.

27th July (2012) Serengeti & Ngorongoro National Parks, Tanzania

Safari customs dictate an early start with a hot beverage only, before leaving. You return to camp for breakfast later and to pack up the tents.

Today we explored more of the Serengeti before heading to the rim of the Ngorongoro Crater to camp for the night. A whole day of safaris. I love safaris. You never know what you might see. You feel excited expectation from before leaving camp until you have exited the gate. Some of my best animal sightings have been while exiting the park.

Today we started with a young baboon showing us his foot. It resembled a human hand. One toe stuck out to the side like a thumb and three fingers curled over, showing nail beds. I snapped a great baboon butt shot while one bent over for a drink.

The hippos remained hiding in the water. We found a group of about twenty submerged. Without the odd ear or eye being present, you'd think they were a pile of rocks. It was hard to tell where one hippo ended and another began, so who's sniffing a butt, or who's smacking lips.

A leopard caused a traffic jam. At least eleven vehicles stopped. One by one, they would move so another vehicle behind could catch a glimpse. You have to be patient and hope the spotted animal doesn't disappear before your turn.

I expected cheetahs to be my favourite cat after lions, but leopards were fast taking over even lions. Their spots are more mosaic, compared to cheetah's spots, often called rosettes. The rosettes have dark mismatched edges and a lighter colour inside. They don't have lines on their faces which have led to the saying "cheetahs cry" as how to distinguish between cheetahs and leopards.

We watched a male lion with his glorious red mane blowing in the wind walk to the top of the rocks for a nap. Round the other side of the rocks lay a second lion, sleeping.

A lion walked through the grass as it tickled his nose. He made his way to the top tip and everyone's excitement grew. There were whispers of, "He's going to do a Mufasa/Simba," referring to scenes from the *Lion King* movie. This lion did not replicate the scene, but no one was disappointed with our experience. A group of lionesses walked between the vehicles not fussed by our presence and we found cubs playing in the distance. They were too far away to see clearly, but always adrenaline inducing seeing cubs.

Elephants sauntered across the road fresh from a mud bath. Splotches of caked on mud covered varying parts of their bodies.

We spotted a long suffering rock hyrax mother carrying four babies on her back. Two were bigger than the others, so we surmised she'd had a second litter before her first litter had moved on. After a while, three jumped off her back and one lay on top with its head resting between her mother's ears. Very sweet.

Once at camp, we thought our animal sightings were complete, but no. At this time, at this particular camp, they had a regular animal visitor. I had read about this during planning, so knew there was a chance. But the sighting shocked the others. I was glad the campsite lived up to its reputation. An elephant regularly wandered through to check out the latest campers. He strolls between the tents while the cameras click away. You can't ask to be any closer.

28th July (2012) Ngorongoro Crater to Arusha, Tanzania

Up early as usual, but we ate breakfast first. The support crew would pack up camp and meet us later to exit the park together.

We descended the steep walls into the open caldera that is the Ngorongoro Crater. The crater sat to our left, but shrouded in mist. As we descended, the mist gave way to open plains and the animal kingdom welcomed us.

A warthog greeted us with his tail half up as he jaunted along.

An alluring scene had a lone water buffalo ambling through the green grass. The surrounding waters enveloped in pink and white hues emanating from a flamboyance of flamingoes. I was happy to see the flamingoes who may have once called Nakuru home. A barely discernible hint of the distant crater wall sat on the horizon. I wanted to drink in the scenery, but a hyena catching up with his pack broke my reverie.

As we moved on, we found a massive herd of water buffalo with their young calves dotting the plains. A pink stripe ran through the otherwise blue-grey sky in colourful contrast to the brown and green grasses and blue tinged water holes.

We finally saw hippo legs, with two standing on the water's edge.

A herd of zebras had their ears at attention as they detected a lioness in their midst. A second lioness appeared. Squeals of delight are released in our vehicle, thinking we may see a lion kill. The lionesses skirt the edge of the zebra herd and continue on their way. No kill today.

With the threat over, the zebras relax. Two start a game of chase while a third rolls in the dirt, kicking up dust.

A couple of elephants peek out above the tall grass.

We spy more hippos with legs. A pod, otherwise known as a herd, crash, school or bloat, of around twenty hippos had full bodies exposed. They basked in the sun after their swim with their babies in tow. Hippos are becoming a favourite.

We were at a known hippo pond, popular for visitors, thus they created a picnic area here. We ate our packed lunch at a safe distance. This signalled the end of our safari. We exited the park and drove to Arusha.

Driving in convoy, there were four vehicles now the supply truck had joined us. The supply truck broke down, making us stop. They couldn't fix the truck, so we transferred the supplies into the other three vehicles before continuing.

We collected our clean laundry after arriving at camp. It's wonderful returning to clean clothes after being in the dirt without showers for a few days. It cost 10,000 Tanzanian Shillings (TSh), just under US$6.

We had a tour of the snake park that gave our campsite its name. It contained various snakes; a snake bite clinic; cultural displays; and a village visit. The village kids knew we'd have presents. The ball I'd bought to donate was snatched from my hands before reaching the village. One little girl attached herself to me and one of the two Australian sisters travelling together. She somersaulted round and round while holding our two hands. I can't figure out how she managed that without breaking an arm.

As we got closer to the village, the grab, grab, grabbing started. Kids were taking items out of people's arms and even pockets. They assumed everything we had was for them. The lack of appreciation made the experience unpleasant. One guy found the circumstances intolerable and refused to hand over what he'd brought, holding it high above their reach.

The Danish girl had developed a cold over the last few days. I offered her my cold medications. She tried to take one tablet. I said she could take the packet, explaining I'd once been the recipient of a fellow traveller's cold medications, hence why I carry some. I was paying it forward and asked her to do the same.

My medication bag has expanded over the years. Each time I needed a medication I didn't have, but someone else did, I added it to the list and forever carried it just in case. The list became extensive.

29th July (2012) Korogwe, Tanzania

We were back in the big truck for a driving day. I boarded early to get a seat, avoiding the front row. I appreciated being near the back benefitting from the air flow from the windows in front of me. Having a double seat to myself meant I could sit in the aisle avoiding the sun, but still have access to the window.

We had 380 km to our destination of Korogwe. Along the way we had a touristy stop at the tanzanite shop. Tanzanite is a blue and violet-coloured gemstone. The colour can change in differing lights.

We hoped to see the top of Mount Kilimanjaro, the highest mountain in Africa. But alas, the clouds blocked its peak.

Our campsite for the night, the White Parrot, had strong internet service. I paid to use theirs while I had the chance. I did not as yet know my Kindle internet was free. 700 TSh later, I had dealt with more house purchasing e-mails. Settlement, being the 12th of August, was getting close.

30th July (2012) Dar es Salaam, Tanzania

Being a second drive day, we travelled 340 km to Dar es Salaam. In the spirit of changing seats daily, I arrived early, choosing a seat towards the back on the opposite side of the truck from yesterday, and settled in. The honeymoon couple boarded last. Seriously, who goes on a group camping tour for their honeymoon? At least have a week in a hotel together first, calling that your honeymoon. Then the camping becomes a trip after the honeymoon. In their defence, they stayed in a fancy hotel after the tour. But still.

The only double seat left was the front row. That's what happens when you're last. You deal with it and make sure it doesn't happen to you again. That's not what this couple did. They saw the empty front seat and me sitting by myself in a double. They wanted me to move. I couldn't believe the audacity. Their argument was, "But they are bad seats with the sun. We don't want to sit there."

Too bad. "I don't want to sit there either because of the sun."

"But you should sit there because you're on your own. Or sit with Jess."

Jess slumped into her seat, pretending not to pay attention to the unfolding situation. That wasn't an option. Other people started saying I should move because they were on their honeymoon. It was their decision to go on a budget camping trip. Why should I suffer because of them? They had received multiple special privileges already by this point.

The vibe in the truck grew dark. Everyone acted like I was the nastiest person in the world for not giving my seat to the honeymooners. They shamed me into moving to the front.

It was horrendous. I was a grumpy sweat ball within half an hour; the sun beating down on me. Such a stupid design to not have an option to block it out. I have zero tolerance for heat, worse than anyone I have ever met. I don't know if it's in my genes, but I have no control over how it affects me. My only option is to avoid heat and direct sun at all costs. I sat on the floor to avoid the direct glare.

After a few hours, one guy travelling on his own swapped seats with me to give me a break. He must have seen how flustered I'd become. Thank you. He tried to make a shade curtain using his towel, but it didn't stay in position for long.

People can be mean, but when groups of people are mean to one individual, it is horrible. Pack mentality can be awful. I've never liked groups, and situations such as this help to explain why.

This was our last day on the truck. Luckily, this tour had more days off the truck than on it.

On arrival at Kipepeo Village, most people upgraded. Jess and I get along when it's the two of us, but she joins the pack mentality when others are around. Here, Jess and I shared an upgrade. The sisters also upgraded, and the four of us felt as though we were walking to the ends of the earth to find our allocated treehouse-style bungalows.

They were cute units built of red mud and thatch. Downstairs housed only the bathroom, with one room upstairs containing a sleeping platform with mattresses. The room was open to the elements with a bamboo gate differentiating the inside from the outside. The gate led to a large balcony, complete with a table, chairs and a hammock. There were no windows or solid doors. A few curtain pieces hung on the balcony side. The sleeping platform was shrouded in one large mosquito net to keep the insects away at night. There was a sign saying to lock the balcony gate as crows come inside and steal belongings from the rooms. I guess the crows are too big to squeeze between the bamboo strips that form the gates.

I spent the last night of my trip here, after the tour finished. It was nicer having it to myself, knowing the others were gone.

We would travel via ferry to Zanzibar the following day, having a tour of Stone Town and a spice farm.

31st July (1998) Around Scotland, UK

Yesterday, the father I was nannying for drove me to the biggest town in the area called Oban. I looked across to the Isle of Skye wishing I was there as I wrote a postcard to my share house in London.

Here I am in Scotland. I've got a couple of days off, so I'm heading up to Inverness to do some more family tree research. I also needed to get away from the house. I hate it. It's worse than London. I've done everything from cleaning cupboards to sheep chasing. It's in a beautiful spot, though, and the house is enormous. Who knows? I might be home before this card if it doesn't change drastically. I'm definitely not going to Ireland, though.

I was not enjoying my Scottish experience. The job ad said:

Scotland/Ireland for the summer? Live-in Nanny/Mother's Help to assist with 1-month-old twins...

I have never enjoyed travelling as a nanny. It sounds good in theory. They offered access to a car during my days off, but when they discovered I'd only recently attained my licence, they reneged on their offer, leaving me stranded.

From Oban, I took a coach leaving for Fort William at 3:55 pm, then on to Inverness at 5:45 pm, arriving two hours later.

I stayed at a youth hostel for the night and had hoped to do family research into my Isle of Skye Stewart ancestors the following day. But the family history centre was closed being a Saturday.

I walked around the town and sat by the water, imagining one day reaching the home of my ancestors. Is it any wonder I suffer in the heat when my genes come from places like Scotland?

I achieved little from my journey apart from escaping the family. I caught the 3:15 pm bus returning to Oban at 7:00 pm after travelling via Fort William. A quick trip. But then the interesting part happened.

The family could not pick me up in Oban. I had to make my own way to their house in the middle of nowhere. There was a small local bus that would get me closer to a town called Ardfern, a forty-five-minute walk. The family told me to hitchhike. They said it was normal in these parts, so safe. I thought hitchhiking was never safe. I've heard countless stories of hitchhiking backpackers never been seen again. With limited public transport, the locals hitched their way around. But the locals would know each other, making it safer. I had no choice. I needed a break from the family and a way to get back.

I started walking in the correct direction, wondering what would happen. I was too scared when the first cars drove by, keeping my head down. Then thought maybe I should try. So I stuck my thumb out when I heard a car. It drove by without stopping. I kept walking. I tried again, and a car stopped. Now what?

The male driver opened the window and asked where I was going. I gave him the name of the house and he knew it. He was a local and knew the mother I was working for. He said he didn't know she was home and was happy to drop me off. How lucky was that? I made it home in one piece before dark.

I remember walking along the grass on the side of the country road. No footpaths out this way. I remember nervously sticking out my thumb, wondering what the consequences might be. It was my first proper hitchhiking experience. And my last. I find it strange that the father who was trusting his babies to me was encouraging me to partake in what I considered reckless behaviour.

August

1st August (2012) Kendwa, Tanzania

We departed Stone Town for Kendwa's beaches, where the majority of the group planned to relax in the sun, but it bucketed rain all day. I organised a scuba dive trip (US$150) for the next day and crossed my fingers the weather improved. Most of the group hung out in the bar and restaurant. I stayed in our room, the nicest accommodation of the tour.

Our unexpected upmarket resort, had three-bed rooms. The two Aussie sisters pounced on me to be their third, which made me happy. I'm interested in why they were desperate to be with me instead of the other younger single travellers. But I didn't push my luck by asking. Maybe not everyone bought into the pack mentality. I don't recall what happened to Jess. This hotel marked the last share negotiations.

The large room contained three immaculate wooden beds with headboards and canopies to the ceiling. Mosquito nets fell from the canopies and tethered to the foot of the beds. The baby blue sheets looked smart, with pillows and cushions to match. A balcony offered a hint of the ocean through the vegetation.

I made the most of the balcony, reading my Kindle in peace.

The food kitty ended when the camping finished. I paid 35,000 TSh, around US$20, for lunch, dinner and drinks.

I was glad when this trip finished. It was the first and only time I received no goodbye hugs. There is one weird person on each group tour. On this tour, that person was me. To be fair, I arrived sporting a black eye and tight cornrow braids; I was well into an African frame of mind after two weeks; and was the oldest in the group. I decided against correcting the girl claiming to be the oldest.

This tour was a reconnaissance mission to choose between two companies. I imagine it's no surprise I chose the first company, Africa-In-Focus, for my longer African trip in 2014.

2nd August (1994) San Gimignano, Italy

We left London on the 31st of July, flying Excalibur Airways to Pisa, Italy. We hired a car to drive to San Gimignano, the city of towers. Our hotel sat outside the town walls facing open countryside.

The pilot announced a thirty degree arrival temperature. It didn't drop below that over our week-long stay. The dry heat proved an improvement over the recent London weather. My one diary entry for this trip mentions the difference:

> It doesn't completely cripple me like it has been in London.

I was travelling with work as a live-in nanny. My work hours in London were from the time Katie woke until her bedtime, roughly 7:00 am to 7:00 pm, and I had a suite of rooms. While on holiday, Katie and I shared a hotel room. Katie did not wake overnight, but I'd need to dim the lights and be quiet after her bedtime.

The family allowed me to swim in the hotel pool, with the baby monitor on, once Katie was asleep. Being after dark, I had the pool to myself. A peaceful way to end the day. I wouldn't do that now. It felt wrong, but I enjoyed it so much I ignored those feelings.

My favourite memory of this trip, though, was breakfast. Katie and I rose earlier than the parents and headed downstairs. We'd often have the buffet breakfast room to ourselves with attentive staff. I would pick a table with a pool view and the staff arranged a highchair. I'd strap Katie in and the staff entertained her while I filled two plates of food from the buffet for Katie and myself.

The staff loved Katie and gave her so much attention that we'd sit at breakfast for an hour to an hour and a half with no complaints from Katie. The staff brought me cup of tea after cup of tea while I just sat there. A perfect start to the day. Once I finished my plate, the staff would ask if I wanted more. I'd go to stand, but they'd insist on getting whatever I wanted, so I didn't have to leave Katie. A second portion of bacon delivered to me. I wasn't accustomed to special treatment so revelled in every minute. I recall Katie to my right and the buffet in the distance as I gazed over the pool, drinking tea. Bliss!

On this date, though, the parents woke early and joined us halfway. They shattered the bliss. Katie refused to eat and acted up, trying to climb out of her highchair. Breakfast ended abruptly. I preferred meals without the parents.

The parents headed out of town, leaving Katie and me to our own devices. We swam in the hotel pool throughout the morning. Then I relaxed by the pool, writing my one diary entry for the trip, while Katie napped.

In the afternoon, we ventured into the heart of San Gimignano. The parents thought climbing the towers was impossible with Katie, doing it without us. But I wanted to see the view. I left the pram at the base and ascended the tower carrying Katie, to discover a panoramic view of the town and countryside. It wasn't too difficult. We also visited the Cathedral where I bought postcards.

I filled the pram's storage areas as I souvenir shopped on my way back to the hotel.

From my diary:

My house is going to be filled with holiday memorabilia. I'm going to ensure it's all nice stuff from now on so that it will look good in the future.

My 1994 self would be disappointed with the lack of travel memorabilia displayed in my current home.

3rd August (1994) San Gimignano, Italy

I spent my pre-agreed afternoon off in pain from sunburn. Heat radiated from me, and all I wanted to do was avoid the sun. The hotel air conditioning struggled with the heat so I could not recuperate in a cool room. With a shaded balcony, I sat there elevating my swollen feet. I hadn't suffered burnt feet before.

I sent a postcard to my Catholic father with a picture from inside the Cathedral of San Gimignano. I thought he'd appreciate the religiousness.

Yes, I have the postcard. I asked my parents to keep my letters, which they returned to me when I came home. The letters became extra diary entries which I am grateful for now. The postcard reads:

> I've gone on holiday with the family I work for in lovely Italy. We went to this amazing church in the town we are staying in. This is the view as you walk in. On the left are frescoes of the Old Testament and right the New Testament. They are magnificent. They were painted in the 14th century. The crucifixion is particularly beautiful.

No mention of the fact I wrote it while my sunburnt feet were elevated on the balcony of a hotel with a broken air conditioner. I remember it vividly. I had a wet face cloth to soothe my burnt body. An intermittent breeze blew over the damp skin, cooling me.

4th August (1994) San Gimignano, Italy

One of my memories from this trip was Katie's bedtime bath. The parents requested two rooms next to each other, and one with a bath. They allocated us rooms on different floors. The parents' room contained the bath. The first night I carried Katie and the bath accoutrements to the parents' room. It was not practical.

Our room had a bidet big enough for Katie to sit in, so I suggested I try that instead. Hilarious. I had packed bath toys, and if my camera had worked, you would see photos of Katie in the bidet with a rubber duck and other sea creatures stuck to the tiles. It proved easier than carting everything in the elevator to another room.

I completed a 36-exposure roll of film, but the film had not loaded correctly, which I discovered once back in London. The family gave me three photos they'd taken of me. Very disappointing. This was the only nanny family holiday I enjoyed. Because of that, I have clear memories, thankfully.

The hotel did not offer dinner. Katie and I would eat at a restaurant in town while the parents ordered a drink. Afterwards, Katie and I returned to the hotel while the parents ate alone. It would have been easier if Katie and I could have dined at the hotel. Having meal options at your hotel is preferable. Even if you don't use it, it's good to know it's there.

5th August (1994) Volterra, Italy

We spent the day together in Volterra, where a tradition started. We viewed ruins of a Roman theatre from above with ropes to keep us out. They weren't the most intact ruins, but my first ruins as an adult, so I loved them.

I expressed out loud my desire to stand on the stage. To my surprise, the mother coaxed me to climb over the ropes. With no one around, the mother insisted. I wouldn't have done it without encouragement.

I made it to the theatre feeling naughty.

The mum yells, "Pose for a photo."

With nerves coursing through me, I extended my arms and legs to the sides. This marked the start of my Roman theatre star pose. It's now a mandatory tradition at every theatre, but began with this rebellious act during work.

A short round local woman came towards me, yelling in Italian, I assume to exit the ruins. I rejoined the family, and we ran until the woman stopped following. I was mortified, but Katie's mother just laughed it off.

I am glad we didn't get caught, and the mum encouraged me to do it. I love the tradition of the pose in Roman theatres. No regrets.

There is a second photo of me amongst the ruins. I'm grateful the family printed me copies.

6th August (1998) Glasgow, Scotland, UK

The father I worked for drove me to Lochgilphead at 8:15 am for the 9:00 am bus to Glasgow. From there I hoped to catch a bus to London. With no tickets available until the 10:30 pm overnight departure, I had to fill in the day.

I have got the headache from hell. Interesting long, long, long day...
I spent about 3 hours in Waterstone's [a bookshop] and bought
The Baby and Toddler Meal Planner.

I had wanted the meal planner since it came out to help me feed my nanny babies.

The palmistry books helped me fill in time by deciphering my palm. I discovered many travel lines, but the signs predicting children confused me, so I was not sure what the future held on that front as per my palm. Children were not in my future, but I didn't know that in 1998.

The travel section entertained me with books about New York. I was excited by the thought of being there soon and of fulfilling my dream of working in America.

Waterstone's was a huge shop with toilets, a coffee shop and:

big fat sofas to sit on... Oh, my head hurts.

I went into a gallery with film props from *Alien, Star Wars* and others. They advertised *Titanic*, but only one life belt worn by Kate Winslet, but had the music playing. I watched some of *Star Wars*, got scared by an alien, and most importantly, filled in some time.

I filled in more time at the cinema seeing *Lost In Space*.

My head. My head. Head. Head. [I did not carry paracetamol in these days.] I hope the bus isn't full so I can have two seats to myself. Lucky I have my pillow but nothing to put over me. I wasn't planning on doing a night run. I'll survive.

By this point, I didn't care. I had stopped working for the family who'd brought me to Scotland. I hated the job, so left. I was relieved it was over, and the parting was amicable.

7th August (1994) Pisa, Italy

When checking out of the San Gimignano hotel, multiple staff said, "Bye Katie," and Katie waved. It confused the mum and dad how the staff knew Katie's name, and mine, but not theirs. Katie and I interacted with the staff a lot more than the parents. They had no idea what Katie and I had been up to. An outward smirk hid my inside laughter.

While packing the car, the mother lamented how carrying baby paraphernalia had limited her ability to purchase local pottery and glassware. I gave a small nod in her direction, hoping my bag didn't rattle as I added it to the pile.

My bags overflowed with souvenirs. They didn't need to know that. I bought glassware and pottery. With my dream of a blue and white kitchen already in place, I'd bought a matching blue and white fruit bowl, mug and spoon rest. The family never discovered how much I brought home.

We explored Pisa before our flight to London.

Pisa brought back flashes from my family's 1983 trip. I have a vivid memory of ascending the circular staircase of the slippery leaning tower in the midst of rain. By 1990, the tower leaned too much, so closed for eleven years of repairs. I felt privileged to have climbed it.

The third photo from the family was taken in Pisa. The father and I each have a hand on Katie's pram. Katie is trying to escape from the pram, so I'm focussed on her.

With an 8:00 pm flight, we didn't arrive home until midnight. My diary for the following day noted I was exhausted and started work in my dressing gown. That's one advantage of being a live-in nanny.

8th August (2002) London, England, UK

With the Commonwealth Games in Manchester over, I travelled to London. The plan was to stay, work and save money. As a career nanny, London provided the highest salaries. I stayed on a friend's couch while getting sorted. My mind was full of Commonwealth Games netball experiences, though, which didn't help me settle.

A friend in Newcastle rang me to say she'd be in London around 4:00 pm. The call snapped me out of my netball reminisces to my previous London life; an instant time warp. I wanted my netball world, and the money of the London world.

London realities hit me all at once. You forget the difficult bits over time, but now they confronted me.

> The crappy showers, dirty/old bathrooms, the amount of dirt on your face and up your nose, and it is really expensive. I don't think I want to live in a dump again.

I mention items I'd have to buy.

Sheets, doona, pillow etc as well as like a saucepan, tea towel, scrub brush, etc. But that all adds up and I have no guarantee of how much money will be coming in.

The job market had changed since 1998. There were two publications with weekly private nanny job listings over multiple pages. However, the current edition contained seventeen jobs occupying one sixth of a page. No baby jobs, which was my expertise. Nowadays, families with babies registered with agencies, making it impossible for me to secure work since I was unable to register.

> It's all a bit depressing, really. There is so much money to be made here and I can't get in... I'm tempted to pack it all in and go home... I'll feel better when I get a job. The problem is, I don't know IF I can get a job. It could take a while.

I had a comfortable life in Melbourne.

> Car, gym, netball, spending money, good food, good accommodation. In London, crappy life plus miss out on netball. Not worth it.

I was questioning my plan. Were my living and working abroad days over? That thought seemed unimaginable.

9th August (2019) Los Angeles, California (CA), USA

My flight being delayed by an hour and a half until 10:30 am was not an issue with free time in Los Angeles before a 6:00 pm train.

After a thirty-minute timeframe for immigration and baggage collection, I located the green "Long Distance Buses" sign and hopped on the Flyaway Bus direct service to Union Train Station. I arrived at my final destination within an hour and a half of landing. Quick and simple.

My booked sleeper cabin gave me access to the Amtrak Metropolitan Lounge, where I could store my luggage. I had nine hours to fill in, with plans to shop at the outlet mall, catching a bus from Union Station.

I found the lounge busy on arrival, but snagged a seat. The crowd awaited a 10:00 am train. Once boarding began, the lounge emptied. I spread out and helped myself to the free food and drinks. I made tea to help wake me up with my favourite Half-and-Half milk available. They also provided juice, soft drinks and snacks such as chips. I was too comfortable to leave so cancelled my mall plans.

My second plan was the Wells Fargo Museum. I had attempted this before but only open on weekdays as housed inside a bank. I often visited on weekends, thus unable to enter. It would be open today, being Friday.

At 2:30 pm I left my comfortable lounge to escape the woman next to me trying to convert me to her religion. I walked twenty-five minutes to the Wells Fargo Museum through Grand Park, a welcome green patch in the middle of the concrete city. The hill highlighted my lack of fitness while the increase in temperature burnt my face.

It didn't take long to make my way around the small museum. I welcomed the air conditioning and flat ground. Finally, I can tick it off my Los Angeles list. I love old stagecoaches, and the one displayed here had a sign above the seats. It read: *Ladies Will Not and Gentlemen Must Not Ride With Their Feet On The CUSHION*. It made me laugh. I loved the old bank notes with a three cent note from 1863 displayed.

I caught the Angels Flight tramway down the hill for fun tapping my Los Angeles public transport card, called TAP, to pay my fifty-cent fare for the short ride. I believe it cost $1 without a TAP card. Two of us caught the tramway down, but a long line waited to go up.

I walked around the familiar streets and through Grand Central Market to Walgreens to buy supplies before returning to the station. I enjoyed the fresh air and exercise. It helped wake me up. Sitting in the lounge made me sleepy.

At Walgreens I bought snacks for the train in the way of Pringles and Cookie Dough Bites. I bought proper food for an early dinner, being a pasta salad, strawberries and a bottle of water.

On return to the lounge I felt dirty. I hadn't changed out of my plane clothes as planned, so I'd been wearing the same clothes for over twenty-four hours. I wrote in my diary next time I should catch the evening flight so I could spend the night in a hotel, then shower in the morning before the train.

When boarding, I walked rather than use the Red Cap service and the shortcut from the lounge. The train pulled in as I arrived on the platform. The double-decker trains are huge when you stand next to them. I was excited about the adventure ahead. Amtrak will always have a soft spot in my heart after my 1992 adventure.

I travel in comfort now compared to 1992 with my perfect little room for one. It's better than sharing. The space would be tight for two.

I had three nights and three days to enjoy my train cabin on the *Southwest Chief*, train number 4, with a change of trains in Chicago after forty-three hours. My final destination was Rhode Island with stops in Washington, D.C. (District of Columbia) and New York.

Dinner was available in the Dining Car which I skipped. I instead asked for my bed to be made. I changed into my pyjamas after a wet wipe wash. Once I thought no one needed anything else from me, I took melatonin and headed to bed. It remained light outside, but I was exhausted. No latent light or noise bothered me, so fell asleep quickly. I later woke cold, adding extra blankets for warmth.

I planned to adjust my body clock to the Eastern Time Zone. 7:00 pm in Los Angeles was 10:00 pm in New York, so perfect to sleep early and rise early.

10th August (2019) Amtrak Trains, USA

I'd planned to store my big bag on the luggage racks downstairs, packing a separate bag for the cabin. However, they'd roped off the downstairs storage, so I had to keep my luggage in the compartment. For one person with one bag the space works. For two, it would be tight. My big bag sat in the doorway, which for overnight helped block light from the corridor and added a layer of security. When in bed mode, it left zero floor space.

The cabin bag contained my essentials. I had comfy clothes in two stretchy ankle-length dresses and a clean T-shirt to wear over my plane skirt. If I wore a cardigan, I'd be warm. Temperatures on trains and planes are unpredictable. I'd packed my toiletry bag and thongs for the shower downstairs; a quick dry travel towel in case I needed it; my small pillow; headphones; playing cards; iPad; chargers; tea supplies; a travel cutlery set; removable tape for blocking any annoying small lights; a bull clip if needed to hold curtains closed amongst other potential uses; and a large foldable map of America to follow my progress.

Awake at 4:30 am, I caught the sunrise with the Arizona desert revealing itself. I would sleep on the train again overnight, allowing a whole day to relax and enjoy the scenery.

With everyone asleep, I utilised the downstairs showers. I was first thus clean, and plenty of hot water.

Breakfast began at 6:30 am with no reservations. Others had arrived before me, and it is customary, well mandatory, to share tables. They sat me with three leaders from a scout group in the seats sections. Amtrak has announced it will phase out shared dining, which is a shame as it's part of the train experience.

I ordered the hot breakfast, enjoying the potatoes and crispy bacon. I requested hot water to make tea and made a second cup to enjoy a cuppa in my room.

I left my cabin in bed mode to stretch my legs out while I drank, watching the desert landscape go by. I placed my big bag at the end of the bed to recover floor space.

By the afternoon, I became sleepy and struggled to keep my eyes open. I wasn't sure if tired or part of my new ability to sleep with motion. I was torn between looking out the window, reading, and sleeping. Great choices though, right? I already didn't want it to end. I loved every second and was pleased I chose the train over a plane.

For lunch, I ordered the Angus Burger with potato chips and cheesecake for dessert. All delicious.

We could alight the train at Albuquerque Train Station with a twenty-minute stop. It is nice to get fresh air and I walked the length of the train taking photos. This is where my passport adventure occurred back in 1992/3. They have built a new station since the last one was razed. No familiarity, of course, but forever a shared history.

I discovered a historical carriage, single storey, with a pop up observation roof called the Sierra Hotel. You can book it for private travel and attach it to any train route. How incredible!

The desert gave way to greener pastures, but I preferred the desert.

I chose steak with baked potato and green beans for dinner. The chocolate dessert was not the same as my last Amtrak trip. I described it in my diary as not worth the calories.

I headed to bed close to 10:00 pm Eastern Standard Time, or 9:00 pm for tomorrow's time zone. It's tricky sorting body clocks.

The afternoon sun poured into the cabin, which I'll assume contributed to the warmer overnight environment. I cooled the room by opening the door to the air-conditioned corridor. I kept the door curtains closed for privacy, though.

11th August (2019) Amtrak Trains, USA

I slept later until at 7:15 am. I showered and washed my hair. The water was hot enough, but needed more pressure. It took time to rinse the shampoo and conditioner. Clean hair improves your mood, but I didn't have a hairdryer and nervous my hair straightener would blow a circuit, so I sported curly hair for the day.

By the time I got to breakfast, the train remained an hour late. I thought we'd catch up overnight with fast speeds noted, but we experienced slow patches, too.

For most of breakfast, we were stopped at the station for Kansas City, Missouri. I knew nurses from here. A meetup would have been nice, but tricky to arrange. At least I thought of them while in town.

The scenery today involved corn fields, rivers and stormy skies with lightning and thunder.

We never caught up arriving in Chicago an hour late. I had kept my cabin in bed mode throughout the trip. They made me pack it up a few hours before arrival, which I was not happy about, as enjoyed stretching my legs. I carried my big bag downstairs and placed it on the luggage rack early so wouldn't have to do it with people in front and behind me eager to alight. I'm not sure why they didn't allow us to use the luggage rack throughout the journey.

In Chicago, I wandered the station attempting to match places to images in my head from 1992. It was at this station my life on Amtrak trains began. The main hall was beautiful with white marble everywhere, but the ticket counters from the nineties had changed, at least based on my memory. I couldn't find where I decided to catch the train rather than exit to a hostel.

I found the large comfortable lounge where I had two hours to enjoy the big televisions, where I watched a documentary on Brexit; read; had a terrible hot chocolate; drank refreshing sparkling water; and ate a banana and banana chips.

When time to board, they escorted us as a group. We formed a long line from the lounge to the platform. The non-sleeper car passengers had to wait until we'd boarded. A little bizarre. We left the lounge just before 6:00 pm. I was well settled by our 6:40 pm departure.

Dinner would be available in the Dining Car soon but you could also get food delivered to your cabin which I chose. A different opportunity to feel special, and the fastest way to get food as delivered before the Dining Car opened.

The lower quality packaged food was substantial enough to satisfy my stomach. The pasta came with a side salad; a dinner roll with butter; a brownie for dessert; and an orange juice. And I enjoyed it in the comfort of my private cabin.

I was travelling on the *Capitol Limited*, train number 30.

I hopped into bed around 9:40 pm Eastern Standard Time, but took a while to fall asleep. It was my last sleep on a train.

12th August (2019) Washington D.C., USA

I slept well on and off. The first time check was 4:14 am. I experienced weird dreams which weren't melatonin related, as I didn't take any. I rose at 7:15 am and headed to the shower. The shower had better water pressure, so washed my hair again to rid myself of yesterday's curls. I took my time with no one waiting. I wondered if anyone else used the showers.

I had breakfast in the Dining Car which was upmarket compared to the previous train. It was newer, more spacious, and comfier seats. Being more European style, it contained a counter to order from and fewer tables. As only for sleeper passengers who have meals included, it was buffet style where you helped yourself to the food set out. They had muffins, cereal, porridge, bananas and muesli bars. You could get other items from the counter such as a breakfast sandwich, boiled eggs, yoghurt, fruit salad and hot drinks. I made my tea and ate porridge, a muffin, a banana and a yoghurt. The train followed a river on the opposite side of my cabin. So I sat on that side for breakfast and lingered. I was torn between staying in the Dining Car and returning to my room. With no communal seating, I enjoyed being there on my own.

I was loving this train trip and dreaded getting off.

We arrived in Washington and I reluctantly alighted the train. My hotel was a short walk from the station and easy to find. The station contained food options and other shops thus useful to have close by.

I made an excellent hotel choice. Besides the convenient location, and being able to see the Capitol Building from out the front, I chose this hotel because of its decor. The hotel's colour scheme was what I wanted for my house. Would I enjoy living with those colours? I took loads of photos for future reference.

I could not linger, as I had a full itinerary planned. I had to squeeze in one site before a pre-booked night tour.

I freshened up and walked back towards the station to the Postal Museum. I enjoyed the Postal Museum and stayed until kicked out when closing. I saw the history displays on everything postal and learnt a lot. You play on sorting machines to discover if skilled enough to work there. I needed more practice. The machines wanted you to move at lightning speed.

I discovered tall buildings had post boxes on each floor, usually near the lifts. You put your letters in the slot and they travelled through the tube to the ground floor where the postie collected them. Brilliant concept. On my return to the hotel, I realised the post and collection boxes remained; though no longer functional. It pleased me they hadn't been removed. I wondered if any letters remained in the tube waiting to be discovered.

I loved the train sorting carriages and the idea of playing with mail while travelling across the country on a train. Sounds like an awesome job.

With its high ceilings and white marble columns, the building resembled the recent train stations I visited, including intricately adorned ceilings with chandeliers. The building alone is worth a visit.

I had a quick dinner at the station of chicken nuggets at McDonald's. I bought supplies at the Walgreens and headed back to the hotel.

I had four nights at the same hotel without breakfast included. I bought a box of Raisin Bran cereal, a large bottle of milk, and a large bottle of orange juice. Breakfast in my hotel room made easy. This would also work as a time saver eating while getting ready. I had a Tupperware container to use as a bowl and a travel cutlery set. It was cheap at just over US$10 for four breakfasts.

The starting point of the "D.C. Monuments By Night" tour was a twenty-minute walk from my hotel, as per Google Maps. I prefer walking to public transport, so I jaunted off. Being summer, it remained light at 7:30 pm. I enjoyed exploring a large amount of the city on my first day.

> Got a little turned around to start with. Totally different on the map in my head and reality, but I made it ok. Great tour guide. Was lovely seeing everything at night. Got bitten three times. [Mosquitoes were out in force.] Lots of scaffolding everywhere. [You could barely see the White House.] Saw Mr Lincoln. [Where I recreated a terrible photo by getting another terrible photo of me with the

giant Mr Lincoln. I always ask the wrong person to take a photo of me here.] Still haven't stopped at Jefferson. Why don't they stop there? Very late at night, though. 11:30 pm after a ride home from the tour guide, which was nice. TOO LATE.

The tour guide made sure everyone found their way home. My hotel was on the way for the tour guide, so we hopped into her private car and chatted back to my hotel–very kind of her. I gave her a generous tip. I can now tick "memorials" off my sightseeing list.

A tour on arrival is a great introduction to a city. You get excited about where you will spend the next few days; you get your bearings; and an opportunity to ask a local questions.

13th August (2019) Washington D.C., USA

I spent hours and hours planning this trip and it paid off today when I saw the Reading Room of The Library of Congress with no one else around. The itinerary changed numerous times but created spectacular results. I had multiple pages of notes in my travel bible for today. I didn't want to miss anything.

I had read underground tunnels existed to transport people between government buildings. An entire network of tunnels you wouldn't know existed unless someone told you. I wanted to explore them, taking notes on where to look. Alas, most are for employees only, but I tried the best I could. One tunnel has a little train to transport people faster. A tour of the underground tunnels would be an excellent V.I.P. tour. I'd pay for that.

I rose early for the fifteen-minute walk to the Library of Congress in time for an 8:30 am opening. This ensured tickets to the earliest tour and seeing the magnificent Reading Room without a crowd.

On my walk, I passed a church with a relevant sign: *God grant Congress the strength to stand up to the NRA*. We can hope.

I passed the imposing Supreme Court Building and made it to the Library of Congress. A handsome building from the outside and magnificent on the inside. The lavishness blew me away. I hadn't expected it to be so intricate. America was showing their power to the world. Marble, gold, carvings, stained glass windows, columns, statues, rotundas. My mouth was agape as I meandered through the opulence by myself.

I headed straight for the Reading Room viewing area. I could have stared at it for days. The red, the marble, the gold, the wood, the books. What richness that combination makes. One day I will apply for a reader's ticket. For international individuals, a specific research topic must be nominated, a requirement Americans are exempt from. I will find a relevant future book topic and relish every second in the library. If these surroundings don't inspire writing, nothing will.

The fact I had recently finished reading a book with scenes set in this room helped my appreciation and it appears in one of my favourite movies, *National Treasure*. Both scenes played in my head as I appreciated the room through the glass.

I was not happy when others arrived. It was my space. "Go away," I wanted to say. "How dare you ruin my time?" Of course I didn't say that. I was lucky to have any alone time. People were bound to come. I arrived at the viewing room at 8:45 am if you want details for a future visit.

I had instructions to seek the conveyor belt delivering books from downstairs and to peer through the archways to the book stacks behind. I could see the stacks, but alas, no conveyor belt. Maybe the conveyor belt works harder in the afternoons.

There are various exhibitions and displays throughout the building, including an informative exposition on the suffragettes' fight for women's right to vote. A map room holds the first known drawing including America, from 1507. It's not the shape we know, but drawn and labelled America. They recreated Thomas Jefferson's library with his book collection. And you literally have to inspect every detail. There are symbols and meanings in each carving on the walls, ceilings, and don't forget to study the bannister's decorations.

My instructions for tunnel discovery revolved around the Capitol Building, but there's a tunnel for everyone's use between The Library of Congress and the Capitol. On the opposite side of this passageway, lies three tunnel branches. The walkway to the Senate houses the tram nicknamed the Senate Subway. I could access none of these. Though, I wandered corridors I don't think I was meant to, trying.

I'd pre-booked a 12:00 pm Capitol Building Tour. Tours are free but require advanced online booking. You had to arrive thirty minutes prior for security and to collect your pass. The tunnel allowed you to skip security as had been through it entering the Library of Congress. I found it loud and noisy after the serenity of the library. The busyness was overwhelming and the building underwhelming. The brief diary entry says:

Capitol quite bland really. Congress not in session.

I had lunch at the Capitol Building in a huge bustling cafeteria. It wasn't a place to linger, but I found a seat. I had chicken pasta alfredo. There were themed desserts I took photos of rather than eat. I was parched, as they don't permit even water bottles through security. Pasta with a bottle of water cost $12.90.

I bought a $1 book containing the full Constitution of the United States and The Declaration of Independence. I am yet to read it.

Outside, the heat was stifling. I used my trusty pink umbrella to create shade. My feet and my old injured ankle complained about walking. I had planned to visit The Air and Space Museum next, but it was under restoration with most of what I wanted to see closed, so saved it till the next D.C. visit.

I stopped at NASA Headquarters checking out the gift shop, then the day's last stop, the Museum of the Bible. This museum looked extraordinary online, so I became a member before leaving home. My main visit was planned for tomorrow, with today being an "if time" scenario. Skipping the Air and Space Museum allowed time today, and I appreciated the two visits.

The Museum of the Bible has six floors of exhibits, recreations, rides, shows and virtual reality theatres. I wanted to experience it all. The bible is the oldest book in the world. I was here for the history.

My tired feet walked me the twenty minutes home via the station for dinner. Chinese tonight with my standard American order of Orange Chicken, and a Sprite for $10.23.

14th August (2019) Washington D.C., USA

I was tired and hot so caught an Uber to the museum. I needed a break from the heat and avoided it most of the day. $9.32 well spent.

Membership to the Museum of the Bible entitled me to unlimited visits, early entry before the public, and free or discounted extracurricular activities. I was happy to pay $49.99 for that. I relish having places to myself. If I can enter before the crowds, that's brilliant and worth paying for. The museum remained quiet after the general hours began. Only a handful of people milled around.

I paid extra to do a Virtual Reality experience of a tour around Israel, which I enjoyed. It was:

> Very cool looking up and down over the desert ruins. Definitely have to go back to Israel!

The museum has been broiled in scandals around how they obtained its exhibits questioning their authenticity. Some items have since been returned to rightful owners. I don't know if I saw real artefacts or replicas or fakes, but I enjoyed my experience and education.

> Watched all the videos at Bible Museum and came up with a few ideas for my book. Needed the double entry.

More evidence of always wanting to write. I have collected ideas throughout my years of travel. What I meant, I have not noted. But I have a rough idea based on my photos. My memory says I took more photos than I can find. Maybe one day I will find a secret treasure trove of ideas for a book on a random memory card.

Here is an idea of what the museum contained, based on the items I have ticked as completed in my travel bible:

- Changing ceiling on the first floor
- Hebrew Bible walk through
- World of Jesus wander through
- New Testament Theatre
- Drive through history film
- In the Beginning
- IllumiNations

- Biblical Garden
- 6th floor restaurant and views
- Bible in America
- Bible in the World
- Slave Bible in the Caribbean
- Wiedmann Bible
- Israel archaeology
- Vatican Treasures
- Washington Revelations flight

Has that got your mind ticking over? I thoroughly enjoyed my interactive visit. I had a grilled cheese sandwich for lunch at the museum while resting my feet.

More book ideas came from The Spy Museum. It was brilliant. Busier than the Museum of the Bible, but never over three people in a line. It's fun because you become an agent and partake in missions. To complete your assignment, you access various forms of technology along the way. Everyone needs the same machines. I visited on a quiet day, so would be difficult in peak season.

Even though it's summer and the American school holidays, August is a low season in Washington D.C. because of the weather. It's too hot and muggy to be visited en masse. Once I experienced the weather, an inkling in my memory said, "I knew that." But I forgot while planning.

My spy mission required finding the client list of a scientist suspected of selling secret nuclear weapons technology. I had a cover of a visiting professor from Canada called Hayden Madrigal. You do various tasks and questionnaires along the way and a report of your results is e-mailed to you after you sign out. It was fun. I've always wanted to be a spy.

The exhibits enthralled me as I discovered spies throughout history and how they escaped capture or were caught. Add the myriad of spy craft along the way, and I was hooked. Photos were taken for future reference for my books.

I came prepared with a wish list for the gift shop, but none of what I'd seen online was available. I found one thing I've always wanted though, a folding metal straw with its own case and a retractable cleaning brush. But no spy souvenirs.

I caught the Metro home. You buy a reusable card for $2 and add credit. The total cost came to $4.35, half the Uber cost.

> Much dirtier than I remember. I think it was pretty new when I used it back in 1992!

I took the Yellow Line from L'Infant Plaza two stops, then changed to the Red Line for two stops to Union Train Station.

I ate dinner at the station–orange chicken again from Panda Express.

Back at the hotel, I wrote a Facebook post, watched an episode of the latest incarnation of *Beverly Hills 90210* called *BH90210* and was in bed just after 10:00 pm. It was later than I wanted, but I couldn't resist watching Beverly Hills while I had the chance.

15th August (2019) Washington, D.C., USA

Today's adventure required hours of planning with multiple e-mails and international phone calls. But worth it to organise what I wanted without paying for things I didn't need.

I started early with a cruise to Mount Vernon, home of George and Martha Washington, departing at 8:30 am. Buffet breakfast was included, which meant one less task to do before leaving. I caught an Uber to the dock for $12.27.

The breakfast exceeded my expectations, with bacon, eggs, potatoes, waffles, sausages, muffins, pastries and orange juice. I ate as we sailed along the Potomac River. A great way to start the day.

You get a full view of the Mount Vernon property from the water. The land entrance is some distance away. But I needed to pick up my pre-booked extra tour tickets from there.

As I made my way, I paid my respects at George and Martha's tombs and discovered a vibrant orange pumpkin patch nearby. I'd never seen a pumpkin patch before and became enamoured by it. I relished seeing the property as a working farm as intended.

On arrival at the front of the house, I took photos, despite the facade being covered by scaffolding. Then watched the orientation film before my first tour.

I was ecstatic to be on *The National Treasure* tour. After seeing that movie thousands of times, I revelled in visiting locations from the movie and, as a bonus, the settings are also part of history. They made adaptations for the movie, but both aspects were interesting enough to produce Cheshire cat grins.

We began in the basement; the cool temperature was a bonus. Although the movie didn't precisely replicate the space, I could see how the real aspects inspired the filmmakers. Being on this tour made me feel a part of the movie, which was my ultimate aim.

Each of my three tours visited the basement, but I savoured each revisit. Every tour had a different theme, so I gleaned new information, plus individual guides tell different stories. I learnt the complete history.

I joined a Preservation Tour visiting off limits locations. No one else took part, so I had one-on-one time with a Preservationist. I got to touch an original piece of house siding from George Washington's day. It had been removed due to water damage. I touched history, and you rarely get that chance. We ventured into the attic spaces where they were working on the roof. That's not on the usual tours.

The extended house tour was the last item on the agenda. I loved repeatedly going behind closed doors. It's a thrill each time.

I squeezed in a hotdog and chips for lunch between tours and stayed until closed.

Getting home proved difficult, and I felt stranded. With no public transport, Uber became the best option, but with internet issues, I couldn't access the app. There was a family also getting a rideshare, but they had a signal.

Eventually, the internet worked long enough to organise the Uber, and I made it home after paying $38.99 for the long ride.

There are cheaper ways than what I often spend. But I want the full experience, so am prepared to pay more. The cruise with breakfast and entrance ticket to Mount Vernon was $70. A further $20 covered the return boat trip, but left at 3:00 pm, which meant no time for extras. I loved the tours and am glad I did them. They totalled $70. I paid over $165 for a day that could have cost $90. No regrets, though. For me, it is money well spent.

The Uber dropped me off at Union Station, where I bought a turkey and cheese wrap from Walgreens for dinner.

16th August (2015) Sydney, New South Wales (NSW), Australia

Jill and I had tickets to the Netball World Championships Grand Final match in Sydney.

We flew from Avalon Airport; a first for me. I was surprised by the easy parking, and zero lines at security.

I had the usual timeframes in my head and got nervous waiting for Jill to arrive. I called her.

"I'm pulling into the carpark now," she said.

"Great. See you soon."

After twenty minutes, Jill had not appeared. The carparks were close by. Where could she be? I rang her again. "Where are you?"

"I had a car accident at the carpark gate."

"What?"

"Just a fender bender, but we had to swap insurance details. I won't be long."

Only Jill could have a car accident at the carpark gate.

Once at the terminal, the antics continued. I never wanted to travel with her again after her performance.

At security, Jill was working her way through her standard Starbucks drink order, which was over 100 millilitres. She slurped her way to the end. With no bin, she placed it on top of the x-ray machine.

As a smoker, she carried lighters and exceeded the personal limit. In front of the security officer, she handed them to me to carry. I wasn't happy.

But it got worse. "I wonder if I have any drugs with me," she says loud enough for the security officer to hear.

I am dying, hoping the floor opens and swallows me. I wanted to disassociate myself from her. "We are not travelling together," I want to say out loud. I'm imagining removal to a separate room for a strip search. She means prescribed medications, but blurts out drugs instead.

We were the only people at security. Everyone else waited at the gate. It was like a comedy sketch. But this was real, and mortifying.

Despite Jill's antics, security let us through.

My earlier panic was unwarranted as our flight became delayed by three hours. We'd planned to travel via public transport from the airport to the stadium. Another passenger was heading to the sports precinct, so we shared a taxi instead to save time.

We arrived just before the game started, found our local friend and watched Australia versus New Zealand in the 2015 Netball World Championships. We won! A close match 58-55. It's always close at the end, but we came through.

Despite the drama, the match was worth it. I love Jill, but I never want to fly with her again.

17th August (2019) New York, NY, USA

I enjoyed a relaxed morning with a sleep in. The hotel had a free guest laundry, including free powder, so I washed my dirty clothes.

> Kind of cool how relaxed I was that I was in New York and didn't think twice about just going out... Follow the map and everything works. Got to TKTS booth and got tickets to *Waitress*. Then hadn't had breakfast apart from an apple and cup of tea (first since the train) so had McDonald's where air-conditioned and toilets. (Tried Starbucks but no indoor seats, so left.) I watched very bad traffic management with construction vehicles crossing the road. They had no control and both cars and pedestrians were ignoring them! Fun watching them from above.

I chose a hotel near Wall Street, so I utilised the nearby South Street Seaport TKTS booth. It opened at 11:00 am, with no reason to leave the hotel before then. My plans for the rest of the day depended on what theatre tickets I bought.

I arrived soon after opening to find a line. I assumed wrong that it wouldn't be busy. But quieter than the Times Square office. I had theatre suggestions in my travel bible *Come From Away*, *Beautiful* or *Wicked* but I bought tickets to *Waitress* instead at 2:00 pm on 47th Street.

Saturdays made everywhere busy, hence why McDonald's for brunch became the best food option. With seats upstairs, I enjoyed the bird's-eye view of the chaos that was the traffic un-control below.

I walked an hour and a half to the theatre. The city blocks change in vibe as you move uptown. That's what I wanted to experience today.

At the theatre you lined up outside. I'd just walked in the heat and looked forward to air conditioning, but waiting inside was not an option.

I enjoyed the show. I laughed and cried. You can't ask for more.

I had pre-bought evening theatre tickets, thus stayed in the vicinity until its time of 8:00 pm. I had designed a walking tour starting at a waterfall tunnel I wanted to see between 48th and 49th Streets. Unfortunately gates locked me out, so I couldn't walk through the plexiglass tunnel with water flowing over it.

I continued to 51st Street where 6th 1/2 Street starts. Yes, sixth-and-a-half street. I discovered it while researching this trip. I love the concept, so had to explore it.

Some parts are outside and other parts traverse buildings. There are sculptures and art installations along the way and seats for resting. I appreciated the air-conditioned indoor sections.

> Much nicer than the scaffolding covered, urine smelling and hoards of people of all the other Avenues. 6th Avenue closed off for a market which was nice. LOVE sign hidden away but HOPE sign still there.

I walked to Grand Central Station, one of my favourite buildings in New York. I cannot visit New York without coming here and have visited dozens of times despite only ever catching one train from here. They used to hold New Year's Eve Balls, which I added to my wish list. The thought of being dressed up and dancing around under the stunning blue and gold ceiling amongst marble columns sounded like bliss.

I planned to visit the Transit Museum at Grand Central Station but got distracted by a Barnes & Noble bookstore, so the museum closed before my arrival.

The food court downstairs provided dinner, then I made my way to the theatre for *Dear Evan Hansen*.

I loved the show, shedding tears as memories from high school came flooding back. I love musicals that make me cry.

The subway returned me to the hotel. A wonderful first day back in New York.

18th August (2019) New York, NY, USA

I caught the subway to the Intrepid Sea Air and Space Museum, housed in a retired aircraft carrier. I didn't linger in the direct front position, as still frightens me. Intrepid's front is partly straight, but even looking at the photos when writing this, produced stomach butterflies.

As planned, I headed straight to the submarine. The line gets long, so arrive early and go straight there, saving time overall. By design, submarines are cramped. You walk through in single file in pace with the person ahead of you. I managed a few photos (in case required for a future book), to the annoyance of people behind me.

You get a wonderful perspective of Manhattan when on the open air section. It's worth a visit for that alone. The old planes on the deck are cool.

I made googly eyes at the *Enterprise* Space Shuttle. It's exciting being so close, but I'd prefer to explore the inside.

After a hotdog for lunch, I had my pre-booked Concorde tour. I loved seeing the Concorde up close and personal even from the outside, but mega exciting going inside. It was on my original wish list but out of my budget, and now grounded. I will never get to fulfil that plan, but today makes up for it.

I didn't realise how small it would be inside and out. It's narrow. The seats are economy size in twos with a central passageway. Inside disappoints given how expensive the tickets were. I guess you weren't on the aeroplane for long, given its speed capabilities.

I sat in the cockpit for a photo. Would that happen as a paying customer? There are advantages to not seeing it until decommissioned.

The website stated you had to wear closed-toe shoes. I preferred walking in sandals because of the heat but I carried closed shoes in my backpack to change into. No one made me wear them. Everyone else wore open-toed shoes, so I didn't need them.

I left when time to see another pre-bought theatre show. I could have stayed longer, but I love seeing shows when I'm in New York. After a twenty-minute walk, I was at *Beetlejuice* sitting next to a girl seeing it for the tenth time.

By the time the show finished, the heavens had opened, bucketing rain. I had an early dinner nearby, hoping the rain would stop. The Melt Shop, which specialised in grilled cheese, made me a turkey and cheese toasted sandwich.

It continued to rain, and it was wet rain. I dashed to the subway, skipping my next activity of walking The High Line. I had four pages in my travel bible of sites to see along the way, including food options, ice cream venues, and even toilet locations, but the weather foiled those plans.

My last activity was spotting mini bronze statues around the 14th Street/Eighth Avenue subway station. The public art works is called "Life Underground" and comprises cartoon like characters in various scenarios around the station. My travel bible tells me to:

look around stairs, up in the air, on the ground, under stairs, between gates and on all platforms.

It created childish joy to explore and search for these little creatures.

I found an alligator in an access hole eating a man; two characters sawing through the ironwork; a police character on a massive money bag; a man giving coins to a child; a homeless man sleeping; a giant ear; a woman who has lost her head; a couple holding hands; drunk punters; an elephant; and a man sneaking under the gates amongst others. I felt like a kid dashing around the different platforms discovering them. Some are well hidden.

At least it kept me out of the rain. People were arriving at the station drenched and stations began flooding. By the time I alighted, the rain had abated.

19th August (2011) Newcastle, NSW, Australia

A social life isn't easy for shift workers. An ex-colleague was having a baby shower in Newcastle and I was on night shifts. I wanted to drive so had access to a car during the stay. Four friends were flying. It's a twelve hour drive from Melbourne to Newcastle, which I was confident to do in one go, but not if tired. I didn't have time to transition my body clock, thus safer to drive overnight.

I finished work at 7:30 am and slept all day. When awake, I packed the car and drove. I'd planned to leave by seven or eight o'clock, but took longer to get ready than expected. When leaving, I received a phone call from my father telling me his partner of twenty years had died.

I already expected to cry throughout the drive because of the latest rejection in my love life, and now a death was added to the mix. One friend had made me a lolly bag to help keep me awake. There's nothing like eating lollies while crying and driving through the night. The rainy weather exacerbated the mood.

I left around 9:00 pm and I'd promised to send updates to a friend, so she knew I was safe. Most people thought driving was silly and overnight driving insanity. I felt weird texting throughout the night as didn't want to wake her, so I posted updates on Facebook. I made four over the night.

The first:

> Checking in. 6 speed cameras, overtaken 10 trucks, seen 1000 rabbits and only made it to Seymour. Had a late start. A sleep in a truck park is in my future!

Second:

> Beautiful cuppa in Glenrowan and now serious one need to be done!

Facebook had auto corrected kms into one. I instantly wrote a comment:

> That was meant to be serious kms need to be done.

A friend replied:

> Haha but one rhymes with done! Stay awake and dig into that bag of goodies… PS blow Ned a kiss for me. [Referring to Glenrowan being Ned Kelly's home.]

Me:

> I'll blow a kiss to the dog on the tucker box now, as in Gundagai. Finally in NSW, after being attacked by a random bird/bat in a roadside toilet, waving to my great-great-grandfather's grave and saluting my town of birth. Wide awake thanks to lolly bag. I've got a few good hours in me yet!

I continued to sing and cry my heart out with the window wipers on full as the rain pelted down.

Third post:

> 700 km down. 300 to go. I'm currently near Mirulan, I think it's called. Still going well. Sun's up now, which makes it easy and no wake up tape needed yet.

My tears had lessened by sunrise. Comments for this post:

> Hope you're travelling well Fran! I find counting road kill helps pass the time? Did you stop halfway at all? xoxo

I didn't need a break, just quick stops for toilets, tea and food.
People unaware of the circumstances were confused by my posts.

> Where/what are you doing Fran?

> I'm driving to Newcastle overnight. About 70 km to go. One more cup of tea and I'll be there! I have my wake up tape on now, which will see me through the last little bit.

> You crazy kid.

> Wow, you've done well Fran!

I got lost as skirted Sydney's edge, taking toll roads by mistake. I panicked as didn't know how to pay. But somewhere in the depths of my brain, I recalled it was the same toll company as in Melbourne. I put my Melbourne toll beeper on the dash and it beeped as I went through the overhead toll cameras. Whatever it cost, it would be better than driving through Sydney.

Fourth and final post:

> After 995 km, and 12 hours and 20 mins, I am in Newcastle at the hotel. Your wonderful snack bag got me through! Thank you!

The friend who supplied the snacks and asked for check ins, replied to this post.

```
Yay!!! I did wake up and find no messages
though which made me think you had an
accident… then I jumped on FB. Phew!!! Glad
you're safe, see you soon!!! Xoxox
```

Oops, I had made her worry, but I was trying to be nice and let her sleep. At least she found the posts on Facebook.

I got lost in Newcastle and had to ring the hotel for directions twice. This was before navigation on our phones. I had written directions, but once you miss one turn, your instructions are useless. You can't re-route like Google Maps.

I made it to the hotel exhausted from being awake overnight; driving for so long; and for crying so much. But I made it. The others arrived by plane a few hours later. What shift workers do for a weekend away.

20th August (2019) New York, NY, USA

Today I ventured to Brooklyn for the first time. I wandered around the waterfront near the Brooklyn Bridge looking across to the Manhattan skyline. I appreciated the different perspective of the city.

To the left you view Manhattan to its tip and the full Brooklyn Bridge. If you continue to the right, you discover an indoor carousel and Manhattan Bridge in an area called Dumbo, Down Under the Manhattan Bridge Overpass. This is an overcrowded Instagram photo stop of a specific block where the bridge peeks through the buildings. I saw the view and took photos, but I didn't enjoy it. It's not special if everyone is there. But I've seen it.

From here I walked to the New York Transit Museum, which, unbeknownst to me, had no air conditioning. It's housed in an old subway station and the platform where the historical train carriages are displayed is exposed to the rest of the subway system, so can't be air-conditioned.

The heat ruined it for me, so not my favourite transit museum. It was also geared towards children.

I did enjoy the old advertisements and public notices on the historical carriages. I met Etti-cat. A play on "etiquette" about behaviour on the subway. One poster says:

> ETTI-CAT says "I'm flabbergasted! All I did was to give my seat to a little old lady and they pinned a medal on me!" (Standing is part of physical fitness, you know.)

A public health message from World War II states:

> *Food will win the war*
> *We observe Meatless days*
> *Wheatless days - Porkless days*

From here, I walked across the Brooklyn Bridge to Manhattan. I didn't know you joined the bridge walkway some distance before the water. If you are looking to cross the bridge from the waterfront, forget it. It's a long walk in its entirety.

I picked the wrong time of day to walk across heat-wise. Add too many people, and I didn't enjoy it. But I've done it. I treated myself to an ice cream at the opposite end and found a shady spot to sit before returning to the hotel.

Because of the heat, I again skipped The High Line to arrive early at Penn Station's lounge. I was hot, tired and needed a rest.

I caught the *Acela* train in first class to Providence, Rhode Island; a three-hour ride with free food delivered to my seat. I had a comfortable single seat and delicious food on crockery with silverware, and a view out the window. I was sad to leave New York, though.

The *Acela* is a commuter train often filled with regulars. I was the only first time traveller. The conductor serenaded me with a song about the train. The regulars smiled to themselves. It was like a family.

We ran thirty minutes late, arriving at 9:30 pm. I had booked a hotel close to the train station. There were seven lines of directions in my travel bible, but I saw the hotel from the station exit. I crossed the road. Google Maps made it look further away than reality.

I had a studio apartment and was regretting not staying here longer. It was a one-night stay before moving to a recommended hotel to meet a friend. I'll know where to stay if I ever return to town.

21st August (1999) New York, NY, USA

I needed an early start to achieve my goal of tickets to climb the Statue of Liberty's crown. You needed to be in line by 10:00 am to guarantee a spot. It closed after 9/11 for eight years. Pre-pandemic, you had to book months in advance to ensure tickets and pay for access. It was closed when I wrote this and open when editing. In 1999, it was free. You just had to arrive early.

My ticket mentions a strenuous climb of three hundred and fifty-four steps. You start with a normal staircase, but the stairs narrow into single file. This takes you to a set of circular stairs that continue round and round until you are inside the crown.

The two interwoven staircases created a one-way system. Their open design exposes visitors to the statue's internal structure, and accentuates the height. It is not recommended for those scared of heights or easily intimidated.

The crown has limited space with a capacity of five or six. Ten people may fit, but not be able to enjoy the window views simultaneously.

The room contains multiple rectangular windows to form the crown pattern. It's not a better view than other areas of Ellis Island. It's about being IN the crown. Whenever you view the statue in photos or in person, you can point to the crown and declare, "I've been in there." If you want a city view, you will be disappointed.

From this vantage point, you can read the words on the book she is carrying "July IV, MDCCLXXVI", the date of the Declaration of Independence signing.

Lift your gaze to see the torch and the balcony people used to climb. It involves ladders as opposed to stairs, and has been closed to visitors since 1916. They replaced the original torch in 1986. It's displayed in the onsite museum.

22nd August (2019) Providence, Rhode Island (RI), USA

Today my colleague and I did something I've seen on television but never thought I'd experience myself. We rode an American yellow school bus to the conference. We saw it approaching and got excited when realised it came for us. On we hopped, wearing big smiles. Even the American attendees enjoyed a trip back to their childhood.

After the conference, we stocked up on breakfast supplies from a CVS store. I bought Raisin Bran, milk, applesauce and a large bottle of water. Breakfast and hydration sorted.

We had dinner in Federal Hill, Providence's Little Italy, which we discovered on the tour we'd taken yesterday. It's full of Italian shops and restaurants. We caught the bus from near our hotel at an outdoor bus terminus. It took us a bit to figure it out, but we made it. And made it quickly. It turned out to be not far.

It was a gorgeous evening to be outside listening to music and eating yummy eggplant pasta followed by a scrumptious dessert at a bakery called Pastiche that had been pointed out to us. I ate more than I needed. But I enjoyed my chocolate mousse cake and hot chocolate to finish the night. We walked home after sitting all day and eating too much for dinner.

Providence may be a capital city, but it's compact. The map makes everything look far away when they're not. It's weird, and hard to describe. We felt silly for catching the bus around the corner.

I enjoyed having a companion to spend the evenings with after a conference.

23rd August (2019) Providence, RI, USA

Another first today, in making it to the Cheesecake Factory. And I'm hooked. We chose an outside table for two. With the extensive menu, I struggled to decide. I ordered two starters: cheeseburger spring rolls and zucchini fries. They were scrumptious. I'm addicted to cheeseburger spring rolls now. My local supermarket has them, making them too easy to get.

The two starters created an enormous meal with no room for dessert. I was at the Cheesecake Factory, unable to eat cheesecake. Disappointing. My colleague had an idea. We'd come back tomorrow going straight to dessert. That helped me go home satisfied.

24th August (2019) Providence, RI, USA

We had a weird start to the day when our big yellow bus forgot to collect us. The organisers had to arrange Ubers. The bus carried us home, though.

Back at the hotel, we explored the beautiful old building. You could sense the opulence as you entered. The lobby greets you with red carpet, wood columns, an intricately carved wooden ceiling complete with chandelier, and marble stairs to a gold and glass elevator. Alas, the elevator is no longer in use. There is a sign that says it's for time travel only. I'm up for time travel, but it didn't happen. Now it's a decorative piece.

We walked to the mall. I stocked up on melatonin from GNC and bought two tops and a summer dress from Macy's. My $5 bargain top in the colours of the American flag receives comments at each wear.

We sat inside at the Cheesecake Factory for our dessert dinner. It was constantly busy. With so many cheesecakes, I struggled again to choose. I kept changing my mind. Looking at them rather than a written list made it extra hard. I settled on the lemon merengue pie cheesecake and washed it down with a hot chocolate. Our brains hurt by now after three conference days, so we welcomed a sugar hit.

25th August (2019) Providence, RI, USA

My colleague flew home today, so I saw her off at the Boston Airport bus stop. It was a practice run for when I'd be on my own. It was close.

I returned to the mall for extra shopping. Then relaxed with a weird dinner of Pringles and applesauce, watching old episodes of *Law & Order* in bed.

Tomorrow I'd collect a hire car and drive to Newport and its mansions.

26th August (1993) London, England, UK

Thanks to a fire at Windsor Castle, the Queen needed to raise funds for repairs, resulting in Buckingham Palace being open to visitors for the first time. What a stroke of luck to be in London during this momentous occasion! It started as a temporary measure. We believed it to be a once in a lifetime opportunity.

I got up at 6:00 am to queue. We had seen the long queues, so knew we needed to go early. The line ran down The Mall. We received tickets to a 9:45 am time slot. As two Australians who'd quit our nanny jobs with unpleasant families, we had the flexibility to queue on a weekday, when less crowded.

We paid our £8 entry fee, expensive for two unemployed nannies, but we were happy to pay for the experience. I have a photo of me with an excited look on my face, clutching my colour guidebook. Another photo has me inside the gate, further than the public had been permitted before. It felt exclusive. No photos were allowed inside the palace.

We followed a defined path with ropes, stopping you from going astray. We walked past the doors to the famous balcony. You couldn't help but imagine the Royal Family waiting to receive the crowd's adoration.

I'm sure the current tour differs from back in 1993. It opened on the 7th of August, so had been operating for less than three weeks. They were still figuring it out, but it did not disappoint.

I bought a Commemorative Cover for £2 at the gift shop, which they placed in a fancy bag. Both are in my scrapbook. I kept a catalogue of the souvenir options. The various collections included: Stationery, Bone China, Jewellery, Glass, Tie and Commemorative. I could only justify paying for the cheapest item, the £2 Commemorative Cover. The most expensive options included a hand-painted enamel box for £85, and a lead crystal bowl for £75.

I felt special afterwards as a clutched my Buckingham Palace Gift Shop bag. No one but us knew it contained a £2 purchase.

27th August (1994) Paris, France

I left at 5:40 am for Kate's house. We each paid £132.50 to French Connexion for a weekend trip to Paris, with a 6:45 am departure from near Victoria Train Station. We travelled via bus to Dover; caught the ferry to Calais; and continued to Paris by bus. We'd arrive in time for a "Parisian" dinner and a night tour.

Reality became a broken-down bus leading to three hours in a motorway lay-by, a late dinner, and a cancelled night tour. My diary says:

> Meal was a joke.

From memory, it was chicken and chips. Everyone expected French food to be fancy. Chicken and chips did not live up to expectation. If they'd called it "dinner", no one would have given it a second thought. But the group was not impressed.

The exact words from the brochure: *Parisian Restaurant Meal. Apéritif, starter, main course, dessert, wine, coffee.* We paid £20 extra to include this.

Kate was particularly bothered by the hotel. I don't remember why with my only memory a flash of the bathroom.

28th August (1994) Paris, France

We visited Euro Disney, which opened less than two years ago, making Disney in Europe a novel experience in 1994. Having enjoyed Disney World in 1992, I was eager to have fun and enjoy rides again.

Not everyone on the weekend tour visited Euro Disney. It was a more expensive version of a Paris weekend. Eight of us travelled on the Paris metro from our hotel. We were given entry tickets, pointed in the station's direction, and left to our own devices.

We took each other's photos at the gate, then separated inside the park.

Based on the photos, we watched every parade, including the after dark, illuminated one. We watched a *Beauty and the Beast* show and had photos with Minnie Mouse. Ride-wise I have photos from It's A Small World, Peter Pan's Flight, the Tea Cups and *Snow White and the Seven Dwarfs*. Space Mountain did not open until 1995.

> Euro Disney fantastic. Managed to get there via French trains. Long day of constantly walking around, but worth it. Saw so much. Highlight of whole trip that's for sure.

1994 had the park's lowest rates of attendance. Following the almost closure of the park in October, they rebranded it as Disneyland Paris. I will forever refer to it as Euro Disney.

29th August (2005) Melbourne, VIC to Narrandera, NSW, Australia

Lottie, the Toyota Arkana, has been fixed and re-packed for a second attempt to drive to Far North Queensland. This time I travelled to a job instead of a relationship attempt. I had more luggage on board, including a desktop computer. I had a week until my job started.

I'm embarrassed, and disappointed, to say I have no photos of this trip. I wish I had a million. My diary has one page of notes. And a notebook has five pages of scribblings on tank fills and mileage details like when I crossed the Nullarbor. I wrote an extensive group e-mail on arrival in Queensland and I have clear memories saying to myself I must save a copy to use as a diary entry. Alas, I never saved it and has disappeared into the black hole of a defunct e-mail account. I know this will be a poor imitation of the original telling. Luckily, it was a memorable trip.

No farewell brunch second time round. I completed my packing, bid farewell to my flatmate, and drove. It wasn't long before things went awry. I'm proud to say, though, I survived each mishap.

I made it to Essendon, a Melbourne suburb, where you merge from the Calder Freeway onto the Tullamarine Freeway, before the first mishap. The roads have changed since 2005. The left lane led to an overpass above the Calder Freeway and turned to the right. As you straightened out, cars merged from the opposite direction of the Calder Freeway. It was not a place to stop.

At the turn, I heard a loud metallic sound from underneath Lottie. I assumed I'd driven over a piece of metal on the road, which bounced off Lottie's momentum. I looked into my rearview mirror to see the spare tyre swinging freely.

The tyre was attached to a metal bar that swung open to access a rear storage compartment. A metal clip held the bar against the back of the vehicle. I surmised the clip had come away, making the earlier metallic sound. This meant the bar swung in and out with the tyre attached. I could see the tyre moving.

Surely this was serious enough to stop in a section with minimal shoulder and no emergency lane. I turned my hazard lights on and came to a stop in the narrow siding sticking out into the far left lane. The cars honked, but I had no choice. I needed to investigate. I knew it was some distance before the next exit or emergency lane.

Concrete siding sat to the left. I had to exit Lottie into traffic. The speed limit was 80 or 100 km/hr along here. Either way, the cars drove fast.

A road safety campaign a few years ago highlighted the dangers of alighting into traffic. It took me back to this moment every time. It was what I pictured in my head as I climbed out of Lottie.

I waited for a break in the traffic as best I could. I assumed cars would move into the right lanes after seeing my hazard lights. I opened the door enough to squeeze out and raced to Lottie's rear.

My suspicions were right; no metal clip in sight. Now what? At first, I thought I'd have to remove the tyre and put it inside, but that wouldn't stop the swaying. I had to re-secure the bar.

I had an extensive tool and repair kit, including a packet of cable ties. Would they be strong enough? It was the best choice, so I gave it a shot. I returned to the driver's seat unharmed and climbed into the back to find the cable ties. I can't remember how many I used, but sure it was more than one. Nothing like cable ties holding a spare tyre to your truck. I added bungee cords and gaffer tape for extra security. But the cable ties replaced the metal clip.

Off I drove, with frequent glances in the rearview mirror, to see if the cable ties held. They worked; no movement. The tyre remained attached for the rest of the drive. Day one mishap sorted.

The notebook scribbles are almost incomprehensible. I may have put 70 litres of diesel in tank two. I left maybe around 12:00 pm and drove till 6:15 pm. Maybe I covered 439 km. I slept at a Narrandera campsite where I continued the practice of the back seat being my bed.

30th August (2005) Narrandera to Narrabri, NSW, Australia

Seems I stretched the truth when claimed daily mishaps. I encountered one mishap the first day and two the second day. I experienced none the third day, then downhill from there.

Today didn't start well. I had a 12 volt kettle to match Lottie's 12 volt sockets.

Kettle blew all fuses. Just wanted a cup of tea.

I surmise this is when I began to use the camp stove to boil water, and the practise of filling the thermos for later. Boiling water in a saucepan on a gas stove involved more effort than a kettle. This started the practice of driving, then stopping later for a break to boil water. The water remained hot for a second stop down the road in the thermos.

I have flashes of me in a roadside picnic location with the gas stove on the table and having a cup of tea as I stretched my legs. I also have memories of buying fuses, so they should have been in my tool kit.

The next mishap required professional help. I drove with diesel tank number one selected. I'd done over 400 km and planned to switch to tank two once through the town I'd entered. Parkes is the town from the movie *The Dish* about the moon landing footage.

I based my mileage on my Nullarbor drive. The problem was the desert had straight roads, and few reasons to slow. The Newell Highway traversed towns, and I drove into a head wind all day. I had my foot hard on the accelerator yet struggled to reach 85 km/hr. Whereas I drove 100 km/hr or more across the Nullarbor. I had not taken the different conditions into account.

I believe the tank gauges worked when I bought Lottie, but now one of them had broken. So there was no warning light. I used mileage as my guide for when to fill up.

I drove through Parkes, knowing I'd flick the switch to tank two any minute, when Lottie shuddered. A railway crossing lay ahead, so I limped the car into a carpark on the left as it stopped. I had zero power.

A few seconds later and I may have stopped on the railway tracks, unable to move. I suspected I had run out of diesel. Conveniently I stopped opposite a BP Truck Stop, so I hopped out and headed over to see if anyone could help me. Could I switch tanks and drive away? That would have worked in a petrol car. A truck driver overheard me say I may have run out of diesel and said that meant trouble. You had to remove any air from the engine. If you couldn't, then bye-bye Lottie, and drive to Queensland.

How stupid did I feel knowing I almost got stuck on a railway line and broken Lottie, because I didn't turn a switch? I had over 70 litres of diesel available, but for now, I was stuck.

I had my top level RACV Roadside Assistance. I called in the reinforcements and waited in the car. The mechanic reiterated the truck driver's concerns. But it was my lucky day. The mechanic found little air and was confident he'd removed it. I switched to tank two and filled the empty tank at the BP truck stop.

My notebook states:

Tank one ran out completely at 436 km. (Oops!)

Oops says it all. I filled the tank with 80 litres. So now I can be confident it's an 80 litre tank. I had not used tank two much, but added 21 litres. Diesel cost $1.31 per/litre, so spent $132.

I stopped for a dinner break at 5:30 pm after 521 km. Then parked for the night at Narrabri at 8:00 pm after 639 km. What a day.

31st August (2005) Narrabri, NSW to Hervey Bay, Queensland (QLD), Australia

Day three was mishap free. I took a detour from the inland highways to visit my aunt and uncle in Hervey Bay. Despite the darkness, the distinct features of old Queenslander style houses in Maryborough caught my attention. I would need to revisit during daylight.

My aunt told me I had the same giggle as my grandmother, her mother. No one had ever mentioned that before. Why had no one ever told me? I am known for my giggle, and my giggle has got me into trouble many times. I did not know I inherited that from my grandmother. She died before I was born. I always believed we would have got along and surely that was true if we shared a giggle.

Hearing that brought tears to my eyes. My aunt apologised, saying she didn't mean to make me cry. I said I was upset no one had told me before now. But happy to have her giggle, our giggle. This trip was worth it for that information alone.

I drove 769 km today. I bought 93 litres of diesel at $1.22 per/litre, spending $114.

September

1st September (2005) Hervey Bay to Yamba, QLD, Australia

I followed the Bruce Highway for the rest of the drive along the coast, continuing north. It was a mishap day, but uneventful until bedtime.

I ate dinner at 7:30 pm at Rockhampton, known as Rocky. I slept in a roadside truck stop out of Rocky, as in a dirt rest stop, as too tired to make the 100 km to the next campsite. To me, other parked trucks signalled safety. I'd feel uneasy if alone. Introducing myself to one of the truck drivers, I clarified if I could park there, and if safe. He told me it was all good except I'd be disturbed by trucks leaving. I could handle that, so stayed.

Lottie had a car door style side entrance. While preparing for the night, the door refused to shut. I'm unsure whether to blame excessive slamming or damage during transit for the malfunction. With a failed latch, the lock was useless.

Bungee cords to the rescue. I used the shortest cord to hook the door latch to the fridge stand. Although it worked, the bungee cord's inherent flexibility created slack. Not ideal while parked in a secluded area. An unlocked door made for a restless night's sleep.

After spending the morning with my aunt and uncle, I only drove 433 km today.

2nd September (2005) Yamba to Toobanna, QLD, Australia

The sound of trucks woke me around 5:00 am. I got up and made tea before leaving.

What would happen with a door that can't shut? My biggest fears materialised. The door flew open whenever it wanted. I continued to drive, casting frequent glances back to check if the door was ajar–resulting in a tense drive. I reinforced it with more bungees, but the bungees became overstretched with the force of the door trying to open. It's scary seeing the door flapping out of the corner of your eye. I worried about the tight single lane road from Cairns to Port Douglas and beyond.

But the door was yesterday's mishap. Today's mishap was stupid and avoidable. I filled the tanks after driving 200 km. 91 litres at $1.19, spending $109. I continued another 100 km before I realised I had no recollection of screwing the caps on the tanks. Did I forget to replace them? Yes. I'd travelled too far to return. The next petrol station had emergency plastic covers, which I put on and planned to buy replacements in Cairns.

I had dinner in Townsville at 5:30 pm, then drove a further 100 km, stopping at a campground in Toobanna. I prepared for bed, berating myself about the tank caps and worried about how the door would cope with tomorrow's drive.

3rd September (2022) Toobanna to Wonga, QLD, Australia

I stopped in Cairns to buy screw on caps for my fuel tanks, keeping the plastic ones for emergencies. I also filled the tanks one last time at $1.12 per/litre.

Driving the cliff road to Port Douglas has left vivid memories. The narrow shoulder meant little room between the car and the rock face. The door flapped with each corner, stretching the bungee cord. If the bungee snapped and the door flung open, a serious accident could result. The fear engulfed me, making the drive horrendous. It's an experience I never wish to repeat.

After completing my epic drive, I arrived at Wonga and settled into my enchanting new home. Adjacent to the pool, my two-bedroom villa nestled next to a miniature rainforest, with the beach behind. I could hear the lapping waves from my bedroom.

I drove 3327 km. My drive from Perth to Melbourne was 3323 km. Four kilometres difference! What are the odds? Maybe Australia's symmetrical after all.

4th September (2018) New Orleans, Louisiana (LA), USA

I left my luggage with reception.

I'd booked a walking tour of the Garden District through Viator. The tour met at a nearby bakery. I caught the tram, or streetcar, number 12, the St Charles line, which travels along St Charles Avenue. The historic tram cars are a joy to ride through an area of New Orleans without bars.

I arrived early to have breakfast; a toasted ham sandwich. No one else arrived, as mine was the only booking. I don't enjoy being alone with a guide.

The weather caused concern as forecasters warned of a hurricane. Most of the Bourbon Street businesses had closed with sandbags outside their doors. Since Hurricane Katrina, the locals don't take risks. As an outsider, I observed the flawless blue sky, brought my umbrella and continued on.

We walked around looking at stunning southern architecture with ornate ironwork. Then the incredible Lafayette Cemetery No 1. I loved everything. As we concluded our walk, the clear blue sky gave way to dark clouds that brought rain. Despite the impending hurricane, I raised my umbrella and returned to the cemetery for further investigation.

My phone rang. The company running my afternoon tour called to cancel because of the hurricane. Not happy. I'd booked a Hurricane Katrina Tour to view the failed levees and the worst hit areas. I wanted to understand the levee system; how it worked and why it failed. Instead, a hurricane cancelled my hurricane tour. They issued a refund.

This allowed me to linger in the cemetery, as the storm clouds added atmosphere. I took loads of photos of the tombs and surrounds. It's a city of the dead with a Romanesque influence. I collected information for a potential future book. The caveau system held my interest. Caveau is a French word describing a burial chamber often used by multiple members of a family. It will appear in a future novel.

I caught the streetcar towards the French Quarter and visited two museums, The Presbytere and Cabildo. The first had exhibitions about Mardi Gras and Hurricane Katrina. It explained the levees, and it appears to be the council's fault for not building them to recommendations. The Cabildo is an 18th Century building where they signed the Louisiana Purchase, resulting in the French selling Louisiana to America.

I walked back to my hotel and moved into my new room. I'd stayed in a Garden Room, the cheapest option, and now moved to the most expensive room with a balcony overlooking Bourbon Street. It was too expensive to have the balcony room the entire stay, thus compromised with different room categories.

Although I found the balcony marvellous, most bars and shops were closed, so I overlooked a desolate street. It never occurred to me Bourbon Street would be barren given the pumping music and crowd I witnessed on arrival. The hurricane prediction scared everyone away.

I bought ice cream and ate it on the balcony as the odd tourist walked by.

I met a friend from work, and her cousin, who'd come to town for the conference starting tomorrow evening. We got lost finding a recommended bar, which wasn't worth the effort. We found an open restaurant and sat on their balcony overlooking an empty Bourbon Street. I ordered a traditional Louisiana meal of po-boy, which I'm glad I tried, but won't order again. The streets, bars and restaurants were devoid of vibe.

The hurricane never materialised.

5th September (2018) New Orleans, LA, USA

Before checking out, I enjoyed a cup of tea on the balcony. And dropped off my laundry at a same day laundrette nearby.

I had Café du Monde beignets for breakfast, becoming covered in icing sugar. But how can you resist these fried pieces of deliciousness? I walked round the back of the restaurant to watch the dough tossed in the oil. It's worth a look.

I joined a French Quarter walking tour, hearing the history of the buildings and their inhabitants over the centuries. John Lafitte's blacksmith shop is a highlight.

I enjoy a pirate story although I find privateers fascinating. It is a fine line between pirate and privateer. Which one was John Lafitte?

We strolled through Jackson Square to the "NOLA 300" sign. NOLA stands for New Orleans Louisiana. This year is New Orleans' 300th birthday or tricentennial.

After the tour, I walked further afield to Frenchman Street. Some call it the locals Bourbon Street. It is less touristy and big on authentic music and buildings. It is also where the television show *NCIS: New Orleans* has its True Tone bar. Its real name is R Bar and Inn. I walked passed the entrance to the NCIS Headquarters but obstructed by roadwork vehicles.

Shop signs said they'd re-open on Thursday, as in tomorrow, after the storm. Another quiet day in the French Quarter. I don't blame them for being scared after the horrific stories I heard from the Hurricane Katrina aftermath, and I'm talking about in the French Quarter. Although images of the area flooded were broadcasted, the narrative focused on the squalled Superdome conditions and the people stranded on their rooftops. The French Quarter residents lived through a different hell.

I collected my laundry, which had just been folded as I arrived. The wonderful laundress would not let me leave without the full treatment. I waited as she wrapped it in plastic tied with colourful ribbons. She would not allow me to leave without the ribbons.

With my $18 fancy laundry, and my other luggage in tow, I got a taxi to the conference hotel situated outside the French Quarter.

The humongous hotel contained a towering glass wall spanning over twenty floors. Visible through the glass elevator, it showcased the illuminated Superdome behind, in a spectrum of ever-changing colours.

I registered for the conference, bought breakfast supplies for the morning from a hotel shop, and headed to my room to relax.

6th September (2014) Cape Town, South Africa

In the previous weeks, access to the internet had been limited. I posted a Facebook update the previous night, with a photo of my upmarket airport hotel room.

```
Not a bad way to spend my last night in
Africa. I will miss the real Africa though.
8 incredible weeks. I wish I could have 8
more! You know I'll be back!
```

At the airport I posted again, with a sad emoticon.

```
I am so nervous right now at the airport??
I don't want to leave Africa.
```

Tears fell as the plane took off and throughout the flight. I watched a movie with an African safari scene twice and the safari scene on repeat. I wanted to go back to Africa and repeat the last eight weeks. After years of planning and yearning, the trip was over. I struggled to accept that.

I posted my arrival home on Facebook.

```
Back in Oz safely. Very surreal feeling
though. I couldn't even remember which
key opened my front door. Brain still in
Africa, I think.
```

I commented I'd forgotten how much sugar I have in my tea.
What evoked those responses? You'll have to wait. Sorry, this is a teaser!

7th September (2018) New Orleans, LA, USA

After finishing the second day of the conference, my work friend, her cousin, and I strolled to the French Quarter. We had dinner at Napoleon House, a traditional Creole restaurant, and shared beignets for dessert at Café du Monde.

The hot and wet weather lingered. The streets remained quiet. Even the conference was quiet with attendees cancelling because of the forecasted hurricane.

We walked through the streets with the NOLA 300 sign and buildings lit in bright colours. I enjoyed New Orleans and was glad the hurricane was not on the radar before my arrival. It would have been disappointing to miss this experience, especially as no hurricane materialised.

8th September (2017) Las Vegas, NV, USA

I got my trip disaster out of the way early. I handed over my paperwork at the check-in counter. She said, "You don't have a visa."

"Yes, I do. I gave it to you." I had a printed copy of my ESTA (Electronic System for Travel Authorisation) visa waiver with my passport.

"This does not match your passport. I can't check you in."

I had mistyped my passport number, voiding my ESTA. Thankfully, the Flight Centre kiosk could arrange a new one, for a fee, once open. I found a line forming and growing. Last minute ESTAs was big business. The visa cost $17.55 and Flight Centre charged $55 for their speedy service.

I got the ESTA, rejoined the queue, and made the flight.

Qantas' flight QF93 to Los Angeles allows you to arrive before you departed. I love that. I arrived at 6:35 am; through the automatic kiosks at 6:55 am; and my passport stamped and luggage collected by 7:30 am. I reached the Delta Terminal at 8:00 am.

However, a miscommunication along the way meant I bypassed the domestic check-in area, arriving airside with my check-in bag. At first I didn't realise what had happened. Two security personnel called me over, saying their way was quicker. The next thing I knew, shops and cafes surrounded me with no way back.

They opened my big bag, which held liquids over 100 millilitres and scissors. Why did they let me through? The whole situation still confuses me, to be honest.

The normal process fills in time and I wanted to ask if I had lounge access. I had a first-class ticket for my domestic flight, but was unsure if it came with lounge privileges.

As first class entitled me to complimentary checked baggage, it could check it at the gate. However, I'd have to wrangle my luggage until the gate opened in three hours' time. I bought a banana and a bottle of water which allowed me to ask for a cup of hot water too (free). I made a cup of tea to commiserate my mishaps.

A storm in my destination of Las Vegas closed the airport for three hours. My flight became delayed, but after we'd boarded. It didn't bother me as I got longer to enjoy first class with free unlimited drinks and snacks. There were twelve passengers in first class with our own flight attendant. The narrow plane had a 1:2 seat arrangement giving me a window seat without a neighbour. I enjoyed the scenery once we flew. I saw Los Angeles's beaches, the Hollywood sign, then mountains and desert, and fluffy clouds.

I caught a SuperShuttle to my hotel and the late arrival meant check in already open. Caesars Palace was a dream come true. I lived out my ancient Roman fantasies here. The building, the lobby, the decor. Roman heaven. A tacky, but oh so wonderful, treat for myself and I planned to savour every minute.

My pool view room sat on the nineteenth floor of the Palace Tower. Incredible lightning strikes, remnants from the earlier storm, were visible from my window. I deliberated for ages over which tower to stay in. I was ecstatic with my decision.

The massive room included a lounge area with an L-shaped couch next to the king-size bed. Tinted windows stretched from floor to ceiling. There were no signs of the opposite tower block's occupants. From this, I inferred they could not see me.

The bathroom was divine, with a bathtub reminiscent of ancient Rome in tiles and decor. My Roman dreams realised.

I grabbed a take-away meal from the food court. I ate looking out the window at the lights, the traffic and the lightning. Perfect!

I could have slept at 5:00 pm but pushed myself to stay awake and forfeited any hope of seeing the Las Vegas lights this first night. I revelled in the luxurious setting and stunning views as the day turned from day to twilight to night. Exhaustion took over at 8:00 pm.

9th September (2017) Las Vegas, NV, USA

I woke at 3:00 am and worried I wouldn't return to sleep, but I dosed on and off getting up 7:00 am. I planned a legendary Las Vegas buffet for breakfast. One of the famous buffets was in my hotel, so I chose the Bacchanal Buffet of Caesars Palace for my first Vegas buffet. At my 7:50 am arrival, a few people waited in line. It opened at 8:00 am on weekends. I took photos around the hotel while the foot traffic was low.

On my return, I walked straight through and the server understood my tea requirements upon requesting hot water and milk. Maybe there are other people particular with their tea.

Oh. My. Goodness. Food everywhere! You cannot help but overeat at buffets with too many food stations to explore.

First plate: sausages; prime rib; scrambled eggs; bacon; and potato gratin.

Second plate: French toast; red velvet pancakes; churros; and fruit salad.

Third plate: Nutella crepe with mixed berries and whipped cream; pineapple; and an egg tart.

Drinks-wise, I had a berry smoothie, orange juice, and three cups of tea. I missed the Italian, Mexican and Asian food stations. If I have no room for spring rolls, you know I'm beyond full.

I ate for one and a half hours and loved every second. I require further practice at how to indulge in every station, though. You can't come to Vegas without partaking in a buffet. I wrote in my diary:

> I'll do better on the next one!

I over did it, deciding tea was my misstep and I should not drink it at my next buffet. I almost vomited during my third plate when the fullness hit me.

I waited for my stomach to settle and scoped out the pool chair availability from my window. I had read you needed to go early to ensure a chair. People were staking their claims, but not in numbers that required immediate action.

I claimed a comfy pool side lounger in the shade. The cool and cloudy weather helped keep people away. Today's plan was to relax. I read by the pool, people watched, and took dips in the water. I'd bought a new swimsuit for this trip and I loved it. My first one piece with a built in skirt. I've bought no other design since.

> My body may be at its worst ever, but I wasn't the biggest body out there. I was so comfortable all day. Fine by myself at breakfast, then by the pool and then in the pool. Yeah! Go me.

I think that signifies I enjoyed my day regardless of any expected insecurities.

I returned to my room to shower and dress for my evening plans. I explored The Forum Shops, had a snack for dinner (no lunch required), and saw Jerry Seinfeld.

> OMG The Forum Shops were incredible. They did such a great job. It feels so opulent and very ancient Rome. I didn't care about the shops. I was looking above them! Then I thought I'd better have a quick bite in case got hungry. So since the buffet I've only had sweet potato fries which were delicious and I met three Canadians also eating before seeing Jerry, so that was nice. My seats were so great. I chose well. So close I almost felt like he was looking at and talking to me so many times. Very funny. Glad I saw him. I was so tired though. The last half hour I really struggled. I was yawning every few minutes and couldn't laugh as much as I wanted to because too tired. He finished at 9:15 pm so wasn't that late! I'm really going to struggle to see the lights! Forgot a great part of The Forum Shops was a circular escalator! I loved it! I'm so easily amused. I was grinning all the way round the shops. I was very happy indeed. Straight to bed after the show!

I found the circular escalators irresistible. I had no necessity for them, yet I took multiple rides for fun. Such a cute touch to an already stupendous environment. I ride them whenever in Vegas. It hasn't lost its specialness yet.

10th September (2017) Las Vegas, NV, USA

I got up at 7:00 am, left my bags with the Bell Desk, and headed to the Cosmopolitan Hotel's buffet, called the Wicked Spoon.

Each hotel/casino has unique decor and attractions. I had fourteen pages in my travel bible detailing each casino and its sights. The Cosmopolitan was two doors away, but they were enormous doors. Here's a sample of my travel bible instructions to the Cosmopolitan explaining what I'd pass, and see, along the way. This is two of the fourteen pages.

At Caesars go past Absinthe + Cafe Americano
R) with Brahma Shrine on L) towards Spanish Steps and lemonade/hot choc stand
Flamingo Rd Overpass straight into Bellagio
R) at Gucci passed Dior
Follow main trail into casino
L) when looks like a circle (ie - biggest passage)
R) at end
First L)
Straight to Registration Desk
Look up at ceiling
R) for *gardens*
Patisserie @ back on L) hand side for *Chocolate Fountain*
Back towards reception just by Concierge (before) passageway to R)
Toilets
Somehow end up to passageway undercover to street
(Or go to front door + R))
R) to Cosmopolitan
Brunch - "Wicked Spoon" to back keeping L)
Casino on R)

Vitals Shop L)
You pass *Chandelier Bar*

Did you follow? That's what I designed after countless hours of watching walking tours of the strip on YouTube, and zoomed in Google Maps. The asterisks highlight a sight.

The Bellagio reception's ceiling houses "Fiori di Como" a hand-blown glass sculpture of over two thousand colourful flowers designed by Dale Chihuly. A spectacular burst of colour above you. Anyone can wander in and appreciate it.

I almost missed the chocolate fountain, even with my detailed instructions, as was not the fountain I expected. I walked passed initially but found it when turned around. It looked yummy, but it did not impress me. It is the world's largest chocolate fountain, and I can say I have seen it.

The buffet was on the second floor, which the instructions missed. I started at the Asian station.

First plate: pork belly, bone marrow, truffle pasta, gyoza, bacon, mashed potato, hash brown casserole and a fortune cookie. My fortune: *you will have many friends when you need them.*

Second plate: French toast and fruit salad.

Third plate: chocolate mousse and peach cobbler.

No drinks. You don't fill up on drinks with the gluttony of food options.

My diary sums up the day.

> Great day! Vegas is like one enormous theme park; adult Disneyland. It was hot outside, but went in and out of air-conditioned casinos which cooled you down. Buffet was good. Hard to call on which one better between Bacchanal and Wicked Spoon. Good bits about both. I loved the Asian station at Wicked Spoon. I didn't eat from there at Caesars, but it didn't have the most appealing choices either. Loved the pork at Wicked Spoon.

Found my way round easily enough. Was still too full by time at New York to even think about the coaster. I'm pretty sure I would have vomited, so will still have to go back and do that. But they did a great job everywhere. It looked like New York or Paris etc. I loved it.

Made it to a Craps lesson at New York, but to be honest, I still don't get it. I missed the first couple of minutes, so maybe that's why? Not sure, but I sort of did some gambling stuff as haven't done any real gambling.

Saw a movie at M&M World which was kind of cute–3D even.

Bought a couple of dresses at Ross Dress for Less. Not as great as hoping, but a couple of extra dresses will be good. I bought a little too little clothing this time round. Good for conference and hiking, but not for general Vegas! Should be good now, though. Also bought a dress from Bubba Gump, of all places. I like that one!

Saw flamingoes at Flamingo's. Wandered around Planet Hollywood–Arabian theme very well done. Saw a bit of Elara where I nearly stayed. From here crossed back over to Caesars and had a last wander through the amazing Forum Shops but so tired and feet sore so caught an Uber to Venetian.

Very grand entrance. I was sad to leave Caesars but oh my, Venetian is incredible as well. Room is lovely–push button curtains though only works fully to open not close?

Had dinner at food court–pasta–after an easy check in and found out I have $150 room credit! I'm not sure I knew that, so that was a bonus. Can be used anywhere I can charge back to my room. Makes the stay a little bit cheaper to get money back.

Had to go out to get some supplies from Walmart and I made it to outside at night a little bit. The Venetian was magical lit up. I need to be able to stay up late enough to be able to go out. So tired though in evening.

I held my stomach while looking at the roller coaster at the New York-New York Hotel. I wanted to ride it, but not after overindulging at the buffet. Disappointing, but the right call.

The Craps lesson went over my head. This was my way of participating without gambling. But it confused me. It's fair to say I will never play craps. I love the casino floor atmosphere, though. Whatever the theme, the vibe is electric, and understand how it can be addictive. I get the good feels without gambling.

I found the slot machines fascinating. They had a theme for everyone. I saw *Game of Thrones, Wonder Woman, Titanic, Big Bang Theory, Ellen DeGeneres.* They wanted to hook everyone.

Walking the strip is akin to traversing the world. One minute you're in ancient Rome, the next modern day New York, then in Paris, a Medieval Castle and the Venice canals. The insides and outsides combine with the New York-New York coaster travelling around the skyscrapers outside and inside the casino's fake subways. And the Eiffel Tower is outside, but the legs sit on the casino floor.

Where else but Vegas can you see a chandelier three storeys high or take a photo of yourself inside a giant red stiletto?

The pink flamingoes at Flamingo's had mist machines to keep them cool. They're easier to spot here than in Africa.

If I thought my Caesars room was nice, my Venetian Hotel room was spectacular. A notch above Caesars for sure. I considered Caesars too expensive for my entire stay, making the Venetian cheaper. If that's true, the Venetian was excellent value. My room had an elegant interior with a sunken section furnished with a lounge suite and table and chairs. The bathroom had double doors, and I opened them with exaggerated fanfare each time. It felt grandiose and made me want to install double doors at home. I delighted in the automatic curtains. To the right, the view overlooked a roof onto the desert; to the left, my next Las Vegas hotel.

The Venetian's forecourt beats Caesars day and night. Their lobbies and casinos are on par. I love The Forum Shops, but the Venetian's Grand Canal shops were sublime. Some find Caesars tacky, but everyone would consider the Venetian sophisticated. It's a tough choice, but for me, the Venetian wins for accommodation, with a walk to The Forum Shops.

My mini night-time jaunt to Walgreens included breakfast for tomorrow, Pringles for snacks and extra sunscreen. A small glimpse of night-time Vegas.

11th September (2017) Las Vegas, NV, USA

I had a 7:00 am pick-up. The hotels have behind-the-scene bellies for deliveries and transport, amongst other services required to run large venues. You need a map to help find your way around each property. I found my pick-up point, an underground loading bay, to realise I'd forgotten my camera. A zoom lens was essential for today, so I ran back to my room. I made it within ten minutes, and two minutes before my pick-up arrived.

I booked an Area 51 tour, centred on aliens and cover-ups. Janet Airways, our first stop, is an airline that doesn't exist, officially. They have unmarked planes with ten flights daily to Area 51. With Area 51 nonexistent, why do they need employees flown in and out? Sounds fishy, right?

We visited Delamar Dry Lake with marbled dry clay continuing to the horizon. This tour had a photography element, so received hints, advice and props. I had photos taken in multiple poses with and without an alien skull. The Delamar Dry Lake is stunning in its dryness. The movie *Independence Day* filmed scenes here.

Multiple strange occurrences have been reported in the area. It's considered a safe landing site for flying vehicles. Are there any of alien nature nearby? Or are unexplained sightings from Nellis Air Force Base testing new technology? They don't answer questions. We heard jet aeroplanes overhead and saw recent landing marks on the lake bed.

Petroglyphs here differ from elsewhere. They depict creatures not fully human. Have they seen something? There's a rock in the shape of an alien's head. Coincidence, or not?

We drove The Extraterrestrial Highway, otherwise known as a stretch of Highway 375. We stopped at the road sign for a photo.

We visited the Alien Research Center and ate lunch at Little A'le'inn. The car's air conditioner had broken, so I appreciated the cafe's air conditioning.

We continued onto a highlight of the day, the perimeter. Area 51 doesn't exist right? Why do you need a perimeter fence? Why is there a sign on the perimeter saying "Use of deadly force authorised"? Barbed wire stretches across the desert. The occupants of a white SUV focus binoculars on us. It appeared out of nowhere just after we arrived. How did they find us? High-tech cameras? A sealed road begins behind the signs. Something is happening here. But it doesn't exist. Or so they say.

A captivating day of "what if". I relished every moment. I've seen every episode of the *X-Files* at least twice.

Shame about the air conditioning. It reached 39 degrees. I struggled. Rolling the windows down could help, but one passenger had facial palsy issues exacerbated by wind, so not an option. I suffered big time.

With the heat exhausting me, I partook in room service dinner in my air-conditioned luxury room. I received the full V.I.P. treatment. They spread out a linen tablecloth and arranged my food, cutlery, napkin, condiments and a vase with flowers on top. Extra special treatment, free with my hotel credit.

The Vegas lights eluded me again.

12th September (1999) Space Camp, Huntsville, Alabama (AL), USA

In a diary entry from the 22nd of May, I've noted the Space Camp week-long programs had sold out, and hoped to join a wait list. I hadn't expected it to be full five months in advance. I thought the camps being cancelled was the only plausible explanation. Weekend programs remained available, but the price was not much cheaper, meaning less value for money.

On the 7th of June, I received a letter confirming my place for the week-long Adult Advanced Space Academy program starting 12th of September.

In a December 1998 diary entry, I mention Space Camp cost $875. In March, I've documented I'd need $1200 to complete the trip. I considered it a reasonable price for a week's worth of unique experiences and entertainment, food and accommodation. In 2022 it cost $1449.

As a live-in nanny, they provided my accommodation and food. I earned a base salary of $140 a week, plus extra if I cleaned the house. So around five weeks' salary to partake in Space Camp.

The cheapest way to get to Huntsville, Alabama, the home of Adult Space Camp, was via Greyhound Bus. I had a voucher from my snowed-in adventure in Chicago on my way to Iowa in January. The bus ticket has faded and is hard to decipher. From my investigative practices, I learnt I paid with a coupon and $31. Add a $68 voucher to total a $99 bus fare. Sounds cheap.

Only the arrival times are legible. No matter what I tried, I could not glean the departures. My bus route started with New York to Washington arriving 1:20 pm on the 11th of September. That date had no significance as yet. I travelled overnight, arriving in Nashville at 5:15 am on the 12th of September. A third bus delivered me to Huntsville, at 7:55 am. If four hours for the first bus, I had a twenty-four-hour transit.

I arranged a transfer from the bus station for a $12 fee. The official program started at 3:00 pm with registration at 1:00 pm. I could wander around the grounds and museum at my leisure until then.

Adult Space Camp was held at the U.S. Space and Rocket Center, the visitors centre for NASA's Marshall Space Flight Center. It is the largest space museum in the world. We had the full property, including the museum, as our playground throughout our stay. They did not lock the museum doors after hours.

I was space geeking out. The space shuttle *Pathfinder*, complete with the external tank and two solid rocket boosters, sat in front of me to walk around and under. It is the only complete shuttle package in the world. Being a test vehicle, it never flew into space, but impressive regardless.

Rockets Saturn I and Saturn V sit amongst others. Most are displayed in an upright position, making you crane your neck to see their tops. The Saturn V has since moved inside to its own building with a restoration needed after being outdoors for thirty years.

Once registration completed, we had a welcome meeting followed by getting suited up. They gave us pale blue astronaut flight suits to wear throughout our camp. You could buy your own to keep, but my budget didn't extend that far. I returned mine at the end of the program.

They separated us into two groups, allocating me to the Tereshkova Team. Valentina Tereshkova was with the Russian Space Program, and the first woman in space. The camp ran three streams: Pilot, Mission Specialist and Payload Specialist. When booking, you nominated your preference, without guarantees. I requested the Pilot Track but allocated to the Payload Specialist Track. A Pilot no longer wanted that, and I swapped with them! The thrill increased when allocated Shuttle Commander; my dream job.

Day one began with an icebreaker followed by a lecture on why we explore space. We watched an IMAX movie in the museum. After dinner, we attended more classes on the STS, or Space Transportation System, which includes the orbiter, the solid rocket boosters, the external tank and the main engines, known to us as the Space Shuttle; and an introduction to scuba diving. Our structured day ended at 8:30 pm.

Most Space Camps are for children, thus accommodation geared towards them. The adult groups are smaller, so spread us out amongst the rooms. We had four allocated to our room with enough bunk beds for eight. I had a bottom bunk and not a fan of the overnight security lights. I moved an unused mattress against my bed to block them out.

I loved the design of the accommodation building named Habitat, built like a module on a moon base. From the outside, it looked futuristic with curved walls, well three cylindrical walls, or paper towel rolls, better describes the building's outline.

Excitement filled me as I drifted off to sleep, eager for the days ahead. My astronaut dreams were coming true.

13th September (1999) Space Camp, Huntsville, AL, USA

After breakfast, we met with the doctor for our scuba dive physicals. She took a medical history and a set of vital signs, as in blood pressure, heart and breathing rates, and temperature. I passed, gaining permission to take part.

I became ecstatic when passed! I had always wanted to scuba dive and play astronaut in a tank practising repairing satellites. This was the activity I looked forward to the most. The neutral buoyancy of the water imitates zero gravity, the environment an astronaut experiences outside the orbiter. Astronauts need to practice satellite repairs and launches under these conditions to be prepared.

Elation turned to devastation. I suited up and hopped in the tank, eagerly awaiting my turn to explore the space themed water. My diary explains the rest:

> What a disappointment. I'm having great fun here but I didn't get to scuba dive and play space servicing. My ears played up at 8 feet. My left ear wouldn't pop and they said I couldn't go down any further. I was SOOOO UPSET. I cried instantly as I came up and then for the next 2 hours or so. It was one thing I desperately wanted to do while here. Have to come back and do that again, well once, and be a Mission Specialist so can go on the end of an

> arm and move satellites... I feel pretty dumb though. Everyone else seems to know so much more than me–not about space etc, but just generally. My brain is turning to mush. I don't know if I'll ever be able to study and get a degree. I don't think it's stuff we seriously have to know to get through the missions and stuff. I just suck at everything. I'm having fun though. The good stuff is all still to come (apart from scuba dive which is out). I'll dive in Florida.

I remember being under the water, unable to pop my ear. The pressure mounted. I had to stop. The tears fell the moment I reached the surface. The desire to cry was too powerful to stem. Why would my ear not pop? I dived with a head cold in Israel without incident. So why not now? I'll never know.

Space servicing refers to the tank's mock satellites you practised repairing in the neutral buoyancy.

Going on an arm refers to the Canada Arm, the white articulated branch extending from the orbiter with an astronaut attached you may have seen on television. The arm belonged to the Mission Specialist Track.

I needn't have worried about my brain, as I attained a nursing degree a decade after this. I didn't dive in Florida thanks to hurricane Irene, but I signed up for a scuba diving course a year later.

A later scuba entry:

> I eventually got over my scuba disappointment, but it was hard to hear everyone discussing it in the beginning and when Jackie asked me how it was at lunch, I burst out crying again. The first day was hard.

14th September (1999) Space Camp, Huntsville, AL, USA

Today we had mission training. We spent time in each part of a shuttle mission. But we spent a couple of hours at Area 51 first.

I was not sure what to expect at Area 51, but it was games like a television show called *Crystal Maze*. We played three. In the first, we had to cross an imaginary void using two planks of wood and two concrete blocks without touching the ground. We aced this one.

They assigned me the leader on the second and hardest challenge. Not ideal. We failed. We got two across in the allotted time. I can't remember the scenario, but it involved me pulling myself along a wire in a harness. I liked that part, but I started without gloves and got blisters.

The third, my favourite, involved two tunnels high off the ground, three in each tunnel. Each side had a plank and a concrete block. We had to cross a "mine field" with only the team leader allowed to talk. My diary notes Doug was a terrible choice to lead this scenario. From his position, he couldn't see what was happening, which didn't help. The rest of the team achieved our goal without Doug, through hand signals.

Today we ventured inside the full size mock-ups of the Space Shuttle (or the orbiter where the astronauts spend their time), the International Space Station, and a smaller version of Mission Control. We trained for a mission in each of these areas called Alpha, Bravo and Charlie Missions.

Entering the orbiter for the first time thrilled me. I'd dreamt of this moment for years. I stepped through a circular door and greeted by four seats to the left and a ladder on the right. Behind the ladder sat the airlock and payload bay entrance. I was Commander to Buzz's Pilot (also known as Ron). As Commander, I climbed the ladder through a hatch emerging in a room of buttons and switches. The main console had two seats. Switches were lit and computer screens displayed data.

We were tasked with designing a mission patch. Inspiration difficulties resulted in leaving it to the two youngest in our group to finish in their own time.

We had a group photo session and climbed the outdoor mock Lunar Module. Once I heard we could climb on it, I raced ahead to get the extra experience of climbing to the top. Jackie joined me. They'd stopped this practice by the next year. We may have been the last group. I love that we did it.

15th September (1999) Space Camp, Huntsville, AL, USA

Mission day.

For Alpha Mission in the Space Station, I was Flight Operator 2, and I found Flight Operator 1 bossy. We started a spinning chair experiment, but she felt dizzy so didn't continue. We moved to a robotics experiment, but ran out of time. Failure thanks to a lack of teamwork. We were not a productive combination.

For Bravo Mission in Mission Control, I was assigned OTC/CAPCOM. CAPCOM comes from the Mercury flights when astronauts flew in capsules rather than shuttles. CAP is short for capsule, and COM short for communications. CAPCOM is the only one in Mission Control who talks to the orbiter, usually the Commander. I had to relay information back and forth and sort out problems. My impressions at the time:

> It was kind of cool except I couldn't work out how to tell which screen I was supposed to be in on the computer, but mostly the information was given to me and I was like a messenger.

I have a problem being on the correct screen on my current work computer.

Charlie Mission in the orbiter was the one I looked forward to the most. I found myself in switch heaven. Procedure books dictated the sequence of buttons to press and when. You followed instructions and pressed buttons. To be technical, you entered commands into the command-line interface, or computer. The Pilot and Commander each had a book. They had velcro to be authentic so they would attach to the panels, to prevent flying around in zero gravity. Inside, the procedures had three columns. The first column showed who did it, such as P for Pilot, C for Commander or MS for Mission Specialist. The next column told you what button or switch to press, for example O8, C3 or L4. O stood for overhead; C for centre console; L for left, which would be me; and R for right, on the Pilot's side. The number specified which button or switch on that panel needed to move. The last column indicated what to do, such as on, arm, or press. If the command was computer related, you'd press the button then press execute, for example, it would say "Item 15 execute".

I'd gained the nickname Scooby, as in Scooby Doo, which has been a theme in my life thanks to my giggle. I embraced it, buying a "Scooby" name tag for my flight suit. So we had Commander Scooby and Pilot Buzz Lightyear with a serious CAPCOM, as in my earlier Flight Operator foe. She excelled at CAPCOM, but I doubt she'd praise Buzz and me. I think she wished we'd been more serious. We were having fun.

With each mission an hour, we had other sessions including rocket making in groups of four. I was with Jackie, Lisa and Elaine. The diary entry made me laugh, especially the last sentence.

> Lisa had made hundreds of rockets as a child, so knew how to do it and, of course, Jackie, being an engineer, also knew how to do it. Elaine and I opened packages and squeezed out the glue.

We would fire them later in the week.

A daytime telescope session allowed observation of the sun. It was a novel concept for me, but just as captivating as observing planets at night.

After dinner, we accessed the simulators on the training room floor.

They designed the Multi-Axis Trainer (MAT) for the Mercury program. It comprises three concentric rings with a chair in the middle. You are strapped in and grip hard as it spins you in multiple directions. The three rings go their own way. It may not appeal if you're prone to motion sickness. Though, they say it's designed to not bring on nausea. Whatever, I survived. It disorientated me, which was the purpose. There must have been a size issue with me being too short, as they strapped me into the children's MAT. Jackie came, armed with my camera. I'm grateful she took loads of photos for me.

The 1/6 chair simulates the moon's lower gravity. It helps you experience the sensation of walking on the moon. I didn't master this. You bounce as have become lighter. A red line marks the path you are supposed to follow. I believe I travelled up more than forward at the start. Sidewards was easier. A photo shows me with a serious face, concentrating hard on my movements. At the end, you have free movement. I did a big starfish with my eyes popping; an "Infinity and beyond" impression of Buzz Lightyear from *Toy Story*. I was enjoying myself.

After the simulators, our structured day finished. Donning the imitation space suits, Jackie and I took them to the museum for photos in the Apollo capsule. We received permission and Buzz came with us as our photographer. The suits were hot and hard to manoeuvre, but we traversed the entire complex in these suits. I doubt we were meant to go outside, but we did. And seeing as we climbed on the Lunar Module earlier, we did it again, but in our suits. We replicated setting foot on the moon from the Lunar Module, taking turns to be "first on the moon". We did a high five for making it to the moon and posed with the American flag. Elsewhere in the museum, we pretended to be on a space walk outside the shuttle. The ultimate game of dress ups; a definite highlight. And the photos are awesome.

16th September (1999) Space Camp, Huntsville, AL, USA

It thrilled me to be appointed Commander for the Extended Duration Mission (EDM). The earlier missions were one hour. The EDM would be six hours. I can't remember how I became Commander, but my diary explains:

> Us Pilots had a bit of trouble, but I managed to get what I wanted and to be with Buzz and Jackie, so that was great. Eric and Heather got upset, but you know, I didn't hear him call out or stand up for himself. I was happy. I'm so glad I got to swap to Pilot [Track], though. Being in Payload Specialist [Track] could have really sucked. There was enough exciting stuff to take away the sting of not being able to scuba. Next time it will be even better doing everything.

I don't often assert myself, but doing so resulted in the coveted role.

We had a traditional astronaut launch day breakfast—steak and eggs.

Breakfast was the first time we saw our team patch design as icing on a cake. We had a team photo with the cake. Jackie and I are front and centre. We said thank you to our team members for their impressive design.

I need to explain a few things so you understand the following diary entry. One of the Camp Counsellors plays the role of "ghost" throughout the EDM. They whisper or hand notes to individuals, with instructions. We have to figure out the problem and fix it. And tunnels link the orbiter and the Space Station, which you crawl through from one to the other, as in pretend air locks.

The EDM was chaotic and fun, fun, fun, fun. It was a madhouse. We ended up with the best group ever. Me as Commander, Ron (Buzz) as Pilot, Mission Specialists—Jackie and Robert, and Payload—Ron B. and Debbie. It all worked brilliantly, and we got along so well. It couldn't have been a better team if I'd got to choose it all myself.

We started out in the Space Station, which I thought would be boring but was absolutely hilarious. It was a laugh a second. We had solar flares and had to evacuate to the module. Then on the way back Ron B [not Buzz] has an epileptic fit and Ron [Buzz] had a broken arm and we lost oxygen and we all started fainting and left only Ron B to save us all. Buzz was last to go, leaving Ron behind, so he was getting us all as close to the oxygen tank as possible by dragging us across the floor by our feet. Robert also had a psychotic episode, which ended up having Ron B riding Robert like a bull to get him tranquillised. It was so funny. I've got a photo of that one. We had a leak at the same time to find. It was SO MUCH FUN!!!! I can't stress that enough. Then we all finished our experiments. Ours was cooking with chemistry and boy did it taste good. Really sweet, so yummy. Jackie's experiment was making crystals, and that was interesting, too. They had mixed the chemicals before the solar flares made us retreat to the escape module. They had started to form and looked cool before we left, but when we came back in, they had grown even more and looked great. I didn't get to see them under the microscope, though. The other experiment was called ooblek and I don't know what it was, but would change instantly from solid to squish-able. I can't explain it very well. It was almost sad when the orbiter docked and it was time to change over. I could have been happy in the Space Station the whole time. Though I loved being Commander. Pushing all those buttons was a dream of a lifetime. Remember, I always used to try to make my own buttons so I could press them? But they never worked that well.

With the new team arriving at the Space Station, we took over the orbiter. Ron had made plans and decorated the cockpit with signs. Besides CAPCOM, there is a video communication link to Mission Control. It was picture only, so Ron made signs to communicate without sound. His contribution added a fantastic layer to the experience.

We had two miniature vodka bottles strapped to the control panels with a sign saying "Emergency Power". We had name tags on each of our chairs. Ron also made one that said "I'm really in charge" to put behind his chair, but one of my kind Mission Specialists put the sign where it belonged behind my chair. We had loads of other signs on hand ready to hold up in front of the camera like, "You want me to do what?" and "Of course we're lost. We've been upside down for the last hour."

Another sign said the mission was cancelled due to a hurricane and a panic button drawn and labelled on the central console.

It was great fun with Ron and great to push all the buttons. They're hard to find because so many of them, left, right, front, behind and overhead. The overhead ones were the hardest as hard to reach and my headsets got in the way.

Anyway, we had a lot of anomalies of course from total power failure and trying to find (all 6) one button to go from AC to DC power, overflowing waste management system with silly string and toilet paper being thrown all over the shuttle. A fire on the mid-deck which made us cough and raise our temperature and lower oxygen levels. Then a Payload Specialist broke her spine while putting fire out, a pilot with a psychotic episode, not allowing me to use his panel while in the middle of an important procedure and he fainted from smoke inhalation, etc. It was great. I didn't want it to end. I went with expectations of great fun and that was all I had. My dreams were fulfilled.

After the mission debrief, which involved cake and discussing our escapades, we fired our rockets. Ours wasn't a champion. We fired it twice. On its first attempt, two engines ignited while two failed, causing it to ascend then veer to the side. The second time it flew up, but not high. I thought it was fabulous, but it disappointed Lisa. I was still on a high from the EDM, heightening my reactions.

The exhilaration of igniting each one and observing their ascent or failure was thrilling. One almost started a fire. One spiralled all the way while another soared upwards. Rockets often land in the perimeter trees. As the sun shone, the trees glistened like Christmas.

After dinner, we had the Space Bowl; a space themed *Jeopardy*. Everyone tried to get out of it, but they made us play. Three teams ended with similar scores, around $1700. Everyone bet the full amount on the final question and as no one got it correct, everyone lost.

Poor Lisa discovered her camera had not been working this whole time, so we headed to the museum and training floor to retake photos. At least she recognised the problem in time to get replacements.

We had a night telescope viewing seeing the moon craters and watched the moon move into view through the scope as it traversed the sky. It made me want to buy a telescope. One day.

We continued the night on the museum simulators. I'm embarrassed to say I never landed the orbiter. Such a cool perk to have the museum as our personal playground. You'd think they'd lock it tight after hours, but no.

17th September (1999) Space Camp, Huntsville, AL, USA

A half day for our last day. We toured the Marshall Space Flight Center, had a picnic lunch, and finished with a graduation ceremony.

I'm glad I toured the Marshall Space Flight Center in 1999 as is now only open to American citizens. I marvelled at the actual astronaut simulators. A ginormous water tank houses life-size mock-ups of satellites where the astronauts train in full space suits. I wanted to be in there.

We visited a building new to the tour; even the guide hadn't visited yet. It housed the Space Station's mock-ups. The astronauts used these to practice and familiarise themselves with the layout and how it works. I revelled in the opportunity to walk around, touch objects and envision being in space.

At the picnic lunch, Heather nicknamed Jackie Scrappy. I was entrenched as Scooby, and Heather said as Jackie and I were always together, she should be called Scrappy. I believe Jackie was okay with this. After the camp, Jackie and I stayed in touch via e-mail. The subject line often read, "Scooby seeking Scrappy."

Then Space Camp ended.

> WOW!!! What can I say? It's all over. Everybody has gone, and I missed most of the goodbyes. It all happened so fast. Graduation went well. Everything went well. I'm totally exhausted, but it was worth it. Better than a week at Disney for less (slightly) money. I'm sad it's all over. I didn't want it to end. I didn't want to say goodbye to Jackie, but it was a good goodbye... We had a great week together. It was like with April in Hungary—people assumed we came together, knew each other before. We clicked.

At graduation, we received certificates and awards. Our Tereshkova Team won the Pilots' and Mission Specialists' Awards, Jackie's Area 51 team won the award for that activity, and Buzz won the "Right Stuff" award. We had a brilliant team.

My certificate misspelled my name as Francis instead of Frances. While organising a new one, people left, and I missed saying goodbye.

I hung out in the museum and the bookstore until my bus departure. I bought a book called *The Space Shuttle Operators Manual* for $17.50. It has pull outs of the Pilot and Commander's panels. It teaches you how to operate the shuttle. I loved it, commenting in my diary I'll be prepared for the next Space Camp. I remember running through sequences on the open panel pages while on Amtrak trains a few weeks later, wanting people to believe I was an astronaut in training.

I can't be sure what time I departed, but I arrived in Birmingham, Alabama at 10:25 pm. I'm guessing I left around 8:00 pm. After Birmingham, I travelled overnight to Charlotte, then to Richmond and New York.

> Forget the good seat. The bus was pretty much already full before getting to Birmingham. I found a seat next to an old lady, as it looked like she wanted to stay in the aisle. She got up to let me in but then wouldn't move her bag and then tried to tell me there were more seats up front. Selfish old cow! Okay, I'm tired and annoyed because I didn't get a double seat to myself. That sucks. I ended up at the very back in the 3-seater with a guy in the window seat. This means the seats don't go back and I'm right next to the toilet. Oh, dear!! This is going to be a long trip. I guess I was just lucky on the way down. Friday is not a good day to travel.

I tried to continue, but the bus's individual seat lights broke and the overhead lights turned off, so I gave up.

Later, I moved forward to a reclining seat.

18th September (2018) Flying home from UK

It was time to leave London after a wonderful few days catching up with friends and attending my first Comic Con. I had a 3:15 pm flight from Heathrow to Los Angeles and onto Melbourne without a stopover.

Are you confused why I am flying via Los Angeles? The New Orleans conference formed the original trip. I had this hankering to attend a Comic Convention in Coventry, England and the dates matched. I looked into round-the-world fares to fly home from England. Then I did the calculations.

For work related conferences, I can claim the expenses on tax or through a work perk called salary packaging. If I bought a round-the-world fare, I couldn't claim any of the flights.

It worked out cheaper to buy separate claimable flights for the conference, and other flights for England. At the end of my trip, it meant travelling London - Los Angeles - Auckland - Melbourne in one transit. But saving leaves money for future travel.

I had to work night shift the day I landed, so unable to break my journey in Los Angeles. And I would return to Los Angeles in twenty-six days for another conference next to Disneyland. I had become a conference junkie.

My American Airlines flight arrived in Los Angeles at 6:50 pm after twelve hours. After a three-and-a-half-hour layover, my Air New Zealand flight left Los Angeles at 10:30 pm. Thirteen hours later, I arrived in Auckland. Another three-hour layover, followed by a four-hour flight to Melbourne.

I arrived home on the 20th of September at 10:55 am. If my calculations are correct, it took thirty-three hours. A long overall transit, but worth it to break up the flight costs. I crunched the numbers to make sure it made financial sense before booking the impractical route.

19th September (2017) Page, Arizona (AZ), USA

On the 18th September, I started a ten day small group tour named the Grand Circle Experience run by Southwest Adventure Tours. I spent hours trawling through tour itineraries before deciding on this tour. It would visit every National Park I wanted to experience in the vicinity.

Joining a hiking tour made me nervous. I researched hiking, hiking boots, walking sticks, how to dress and avoid sore feet. I didn't want to be ill-prepared and scoffed at.

Hating hiking boots, I didn't buy any. I read you needed to use walking sticks correctly or no point, so I didn't buy them. I learnt how to keep feet safe while hiking, which led me to buy multiple packs of moleskins. And I bought a hydration backpack to carry large quantities of water. What had I got myself into? I can walk all day, but I perceived a walk and a hike as distinct entities. In America, they mean the same.

I was the youngest in our group and everyone booked for the same reason; the scenery. We weren't interested in specific hikes, or proving our skills or stamina. When the guide asked what we wanted, we'd say choose based on the scenery. Only twice throughout the trip did we separate in different directions at the same park. They designed the tour so people *could* do different walks. The guide knew the walk options and made recommendations based on people's abilities and desires. None of us had visited these places. With knowledge, you avoid uphill directions, and with a guide, you never walk the return journey.

By this point, I'd been away for eleven days and had stopped writing in my diary, leaving me little information to draw on. I'm relying on the tour itinerary, my photos and spending scribbles. I can tell you what I wore every day, but little else.

We spent the night at the Holiday Inn Express near Zion National Park in Utah. I had a buffet breakfast at the hotel and we left early to drive to the Grand Canyon. The road uses switchbacks to climb 3000 feet in three miles, then traverses the one-mile Zion Tunnel. On the other side, rock and sand formations surround the road.

We visited the North Rim of the Grand Canyon. My one diary entry summarises the day.

Great day at the Grand Canyon. It's absolutely beautiful. Lovely, easy, relaxed, wandering along walkways with incredible views. North Rim has a lovely lodge and cabins right on the edge. Cabin 306 and 309 are the best. Not as hot today, which was nice. Actually cold at times, needing shoes for warmth but not for walking. Cardigan was also required. Long day as back to Las Vegas time and not at the hotel till nearly 7:00 pm.

I know where I will request to stay if I come back, Cabin 306 or 309 please. Individual requests shouldn't be a problem, this being the least visited rim of the canyon, with only ten per cent of canyon visitors coming here. I have now been to the North, South and West Rims.

Utah was one hour ahead of the two states we travelled through, being Nevada and Arizona. We zigzagged through the time zone change with Colorado the same as Utah. The constant minor changes accumulated.

We spotted female Desert Bighorn Sheep sunning themselves against backdrops sculpted by the weather over centuries. I appreciated the Checkerboard Mesa with its horizontal and vertical lines crisscrossing. We observed a grazing bison herd, and reached over 2000 metres in altitude at Le Fevre Overlook, then over 2400 metres at the canyon.

How to describe the canyon? The colour variations are out of my vocabulary's reach. They change depending on the position and strength of the sun. The canyon's splendour lies in its abundance of juts. It's the ultimate jut kingdom, and breathtaking.

The wind howled, and I purposely put myself into its pathway over a jut, letting my hair go wild. There is nothing better than unfettered hair to add to the scenery. The photos here show me wearing my hydration backpack. The thought of it makes me cringe. It makes me feel like an imposter posing as a hiker. Did I look pretentious? I feel pretentious thinking about it now.

We walked to the viewpoint for Angel's Window; a window like gap in the rock.

We crossed the Colorado River on the historic Navajo Bridge, which adds to the landscape's charm. Walking across allows time to soak in the surrounding wonder that is Marble Canyon. Our delightful guide drove our vehicle across the car bridge so we didn't have to cross twice on foot and again via car. Convenient.

We spent the night at the Courtyard Marriott in the town of Page. We would be here for two nights.

20th September (2017) Page, AZ, USA

We started our day visiting the Glen Canyon Dam further along the Colorado River from Marble Canyon. Yesterday, we viewed from above, but today we are below gazing upward. There's a noticeable contrast between the two perspectives. With the sun at a different angle, the colours have changed.

We rafted along the Colorado River, stopping to view petroglyphs. A gentle float with sandstone cliff faces sheltering us from the sun's heat.

I have seen rock art around the world and it's amazing to recognise the similarities in them despite these ancient people being unaware of each other's existence. Basic life was the same wherever you lived. Animals dominate with bighorn sheep prominent here.

We spent the afternoon at Antelope Canyon; a magnificent slot canyon. I didn't know what a slot canyon was, but I revelled in it from start to finish. I didn't want to leave.

As you meander along, the guides point out formations, showing you where to stand and which direction to point your eyes and camera to visualise them.

I couldn't always envision the formations, but they made me take a photo. I remember thinking I should document the details, but I never did. Can I decipher the shapes in my photos?

I examined each photo, hoping an image jumped out at me. But nothing. I did a Google search for labelled photos with these supposed formations. In one video, I identified a clear seahorse and looked through mine again. I found a photo with the same characteristics, but I couldn't spot a seahorse despite flipping it in multiple directions. A bear featured somewhere, and one website labelled a growling bear rock photo. I discovered the bear after adjusting my eyes. I discerned similarities in mine, but no bear. Maybe rain had altered the formations in the two years between visits. She had photos named Indian Chief, woman in the wind, the buffalo and the lion, amongst others, but I couldn't see what she saw in hers, let alone mine. From the photos, it's the swirls, light, shadows, colours, closeness and heights that I cherished. It was stunning.

The sensation of insignificance in the surrounding grandeur enamoured me. These juts were of a whole extra dimension and spectacular. The light shone through, creating shadows and colour ranges amongst the rocks. You needed nothing other than the scene in front of you. Nature at its best.

The day continued with a hike to Horseshoe Bend. The sign says there's no shade. I utilised my trusty pink umbrella to create my own for the 1.2 km walk. At the end, a 270 degree bend in the Colorado River greeted us.

I struggled to capture the full bend in my photos. I achieved the full bend once, but had to include ugly other bits. I needed to be taller, or maybe on a viewing platform.

21st September (2017) Monument Valley, AZ, USA

A dream come true today; Monument Valley. How many times have these rock formations featured in movies, television shows and commercials? It's an iconic view that shouldn't be missed. It's even more incredible in person. The formations appear to jut out of the ground in the middle of nowhere. Can you tell "jut" is my new favourite word?

We transfer into 4WD vehicles and taken out by a local Navajo guide. The itinerary says it will be bumpy with jostling. Excellent. We make various stops recreating famous movie scenes like John Wayne on his horse surveying the vast desert. I rarely take photos of myself in locations, but I couldn't resist here.

Two of the most famous rocks are called Left Mitten and Right Mitten. I'll let you guess which one is which. I'm not sold on the name choice.

The desert boasts a landscape akin to Mars with its vivid red hues. The breathtaking expanse of crimson stretches in every direction.

We discovered the Navajo Code Talkers that encrypted messages during World War II. What better unbreakable code than a language spoken by, unfortunately, so few? How would the Japanese find a native Navajo to translate? Brilliant.

The Four Corners landmark was a jovial stop, where four state lines meet. I performed a Downward Dog yoga pose allowing for four parts of my body to be in four states simultaneously. My left hand is in Utah; my right is in Colorado; left foot is in Arizona; and my right foot is in New Mexico. As the camera snapped, a breeze blew my T-shirt up and hello midriff. I tucked my T-shirt into my shorts taking a second photo. Then I sat in the middle making my butt cheeks traverse four states.

We continued to our hotel in Mesa Verde National Park, Colorado.

22nd September (2017) Durango, Colorado (CO), USA

Today's hike was out of my comfort zone. Fear creeps in while looking at the photos. It began with sheer cliffs aside a narrow path with people not watching their steps. Towards the end it was the ladders we climbed to the exit. My heart pounded, and I lagged, leaving me amongst strangers. I remember thinking I could never come back. Ladders aren't my strong point.

What we explored in between was my scene, though, so I'm glad for the visit. Ancient village ruins on, and in, a shallow cliff cave; the Pueblo cliff houses. They are impressive from afar, but milling amongst them is better.

Then the ladders appeared.

We visited other ruins nearby and the entire region is reminiscent of Peru, just with different coloured building materials.

We drove to our overnight hotel in Durango, Colorado, arriving early enough to wander around town. Durango was an atmospheric, stereotypical western town with history galore. We stayed at the historic Strater Hotel built in 1887 with confusing corridors making getting lost easy and fabulously fun. The rooms were decorated in olde-worlde charm.

The hotel backed on to the railway line and station. I saw tomorrow's train arrive, the Durango and Silverton Railroad. In planning, I focused on the National Park details of the itinerary missing the train inclusion, so an enchanting surprise.

23rd September (1996) Waterford, Ireland

I had left Denmark, ecstatically secured a nanny position in London with five-month-old triplets starting in two weeks' time, then headed to Ireland.

The overnight bus and ferry combination left at 8:00 pm last evening, arriving in Dublin at 8:00 am this morning. A double seat to myself on the bus portion allowed enough sleep. I missed Denmark and hoped seeing an Irish friend who I met in Denmark would help ease my angst. I rang the Limerick phone number to be told she'd moved to Cork. She was out when I rang the new number.

I continued with my planned itinerary, buying a bus ticket to Waterford at 9:00 am arriving at 12:00 pm. It was cheaper than I'd expected, which made me happy. Dublin didn't impress me, though to be fair, I'd only seen the bus station.

> So far seems to be quite dirty and rundown. There's litter everywhere. Houses need painting or cleaning. It's all very dull and droll.

On arrival in Waterford, I walked to my chosen hostel across the river and along the bank. The wonderfully named Viking House sat in the old city centre surrounded by history, including the original Viking city walls built in 1000 CE (Common Era). A bargain at eight Irish pounds per night.

> The hostel is great. Very clean, well equipped, friendly staff, loads of information, bus tickets available etc. It's just a little too big for mine but very similar in facilities.

I had been designing the perfect hostel in my head throughout my travels with plans to open a hostel in Sydney for the 2000 Olympics. That never happened.

I couldn't access my room until 3:00 pm, so proceeded to the Waterford Crystal Factory after storing my bags.

I enjoyed the factory tour. We viewed the full cycle from blowing the molten crystal mix to cutting and sculpting the designs. I loved the magnificent sparkling crystal, so I had to buy a souvenir. I'd always desired a fancy perfume atomiser. So why not one from Waterford Crystal? I treated myself by spending £41.

I have the atomiser, though unsure if it's ever housed perfume. As a dust-able souvenir, it's in a cupboard.

24th September (1996) Cork, Ireland

The 8:45 am bus arrived in Cork two hours later. On leaving the hostel, I forgot my Irish £5 key deposit, which annoyed me, then over spent throughout the day. I've noted £7 for accommodation, but I stayed at my friend's place. With bus fares, entry fees, stamps, film, phone calls and food, I spent £22.50 plus the £7 accommodation, making £30. Based on scribblings in the Ireland guidebook, I aimed for a £15 daily budget, so I spent double.

On arrival in Cork, I caught a bus to Blarney Castle. I wanted to kiss the Blarney Stone. Depending on when you met me, you'd say I either did, or didn't, need to kiss the stone for the effects. At the time, I needed to kiss the stone.

Along the way, I met a fellow Aussie who had also lived in, and loved, Denmark. I loved having a reason to talk about Denmark and looked forward to talking more when I finally caught up with my friend later on this day.

I've kissed the Blarney Stone. It's a little bit scary but I've done it.

Reaching the stone wasn't straightforward. You lie on your back, stretching out behind you with a metal grate over the hole below. Arching backwards, you are upside down while kissing the stone. There is a staff member to guide and hold you. I've done it, and I have the photo and certificate to prove it.

Back in town, I got in touch with my friend and arranged to meet.

> Finally got in touch with Annette. I'd been ringing the wrong number, but she said I could stay with her no worries and met me at the bus stop and walked me back to her bedsit. It's a nice room, but the bathroom is disgusting. Hot water meter costs 50 pence and is useless, and doesn't really get to meet people but only costs £27 per week plus electricity so that's good. It was great to see her. I was back to my normal self, talking non-stop. It was wicked. I miss my friends from Denmark. Stayed up till 1 am talking.

I had forgotten how hard it was to leave Denmark. I loved my Danish experience.

I'm guessing I'd paid for my accommodation before getting in touch with Annette, which gave me somewhere to leave my luggage instead of taking it to Blarney Castle.

At the top of my diary page for today I have written a heading: *IRISHNESS*. After it I've written two lines:

> Cross the road whenever you want [and] buses stop, pick-up and drop off whenever you like.

25th September (1996) Cork, Ireland

Annette had orientation at Cork University this morning, and we spent the rest of the day together. She gave me a tour of the University and Cork. Knowing a local is always beneficial.

My diary recaps the events and the emotions of the day.

> It was great. Talking the whole time. It was brilliant. Slept on the floor last night and I think it somehow caused a really bad muscle ache in my left leg so a bit sore going up all the hills but we did it. Walked round the shops. Had a nice lunch and a pot of tea. Then went to the movies, *A Time to Kill*.... Had dinner at Annette's place, then met her sister Rose and her boyfriend from Israel, and went back to their place. I went really shy again but not as much as normal. I could see Annette went quiet as well. We went to a pub for a drink and then home by 12:00 am, but talked again until 2:30 am. It was great. She's shy as well, so we talked about that and getting better, how I used to be, astrology, everything. I loved it. I hope I can make friends like I had in Denmark wherever I am.

I had a cheap day which helped make up for yesterday–£7.20. Free accommodation helps to cut costs.

26th September (1996) Killarney, Ireland

Annette waved me off at the bus station, which was nice. It was sad to say goodbye again but has been great to see her and catch up. The scenery on the bus was lovely. I was tired but made myself keep my eyes open. Booked a tour tomorrow for the Ring of Kerry and then tried to get out to Muckross House but no way of getting there. Luckily, a man heard me and offered a ride there as they were going as well. Great timing.

What is it with me and getting into cars with strangers? I believe this happened at a tourist information office, and I rode with a family, making it somewhat safer compared to previous encounters.

At Muckross House:

I went to the farm first and learnt a lot about farming and cooking. Had some delicious bread I'd seen being made and cooked on the old stove in the old style with homemade butter on it. It was delicious. I stayed for three helpings.

The house was magnificent. Exactly what I want my home to be if I managed to get really rich. The gardens were beautiful as well. Pity about the rain showers. Then treated myself to a horse cart ride back to town, which was nice. The driver seemed to like me and offered to take me out for a Guinness tonight, but I declined.

He was more than double my age.

I stayed at the Killarney Railway Hostel, across the road from the bus station.

I went out with a Kiwi girl for some chips. She let me talk for ages about my USA trip and all my travels, etc. It was great, except my chips went cold.

Hot food is an advantage of talking less.

I penned six postcards. I wish people still sent postcards as they were always a joy to send and receive.

Over did the budget again. £10 for tomorrow's tour will help with tomorrow's total. Otherwise my hostel cost £6.50, bus £8.80, entry fee £4.50, postcard £1 and my horse cart ride treat back to town £18 (a whole day's budget). Sometimes you have to do touristy stuff, though. A total of £49.

27th September (2017) Bryce Canyon, Utah (UT), USA

We rose early for sunrise at Bryce Canyon. Alas, the clouds rolled in, but what a view! We saved a magical place for our last day. Hoodoo city! What is a hoodoo you ask? When cliffs erode, they form narrow walls called fins. Frosty weather can cause the fins to crack, creating holes. The holes get bigger over time and their tops collapse, leaving columns. Rain does its magic, moulding the limestone columns into spires called hoodoos. Got it? They are like chimneys sticking out of the ground. Bryce Canyon has hoodoos en masse and is glorious.

We climbed into the hoodoos world. We achieve the descent through multiple switchbacks and stairs. It's a walk where you gaze at your starting point and ponder how you descended from there. There are warning signs to be vigilant of rock falls. But who cares when magnificence emerges at every step? The white sky accentuated the vivid red rocks and splashes of green trees. You traverse mini canyons and forests.

The hoodoos are hilarious in their novel, bulbous shapes. No two are the same. Some cling together while others stand on their own. A spectacular result.

The tour ended in Las Vegas and I headed to my fifth Las Vegas hotel; the Luxor. It's near the bottom of the strip. I started with ancient Rome, and now I'd finish with ancient Egypt. I chose an angled pyramid room on purpose. This is my sole opportunity to sleep in a pyramid. I desired awareness and visual confirmation I was in a pyramid. I hit my head a few times, but worth it.

I had a simple dinner of chicken tenders and Cinnabon for dessert before exploring this end of town at night.

Excalibur is magical, with its coloured turrets lit against the white of the building. Straight out of a fairytale. I walked to the New York-New York Hotel on one side and M&M World on the other before returning.

28th September (2017) Las Vegas, NV, USA

I explored the hotel. Inside houses Egyptian temple replicas. It's nice to visit temples in air-conditioned comfort. Outside, where the temperature replicates Egypt's, stands a sphinx, obelisk, Ramses II and rams, and of course the giant sparkling pyramid. It's hard to comprehend one of those thousands of windows was my room.

I caught the hotel tram to the Mandalay Bay resort for a look. From this hotel, in three days' time, a gunman would open fire on festival crowds across the road, killing fifty-eight people (the total revised to 61 by 2023). They have security footage dated today of the perpetrator carrying in his weapon. I may have walked right past him. An eery thought. I'm glad I'd left Vegas before this happened. My hotel was next door.

I figured out the bus to The National Atomic Testing Museum. It's hard to believe the tests became tourist attractions and people set up deck chairs and picnics to watch the show.

I marvelled at The Grand Canal Shops at the Venetian and The Forum Shops of Caesars, and caught the monorail to experience the view.

As it darkened, I watched the Mirage Hotel volcano erupt. I climbed The Eiffel Tower for the night-time view and the Bellagio Fountain overview, determining where to stand and stood there until the next show. I waited half an hour to capture the full show on video. If you think the fountain show is wonderful from ground level, viewing from above is a whole different level of spectacular. You experience the full design, thus worth it. I have now watched the show from the front, behind, and above. I finished my night, and my Vegas visit, with the Bellagio Fountains at ground level.

29th September (2017) New York, NY, USA

I took my time at the Luxor's buffet breakfast. They offered a good hotel breakfast, but pales compared to a Vegas buffet. I managed two platefuls with everything from French toast to bacon; delicious plantains; and apple and sultana pancakes.

My New York flight departed at 11:20 am. An Uber to the airport proved easy. Security didn't take long, allowing time to buy magazines and wait.

The full flight had seatback screens, but mine decided not to work. Someone left three magazines in the seat pocket which I read and did the Inflight Magazine Sudoku puzzle, which passed the five-hour flight.

Then came the hard part. With a three-hour time change between Las Vegas and New York, I arrived at 7:30 pm local time. I decided I'd take public transport to my hotel to save money.

I caught the AirTrain to Jamaica Station, then connected to the subway. Here the E line would take me to within five blocks of my hotel. Sounds easy. Reality involved cursing my decision, saying I'd never do it again.

The chief stressor was luggage. The transit included multiple stairs and full height turntable gates in which luggage could get stuck. Profanity occurred. Unbeknownst to me, exits close at different times. At another hour, it might have been easier. Great in hindsight.

The empty streets between the AirTrain and the subway made me uneasy. A stench of urine filled the night air. Not ideal for a woman alone. But I made it for the bargain price of $8.50.

I'd booked three nights at The Lexington Hotel on 48th Street because of its proximity to the theatre district. I added this section of the trip after I discovered Bette Midler was performing on Broadway. The dates matched, so I stretched my budget and came to New York.

After the lavish and expansive hotel suites in Las Vegas, Manhattan hotel rooms are a shock. With the bed snug against the corner, I could just manoeuvre around the room. Space is at a premium in New York. With an elegant lobby and a practical location, who cares about the rest?

30th September (2017) New York, NY, USA

I made my way to the E Subway line and The World Trade Center. They'd opened the memorial and museum since my last visit, so I wanted to experience both and to pay my respects. I did not know anyone lost on 9/11, but I knew someone missing for three days in the chaotic aftermath. He attended an out of the office meeting that morning, thus walking towards the building as the events unfolded. His office was in the World Trade Center, though. I was back in Australia.

I knew the district well. On my 20th birthday, I visited the observation deck. I celebrated my 25th birthday with dinner at the Windows on the World restaurant on the 107th floor of the North Tower. No restaurant staff present the morning of 9/11 survived. The building no longer existed by my 30th birthday.

I visited the area a few weeks before the first anniversary. It remained a giant hole in the ground, with scaffolding holding people back and posters for lost loved ones attached to every surface. I'll never forget the gaping hole.

With the fountain memorial and museum complete, it instantly came to mind when New York joined the itinerary. I was pleased to see the re-built atrium as was the only part I recognised. Tears fell as I wandered.

Afterwards I meandered my way to Times Square on foot, soaking up Manhattan. I bought a hotdog every few blocks, totalling three. One hotdog does not make a meal. But who can hold multiple hotdogs? And no one enjoys cold hotdogs. I did my old trick from when I lived here, of hotdog grazing. They cost $1-$1.50 in 1999. In 2017, I paid $3-$4 each.

Then showtime! Mega exciting! Bette Midler live on stage in *Hello Dolly*. I paid a fortune for seats in the Orchestra level row L. I wanted to revel in every expression on Bette's face.

Goldie Hawn sat two rows in front of me. Now and then she'd turn to her companion, not Kurt Russell, and I'd see it was her. That raised tonight's stakes.

I snapped a head shot from behind. The unsubtle girl next to me held her phone camera ready to push the moment Goldie turned her head. Even though we weren't together, I found it embarrassing.

I loved every second of *Hello Dolly*. Bette blew me away. I'd forgotten how comedic she can be. I laughed to the point of tears. My stomach hurt. There she was, large as life before me, performing for me. I was in awe. I lost myself in the music and the story and in Bette. She still has it. So worth it.

Once the final number sung and the audience clapped, an usher collected Goldie. "Follow me Miss Hawn." I felt sorry for her. She wanted to clap for her friend. She stood as instructed and turned to the stage for an enthusiastic clap as dragged away. The price of fame is being whisked away to avoid the crowd. But you miss the bows and curtain calls and a chance to yell out to your friend.

I was on cloud nine; as light as a feather floating back to my hotel. I didn't want the feeling to fade. I wanted to dance down the street. In my head I was. I mused on my wonderful life and how lucky I was to witness Bette Midler live.

Along the way, I passed homeless people sleeping in doorways and I wanted to make them as happy as me. I wanted to share the joy and happiness overflowing in me. I got a $20 note and wanted to leave it to so they'd find it when awake. But how to place it without disturbing them, it being stolen or blowing away before discovered? I kept it folded in my hand as I walked, hoping to find a way to make it work.

I had given up when less than a block from my hotel, a man approached me asking for help. I thought he wanted directions. What followed became a drawn out sob story of his release from hospital and subsequent loss of his wallet and phone in a taxi. The Jewish Center facilitated a call to the taxi company, but could not offer any further aid. The taxi company said they found no wallet. He was wandering the streets, trying to get money to get home. He wore a hospital band, but sounded fishy. Most importantly, he ruined my buzz. I gave him the $20 note in my hand. Instead of being grateful, he said, "That's not enough. I need $40 for the train home." The hotel entrance was close enough to reach safely, even if he followed, so I left.

He yelled after me, but didn't follow. I was fuming. I had an incredible buzz going on and he ruined it. If he truly was stranded in the city with no money, that's terrible. But how can I verify his story? My wonderful floating in the clouds ended, and I climbed into bed with angry thoughts.

October

1st October (2017) New York, NY, USA

I had one more day in New York. I'd looked into tours but chose to improvise. In my travel bible I've listed three places: Rockefeller Plaza, Central Park and the Plaza Hotel.

I enjoyed a relaxed morning before walking to Times Square and buying a last-minute theatre ticket for a 3:00 pm performance. I continued along Fifth Avenue to the Plaza Hotel and Central Park, meandering around with no destination. I passed the fountain and the playing fields and sat on a bench overlooking the lake with glorious historic buildings in view. The sun shone high in the blue sky. The idyllic way to wind down before flying home.

I enjoyed *Anastasia*. They adapted the story but performed well with sumptuous sets and hummable songs. A splendid choice.

Then headed to Top of the Rock, a newish observation deck at the Rockefeller Plaza. I reserved a 6:30 pm entry time to catch the sunset twilight with views overlooking Central Park and The Empire State Building. The sky turned orange and yellow onto dark blue. The lights appeared, and the city twinkled as it turned to night. I'd planned my entry to capture day and night. Everyone wants to see the city at this time, making it difficult to snag an optimal viewing spot. But I waited, moving closer as people left. I had nothing else planned for the evening, so could stay as long as my stomach allowed.

Glass panels, higher than even the tallest of people, frame the deck. Photos through the glass contained reflections. If patient, you could secure a spot at the narrow gap between the panels. A camera lens could squeeze in, capturing photos as though the glass didn't exist. A delightful way to say farewell to New York.

I returned to the hotel, stopping at a deli with a hot and cold buffet. You filled a container with your choices and paid by weight. I piled in a mismatch of food to eat at the hotel while packing. I arranged a transfer to the airport with SuperShuttle for $25. Three times what I paid to get to my hotel, but happy to pay after my fraught arrival.

2nd October (1999) Boston, Massachusetts, USA

This story proved difficult to write. I researched the hostel I may have stayed at attempting to trigger memories. They took the Google Maps photo of the address in October 2020 and shows a construction site fence. No memories gleaned. Disappointing after the excellent detective work which led to the hostel's discovery.

I found a Greyhound Bus ticket from New York to Boston leaving at 8:30 am and arriving at 1:00 pm. To decipher the faded ticket, I shone a light from behind and in front. Then I took a photo to zoom in for clarity. I looked through my "waiting to go in a scrapbook collection", my photos, diary and receipts to discover anything extra from Boston. I had evidence from Salem dated the 3rd of October.

I scoured the 1998 USA Rough Guide for the Salem entry. Did I spend the night in Salem? But the guidebook was clear on Salem's lack of cheap accommodation.

I searched Boston's hostels to see if recognised any. I sensed a connection with The Irish Embassy Hostel. It wasn't marked on the guidebook's map. I'd circled one site on the map a block away from an official International Hostelling Hostel. So it made sense if I'd stayed there.

Then I remembered I preferred private hostels. So I Google searched The Irish Embassy Hostel to see if it still existed. We know it doesn't. But I found its 1990s website and opened the Directions tab. From South Station, where the bus dropped me, catch the Red Line to Park Street, then the Green Line to North Station. I recalled seeing scribbles on the guidebook map.

I'd noted:

red line park st green ? North Station. Dunkin Donuts Friend 222

Looks like the directions from the website. I checked the address; Friend Street 232. I'd explained food options or noted a nearby landmark.

I have no doubts I stayed at The Irish Embassy Hostel. I love how I left clues for myself. It was a hoot putting it together. Do you think I'll make a good mystery writer?

I searched directions from the hostel to the Salem Witch History Museum; direct trains depart from North Station to Salem. It makes total sense to me.

I investigated further, looking up directions to the circled site on the map. It can be reached on the Red and Green Lines. It sounds like proficient planning to me.

I have visited the Mapparium, the circled site. The guidebook mentions free entry, hence no payment evidence. (In 2022 it cost $6.) You walk through a three-storey glass globe built in the 1930s. I believe I visited it while staying in Boston before a day trip to Salem the following day.

3rd October (2016) Goulburn, NSW, Australia

For the third year in a row, I headed to Netfest, a netball festival, in Queensland. For the first time, I drove, rather than flew. Why? Because I love driving, it provided access to an extra car and allowed transport of gear we'd never take on a plane.

This was our most ambitious year, entering two teams in the competition. A minimum of fourteen people with two non-playing managers. We found a house that catered to sixteen. An extra local player made us seventeen girls on a netball trip.

We played outdoors with negligible shade in the hot and sunny Queensland weather. I piled my hatchback high with a marquee for shade; coolers for cold drinks; foldable chairs; physiotherapy rollers; and a netball goal post for shooting practise. For myself, I carried a tent and mattress in case camped along the way.

I was on an early schedule after going cold turkey from night shift. I rose at 4:30 am and drove at 6:15 am. McDonald's fuelled me throughout the day with hash browns in the morning and later hamburger and fries. I drove 654 km to Goulburn, New South Wales, arriving at 2:30 pm. I checked into a hotel one block from the highway and napped for an hour.

With a microwave in my room, I made macaroni and cheese for dinner. I stayed awake until 9:00 pm.

4th October (2016) Coffs Harbour, NSW, Australia

Again I rose at 4:30 am. The hotel buffet breakfast begun at 6:00 am. I ate well, leaving by 6:30 am. I drove an extra two hours, reaching my pre-booked accommodation at 4:30 pm. When you pre-book accommodation, you keep driving even if you'd rather stop.

Food-wise, I ate crackers and avocado throughout the day. A healthier option than McDonald's.

I stayed near the Dorrigo National Park on Waterfall Way. I planned this minor detour without realising the driving conditions; curvy, narrow and surrounded by trees. Not ideal for a tired driver after a ten-hour drive. I made it, bypassing the waterfalls.

The hotel didn't have a restaurant, but offered room service dinner. I ordered when checking in. They asked what time, and I replied, "As early as possible". Two new owners were doing everything themselves and still finding their way. They were thrilled with an early dinner request. They cooked me a yummy steak to end my day.

5th October (2016) Gold Coast, QLD, Australia

I woke early and read in bed surrounded by mountain views. Reading in bed with tea is an indulgent start to the day. I was adventuring this morning, so couldn't leave yet.

I entered Dorrigo National Park before it opened, sneaking in through a carpark away from the main entrance. Extensive research revealed how to approach my desired site via this back entrance. I didn't have to wait until opening time; I had a shorter walk; and I'd be guaranteed to have it to myself.

I've wanted to walk behind a waterfall since watching *Last of the Mohicans*. The spider webs across the path confirmed I was first. My grandfather taught me to carry a walking stick to combat this. He must have made a persuasive impression, seeing as he died when I was four. I will forever call a stick found at the start of a walk a "granddad stick".

I reached Crystal Shower Falls before anyone else. Your first glimpse is from above with the obvious boardwalk behind it. You wander round and down. It's not a spectacular set of falls, but you can walk behind it, and that's what I wanted. With no one around, I could act as goofy and over excited as I liked.

It's a dead-end path. You proceed behind the water and pivot to exit. I entered and peered through the water at the bush beyond, beaming mischievously.

It's a challenge to capture footage in the moment when alone. I searched for a place to prop my phone to use the timer function. My phone had a twenty-second timer. After multiple failed attempts, I got one photo of me *near* the waterfall. Then I tried a video, which worked. The video proves it was impossible to capture a timer photo as it took twenty seconds to reach the falls; thus longer to walk behind the waterfall.

Based on numbered photos, I deleted twenty attempts before the photo of me near the waterfall, and another twenty-five later. You can't say I didn't try. A tripod with a remote control would have helped, but not a selfie stick.

I enjoyed the falls alone for twenty minutes before a father and his kids arrived. Having achieved my goal, I left. I ambled the Wonga Walk trail to the Rainforest Centre, the official entrance. I walked onto the viewing platform for an overview of the park and bought food before returning to the car. A brilliant mini detour. I appreciated the exercise after the long drives.

I drove back along Waterfall Way and to the Gold Coast. The rest of the netball team would arrive tomorrow. I had one last night on my own in a beachside apartment. Every room had a view, including the toilet. I watched the exquisite sunset from bed. A blissful setting to end my drive from Melbourne.

6th October (2016) Gold Coast, QLD, Australia

We needed a mansion to hold two netball teams plus support staff. We booked Commodore Palace, and I arrived first. Oh. My. Goodness. Heaven. It had bedrooms everywhere, and entertainment rooms in abundance. With the basement included, the property stood at four storeys. It boasted a steep driveway to a four or five-car garage; a man cave complete with a billiard table; a cinema room; a lift; a grand piano; a luxurious pool; a rejuvenating spa; and a sprawling deck. I relished my solitude with the amenities before the others arrived.

I played the grand piano. My favourite piece is *In the Hall of the Mountain King* by Edvard Grieg. It's satisfying building the crescendo, but I struggled to remember the chords. I figured them out and took photos of my hands playing the chords for future reference.

The girls started arriving. One large group on the same flight hired a minivan and presented together. I delighted in seeing everyone's expressions at their first glimpse of the house. We'd seen photos, but surreal in person.

We performed the official netball registration requirements and soaked up our new environment.

I'd promised to do airport pick-ups making multiple trips over the evening until the group was complete.

We made sparkly name transfers for our uniforms, but they required ironing to attach them. The girl who'd organised them had a marathon ironing session in the cinema room. She did an excellent job.

7th October (2016) Gold Coast, QLD, Australia

Today our netball tournament began. We had a stellar start winning each game. Our teams were "Mel's Belles", Mel being our manager, and "Young Sharelle's" after Australian netballer Sharelle McMahon.

Courtside was luxurious compared to previous years. We unfolded the marquee, providing welcomed shade, adjusting the position as the sun moved. We had cool drinks and snacks, such as cut fruit. It was nice to have healthy snacks between the kiosk ice creams.

I struggled with the heat. It's hard playing four or five games of netball with the sun beating down, especially for a redhead. It's constant sunscreen being put on, hats on and off, and a water sprayer sprayed.

We placed the goal post outside the garage for shooting practise between games. We had to be careful not to get the ball over the neighbour's fence or in the river.

The extra equipment and comfort made the drive worthwhile.

8th October (1998) Isle of Wight, UK

To reach Queen Victoria's house on the Isle of Wight called Osbourne, I caught a National Express bus from Victoria Coach Station to Southampton. From there, I boarded a ferry to the Isle of Wight. I believe I took a local bus the rest of the way. It wasn't a simple journey with three hours' travel in each direction. Hence why I hadn't yet visited. I'd leave Europe in a few days, so I had to visit now.

Queen Victoria was my childhood royal favourite. I idolised her until I discovered more about her. In 1998, I did not know how mean she'd been to her children.

I was in awe because it was hers. They designed it with the modern conveniences of the day, influenced by Prince Albert's ideas, as a country retreat away from ceremonial London. The external architecture was not my taste, but the grandeur and size were my style.

I spent a couple of hours imagining Queen Victoria and her nine children enjoying it as their home, and then as my grand home with my children. At this stage in my life, I assumed I'd have a large family and be rich.

I bought four postcards for myself; a young Victoria, an old Victoria, one of Prince Albert and one of the Franz Winterhalter's famous family portrait. And I purchased a colour guidebook for further perusal.

I was frantically ticking experiences off my list before leaving England to work in America. Even though it meant a long day, I'm glad I crossed off Osbourne House. I returned to London in time for an evening babysitting job.

9th October (2017) Wodonga, VIC, Australia

I started with a four-hour drive to Wodonga, not wanting to push myself. I had ample time for the drive to Queensland and another year of Netfest.

I finished work at 7:30 am, drove home, drank tea, showered, packed the car and left at 11:30 am.

By 3:30 pm, I arrived at my pre-booked hotel. I tried something new with a self-check-in machine and no reception. We completed everything via e-mail, no keys in sight. I followed instructions on a driveway touch screen and my room number arrived in an e-mail. My phone number formed the entry code, followed by the hash key. To check out, I just left. I didn't talk to one person, which I appreciated after being awake for close to twenty-four hours.

I was sound asleep by 6:00 pm.

10th October (2017) Gosford, NSW, Australia

I managed eight hours of sleep, but an early bedtime meant awake at 2:00 am. I tried to doze but up by 3:30 am and left at 4:45 am.

I ate hash browns for breakfast down the road. I bought petrol after 454 km in Gundagai. The tank took thirty-six litres at $1.25 per litre. Wouldn't you love to pay $1.25 now?

I stopped at Bunnings, adding extra comfort pieces for Netfest: a tarp to attach to the marquee to increase shade; a box of bull clips to aid attachment; a picnic rug; and an ice block.

I stopped driving by 12:00 pm on arrival in Gosford. It sounds premature to stop, but I drove over seven hours. With check in not yet available, I ate Kentucky Fried Chicken to fill in time.

I managed to stay awake until 8:00 pm.

11th October (2013) Amsterdam, The Netherlands.

I arrived in Amsterdam via Singapore on Singapore Airlines. In 2013 I hadn't yet started travel bibles so I don't have one for this trip. I did extensive research with random notes to look at and a staggering pile of paperwork I collected on the trip. Add in around 1500 photos and the memories flooded back.

I caught the airport train to the main train station and walked to my hotel by 9:00 am. I remember being exhausted. With a day's worth of activities planned, I approached reception to drop off my luggage. But I was lucky as a room available to access straight away. I jumped at it.

How could I resist a nap? I picked a must do sight, which I expected to take two hours. Working backwards from its closing time, I set an alarm. I struggled to get up.

I walked to the Dutch Resistance Museum following a hotel map without incidence. World War II resistance stories fascinate me, but I didn't allow enough time. I wanted to read everything but got chased out as the museum closed, and I hadn't finished. I disappointed myself by not getting up earlier.

Here I discovered I needed longer in museums compared with other people, so I should adjust for that. Now, when I plan, I read multiple pages of TripAdvisor reviews. To allocate enough time, I find the longest time someone mentions being there. If it's a topic I'm intrigued by, I add an hour or two. That forms a more accurate length of time needed to read everything.

From the map, I can't understand how I took the wrong street home, but I did. I can picture the street, the shops, the bridge and yet I got lost. I hadn't eaten since the plane so frequented a hot chip van, thinking chips may boost my brain power to find the way back.

I believe I took a boat cruise along the canals. I have flashes of memory looking into the dark, but nothing to confirm them. It's circled in my notes. There's no ticket stub, but I think I pre-paid it. In fact, I have no photos, but I'll assume they wouldn't have worked from behind glass at night. I have no photos from this first day, though I slept through most of it. Without a credit card, I searched my bank statements to discover no payments before or during this trip. Maybe I didn't go on a boat trip? But I think I did. Another example of why I should keep a better travel diary.

My one definitive record is what I spent. That's what I recorded at this time in my travels. I mention the shuttle from the airport, the Resistance Museum entry price, the chips, water and money spent at a supermarket. €34 spent, equating to $51 Australian. But no mention of a boat.

12th October (2013) Amsterdam, The Netherlands

This trip has become even more perplexing because I know I pre-booked my Anne Frank House ticket. I found no proof of payment for that either. Booking was the only way to guarantee entry. You could queue on the day, but the queues were infamous for their length. If you weren't early, you'd miss out. I remember standing outside the special entry door watching the line to the right of me build before open time. How did I pay? I checked every bank statement back to when I paid for the cruise I would join, as I wouldn't have booked entrance tickets before the cruise. Nothing but the flight and cruise. I'm very confused.

Thanks to the time difference, I woke early and meandered to the Anne Frank House. I crossed a canal, walked one block to the next canal, and turned left. My destination would be on the right. I booked the earliest entry on a Saturday, so the streets were empty. I recall wandering the picturesque streets along canals. The tall buildings leaned in. Window sills held flowers and bicycles parked out the front. I had traditional Amsterdam to myself. A wondrous start to the day.

The crowds built as I approached the museum, but I had the magic paper granting access. I relished the moment the door swung open to welcome us special ones. Research and planning will ensure you achieve more in your available time.

We visited the Anne Frank House in 1983. Some memory flashes remain, but too much had changed. We walked through the front door. Now you enter next door with access to a museum complex. I expected familiarity, but was disappointed.

It's hard to imagine what they endured once you see the rooms they could never leave. But the crowd size made it difficult to pay respect. The bookcase was an ingenious idea.

After my two-hour visit, I climbed the tower of the Westerkerk. From above, I saw the city's layout. Brown buildings with white windows and red roofs run along the canals with a green tree or two. How the buildings bend, with the body at an angle to the facade, fascinated me. You don't notice that from ground level. The rooms would have awkward shapes. When visiting, make sure you climb a tower, and stroll the streets to immerse yourself in the distinctive environs.

I arrived at the tower's top for a bell ringing demonstration to add to the atmosphere. The bells were thunderous, but enthralling to watch the movement back and forth, making music.

I peeked at the House Boat Museum. I enjoyed the photos of canal life. One showed the owner mowing his grass roof. Another captured a frozen canal with two chairs, table and lamp in the centre.

I had a reunion over lunch. In September, I posted on a friend's Facebook page:

```
Hello from Australia! Feel like coming to
Amsterdam for lunch on Sat 12th Oct??? I've
got just a quick visit in your neck of the
woods....
```

My friend known as Dutch Suzanne, to distinguish her from German Susanne, both friends from Denmark, replied. We caught up over lunch laughing at the photos Suzanne brought of our Danish adventure in 1996. Upon leaving Denmark, we wrote snail-mail letters and Christmas cards and later reunited on Facebook. But we haven't been in touch for years and haven't seen each other since Denmark. It was brilliant to catch up on my brief visit.

I collected my bags and checked in for my river cruise.

I booked the cruise during a "no single supplement" promotion. Often cruise single supplements are the equivalent of paying for two, making this half price thus affordable. I paid for it from a second job while working full time. Such a fabulous reward after my hard work.

At registration, they whisked our bags away, and we took buses to our boat. This was my first cruise. I joined Avalon Waterway's fifteen-day Magnificent Europe Cruise from Amsterdam to Budapest.

As expected, the passengers were older, with the occasional younger person. Not a problem for me. Why can't I cruise while I'm young? Maybe the river levels will change by my retirement, making cruises no longer possible. It bothered me then, and bothers me now, that no alternatives exist to the companies marketing to the older crowd. Why isn't there a cheaper version younger people can afford? I'm not sure I'll be able to afford one during my retirement.

I was fascinated by having the same bedroom for fifteen days. For the first time, I unpacked my bag; hung clothes in the wardrobe; placed items in drawers; and hid the backpack under the bed. A new phenomenon for me. It had an air of sophistication.

To increase the affordability, I chose the cheapest dates on the cheapest ship. *Tranquility* was slated for refurbishment after this trip. So her last sailing for the season and with the current cabin layout. The dates were cheap because of the potential for unpredictable weather. I can deal with that to save a couple of thousand dollars.

I semi-upgraded, though, in paying for a mid-grade room. We'd be sailing on picturesque waterways. The cheapest rooms had port holes I'd have to stand on furniture to reach. No, thank you. I went for the floor-to-ceiling windows with a French-style balcony. I had to Google what French-style balcony meant, but the concept worked. The windows slide open and a barrier stops you from falling out. No extra space, like a balcony, but fresh air with a balustrade. If the room gets cold, you hop under the covers and you're warm again.

Tonight's program lay on the bed. We had the mandatory Life and Safety Exercise, followed by a Welcome Reception and Embarkation Dinner, and live music in the Panorama Lounge. It's a bit posh sounding for me.

I met my next-door neighbour, also by herself, and had used the no supplement special. She was 83. Her recently deceased husband had no interest in travel and she was wasting no time in seeing the world. Besides her husband dying, I thought it was fabulous she was making up for lost time. I'll never understand people who have no interest in travelling.

We headed to the dining room together for our first dinner. Everyone was more dressed up than I expected and realised I may not have packed the right clothes. It was open seating with one sitting. I'm glad I had someone to walk in with. We started a new table and people joined until full. Most tables held eight, with a few smaller tables in the middle and one larger table holding ten. I preferred to be near the window.

What a magical day of experiences and emotions. It turned out cheap as well. No mention of paying for the Anne Frank House. I don't know how or when I paid. With entrance fees for the tower and houseboat, lunch, and two postcards, I spent €23. I ate Pringles from the minibar, which I would pay for later.

13th October (2013) Amsterdam, The Netherlands

While at dinner, the crew deliver the next day's *Daily Newsletter*. It gives your location and the day and date. These are difficult concepts when holidaying in a moving hotel. It set out the day's program in meal services, when docking, details of included shore activities, onboard activities, helpful hints such as how to tip, exchange rates, the weather, a Quote of the Day and so forth.

Today's newsletter has a helpful hint on collecting Shore Passes before alighting, as they can leave without us if we failed to collect one. Don't forget your Shore Pass. It's easy as they stand at the exit handing them out.

Breakfast can be a drawn-out affair depending on when you awaken. There's the Early Riser Breakfast from 6:00-7:00 am in the lounge, the Champagne Buffet Breakfast in the restaurant from 7:00-9:00 am, followed by the Late Riser Breakfast in the lounge from 9:00-10:00 am. That covers most people's morning habits.

But no lingering over breakfast with an included canal boat ride departing at 8:45 am. We had moored in Amsterdam overnight.

As further evidence I took a night cruise, I remember being glad I'd already seen everything. It poured rain throughout the canal cruise, masking the view. We got drenched while boarding.

Despite the option to stay in town until mid-afternoon, most people retreated to the boat, given the weather. I always returned to the boat for meals, seeing as included. An early lunch at 11:45 am involved a choice between a buffet in the restaurant or a light lunch in the lounge. Buffet for me.

We set sail at 3:45 pm in search of the Rhine River. It would be twenty-four hours until our next port.

It rained throughout the day. I lounged in my bed as the rain fell and I watched Amsterdam and The Netherlands pass by. At times like this, I utilised the permanent hot drink station, which included biscuits. I'd indulge in a hot chocolate while admiring the ever-changing scenery. Bliss!

Dinner this evening was a Welcome Gala Dinner. Alas, I can't give you details as I have no memory and no photos. I searched through the fifteen hundred photos from this trip and I'm horrified to admit, besides side on views out my cabin window, I don't have one photo of inside the boat. None in the dining room, the lobby, my cabin, the lounge, nothing. Terrible. When arriving at a hotel room now, I take photos from every angle. Even if I'm desperate for the bathroom, a drink or food, photos come first, before I mess it up. I could not tell you the colour of my bedspread or carpet. I could not describe the bathroom. No photos and no memory. I remember the bedroom layout, but nothing more. I'm disgusted. Also, zero photos of people. I've never been proficient at taking people photos, but still. I have changed photo habits since, and changed them again after writing this book.

I remember the bed faced the wall separating the cabins, with the window to your right. A small table and chairs sat by the window. Reconfigured boats had the bed against the bathroom wall, looking straight out the window. *Tranquility* would have that after its refurbishment. That would be wonderful as you get a sore neck after awhile.

My spending money will be minimal throughout the cruise, with meals and most tours included. I spent €3.25 on snacks and tipped someone 70 Euro cents. I consumed a minibar cola for payment later.

14th October (2013) Köln & the Rhine River, Germany

Not docking until the afternoon, I slept in and had breakfast delivered to my cabin. This allowed me to choose the latest delivery time and remain in my pyjamas on its arrival. Getting dressed is overrated on holiday.

For a €2 delivery surcharge, I had breakfast in bed with glorious Germany going by as we cruised the Rhine River. Perfection!

There weren't many opportunities to languish in bed with morning shore excursions. Once I realised how brilliant it was, I organised it on two more occasions with morning cruising.

You didn't choose your food. A selection was delivered with variable options dependent on who made it.

Today's tray contained a pot of tea; a jug of milk; a glass of orange juice; a bowl of fruit salad; a basket of various pastries; and a plate of condiments. What more do you need? I hung out in bed, eating and drinking tea as Europe went by.

I semi-dressed and sneakily refilled the room service teapot with hot water from the hot beverage station and had a second pot of tea in bed. This is the way to travel.

After working two jobs, I was exhausted. I needed a relaxed start to the trip. Some cruisers didn't appreciate the quietness, though. When I enquired why, I received a plausible explanation. Being of the older age variety, they were retired. They relax at home as their normal state. On holiday they want to go-go-go. It's their time to be energetic. Us workers are go-go-go as the normal state, so we want to relax.

We had a 4:00 pm included city walk on arrival in Cologne, or Köln. We broke into three categories of groups based on abilities. I joined the energetic tour. I don't remember what the two fastest categories were called, but I loved the name for the least athletic cruisers called "The Gentle Walkers Group". Such a cute name. The people in this group required walking sticks and frames. But they always alighted. Sometimes they'd have vehicles of varying styles to deliver them to the sights. We energetic people walked into the town centres. I hope I'm travelling when I'm a gentle walker.

There were two walks. Being my first visit to Köln, I chose the general tour over the more specific Jewish Heritage tour. Before alighting, you pick up headsets, but you had to pick the correct ones for the tour and speed you desired. White was always for the Gentle Walkers. Blue was for the Jewish themed tour and five colours for the rest.

Being more energetic than most of the group had its advantages. I'd either race ahead to get photos while they caught up or stayed back knowing I could catch them. I'd be apart from the group, but hear the commentary via the headsets. This was my first headset tour. I used to laugh at people on those tours, but I discovered their advantages. If the voice disappeared, I knew I'd gone too far, and either waited for them or ran faster to catch up.

European towns are beautiful compared to Australian towns. They're not afraid of colour, which makes everything appear as from a fairytale. In a row of five houses you go from a green house, to orange, cream, yellow and pink. You would never see that in Australia. Add the stone round turrets behind them and it's romantic, even by yourself. You can't help but smile, be happy and grateful to be there. And don't forget the cobblestoned streets, elegant lamps attached to the buildings and the intricate shop signs showing in pictures and designs what's for offer in the store; a tradition dating to when people couldn't read. I love how the tradition continues.

In the Alter Markt, or old square, City Hall has one hundred and thirty statues on its facade, and the Platzjabbeck, a wooden carving where a red tongue pokes out every hour.

We walked around the magnificent Köln Dom or cathedral. This is Köln's famous landmark. A cathedral has existed here since 818 CE, expanding throughout the centuries. We ventured inside to marvel at the exquisite medieval stained-glass window. I bought a postcard to ensure I had a picture that did it justice.

I took a photo showing the historic hotel next door. This was for future travel planning reference. What an incredible place to stay. It was closed for refurbishment during my next visit to Köln. It would be expensive, given its prime location.

Our official tour finished here, but I paid entry to see the Cathedral Treasury. I would have preferred to climb the tower, but it closed at 5:00 pm.

I walked over the railway bridge to look back at the city view and a full circle to the boat for a 7:00 pm dinner. The boat didn't sail until 8:15 pm, allowing time for dinner in Köln if you wanted. Couples often did this to add to their experience and have alone time. Given my interesting history of meals while travelling alone, I returned to the boat. We docked below the cathedral, thus easy to navigate your way back.

After dinner, I took night photos of Köln from the rooftop deck as we sailed. The movement and darkness blurred the photos. So blurry that people who aren't me would have deleted them. The colours look great in thumbnails though.

I bought a map of the Rhine River to follow our progress. It's a flip map taller than me when open. It starts in Köln and continues to Mainz, depicting every town, castle and sight along the river bank. There could be no more detailed guide to what I'd witness from my bedroom window. Though it highlights what you'll miss while sailing overnight.

The map cost €3.50, Treasury entry €5, postcard 90 cents, totalling €9.40 with €2 for room service to be paid later.

15th October (2013) The Rhine Gorge, Germany

There was one site I wanted to see at Koblenz, but pitch black when we'd pass by in the early morning hours. Other cruise lines docked there, but not Avalon. A statue of Emperor William I sat on a strip of land called the German Corner where the rivers Rhine and Moselle meet. It was on my side of the boat, so opened my French balcony. The statue was semi lit but too dim and distant to capture a photo. I saw it though and put my binoculars to use. I arranged a wake-up call to let me know when near the site; a handy service.

We cruised this morning, but I did not languish over breakfast in bed. We traversed the most picturesque segments of the Rhine and the rooftop deck had live commentary. The 360-degree view from the deck was better than the one-sided cabin view. The commentary broadcasted into the lounge for those inside.

It was a wintry day, but I dressed for the weather. There is a hilarious photo of me wearing my big blue coat zipped to the neck, hood on, and gloves, looking through my binoculars with my camera strap around my wrist, my sunglasses hanging over my mouth and my nurse's bag strung across my body. I appear to have telescopic robot eyes, a pinhole nose and a moustache from ear to ear. People found me entertaining, hence the photo. It was sent to me after the cruise.

It's a castle a minute as you float along the river with narrow towns on the bank with hills behind. It's magical, despite the white sky and frosty wind. Some castles are ruins, and others inhabited. It's a little girl's dream where everyone lives in a castle. I'd love to buy a ruin and make it liveable again.

We saw a flag in the distance. This was the first sign we were getting close. The Loreley. Loreley is a 133 metre rock where, legend says, a mermaid sat and sang sailors to their deaths. It's a narrow point in the river with whirlpools and cross currents. Boats, thus sailors, were lost here, distracted by the sweet music luring them to their death. It is part of the Romantic Rhine folklore.

We didn't see or hear a mermaid. Our boat passed without incident. The sun emerged as we rounded the curve.

A train line runs along the banks, which must have incredible views. It traverses a multitude of tunnels along the way, with entrances and exits built as castle turrets. I loved them. The train signals intrigued me, taking multiple photos. I must return for the train ride.

The river bank contained mile markers useful in figuring out where you were. It aided in labelling photos once home. We neared the 555 mile marker when we saw The Loreley flags and by the time I took a photo of the 550 marker (we cruised downstream), I'd snapped thirty-six photos. An entire roll of film in the old days, in a five-mile stretch. Aren't digital cameras helpful? It took us thirty minutes to cover those five miles.

At mile marker 549 you'll discover Castle Schoenburg, a hotel. What an enchanting place to stay.

At 546, an adorable toll booth sits on an island in the river's midst. It dates to the sixteenth century, and its cuteness will produce a smile.

After three hours on deck, lunch was served, followed by our arrival at Rüdesheim.

We toured the whimsical Siegfried's Mechanical Musical Instruments Museum. Artworks that create music. The historic building added to the tour. They picked me to wind one and the same person who took the rooftop photo took one here of me making a ridiculous face while turning the crank. I have five forehead wrinkles, three chins and eyes popping out. But I'm glad she sent it to me.

I left the group heading off to coffee tasting to ride a scenic chairlift to the German Monument. You glide over grape vines with views of the river and castles. The monument, built in 1883, commemorates the unification of Germany in 1871. Germany is represented as a lady holding the Prussian-German Empire crown and a sword. The monument is colossal, and the views endless.

Clouds filled the sky but cleared after ten minutes, revealing a deep blue sky. I re-took photos with the new backdrop, glad I hadn't rushed to leave. I meandered back to the boat before it's 4:45 pm departure.

A big spend day totalling over €38 on the chairlift, souvenirs and drinks.

16th October (2018) Los Angeles, CA, USA

I have meticulous notes on my arrival from a 10:00 am flight to Los Angeles.

6:20 am: landed
6:40 am: deplaned
6:50 am: in Immigration line

7:05 am: at the baggage carousel (after visiting the bathroom and brushing my teeth). I decided to change into a dress, returning to the bathroom, and my bag sat on the carousel at my return.

7:20 am: waiting curb-side for a SuperShuttle.

No one should complain about Los Angeles Airport at this stage in its history, but they did.

I dropped my bags at The Anaheim Hotel and made a beeline for Disneyland. Within three hours of landing, I was at Disney. Love it!

The plan as per my travel bible:
- check in to hotel and leave bags
- change into shorts
- go to Disneyland, closes @ 6:00 pm
- off to Adventure Park if still awake, closes @ 9:00 pm
- parade @ 8:50 pm
- bedtime

What happened:
- I changed at the airport
- at Disney from 9:20 am until 6:00 pm
- then at California Adventure Park
- the parade started early
- at Adventure Park until closing
- I sat out in the forecourt to watch the fireworks from 9:45 pm-10:00 pm
- five-minute walk to the hotel
- bed by 11:00 pm

With Halloween two weeks away, themed decorations created a spooky ambiance. Bright orange pumpkins everywhere. Everything, and everyone, was depicted in pumpkins. There was Minnie Mouse, Mickey Mouse, Donald Duck, and Goofy pumpkin-fied. Colourful, playful and smile inducing.

My data collection was at an all-time high on this trip. I kept a ride tally. I rode Space Mountain, Star Tours and Indiana Jones twice each, being my three favourites. Then everything from Story Book Land Boats and the Haunted Mansion to Peter Pan's Flight and It's a Small World. At Disneyland, I totalled twenty-two rides before it closed.

Crowd numbers were low, so didn't need the Fast Pass system. Fast Passes allowed you to lock in a particular time to return to a ride without waiting in line. Once you held one, you were locked out for two hours before obtaining another one. They retired this system in 2021.

I used the single rider lane attached to Indiana Jones. This is a separate line where riders fill in empty seats. Rides with rows of three often operate this system. A single rider will fill the space next to a couple riding together from the regular line. It's brilliant when on your own anyway.

California Adventure Park had smatterings of purple-coloured decorations. The orange and purple complimented each other. As the sun set, the lights flickered on. Throw in green lights to the purple and orange and atmospheric plus. I got into the Halloween spirit and bought a necklace of glowing pumpkins.

I was fortunate to discover California Adventure Park for the first time after dark. The park was a sight to behold with its vibrant array of coloured illuminations. Even without the Halloween lights, the park was enchanting. The *Cars* ride, Radiator Springs Racers, stunned in green, purple and red. The lights of the Pixar Pal-a-Round–a Ferris wheel on steroids–reflected in the water.

I squeezed in eight rides before the parade.

As leaving I noticed people sitting in the forecourt, and I joined them. We had to wait but were rewarded with the Disneyland fireworks high in the sky. We weren't crammed in like you expect when inside the park, so nice to have a novel view, and a quick getaway.

Disney is an effective way to keep yourself awake after a fourteen-hour flight. I walked 22,379 steps.

I had lunch and dinner in the park, $19.37 and $16.68. The pumpkin lights necklace cost $16 and my shuttle from the airport cost $20. My Disneyland ticket had been pre-purchased.

17th October (2018) Los Angeles, CA, USA

I set the alarm for 8:00 am but up beforehand and entered California Adventure Park around 9:00 am. I found the park boring during the day. The atmosphere from last night had vanished. Brioche beignets formed breakfast before riding the biggest attraction while its lines were short: The Guardians of the Galaxy, a version of the Tower of Terror.

My tickets allowed multiple entries to both parks on each day. The flexibility was worth the extra money. I moved to Disneyland and returned to California Adventure Park after dark.

With bigger crowds, it was worth buying the Max Pass. Even the single rider lanes were long. The Max Pass gave you shorter lock out times for Fast Passes and free ride and character photos.

I achieved so much yesterday I rode the little rides I rarely bother with today. For example, I took the full circle of the Disneyland Railway.

I left at 3:00 pm to check in to the new hotel to attend a conference named NANNaheim, a mash-up of NANN (National Association of Neonatal Nurses) and Anaheim. Further away from the parks at a twenty-minute walk and luggage in tow, I used Uber to save my feet.

I'd eaten an ice cream before leaving the park and dripped the chocolate on my top. So throughout hotel check in and conference registration, I sported ice cream stains. That's what happens when you hold a conference next to Disneyland. I also ate a soft Mickey Mouse Pretzel, which I have every time now I've discovered how delicious soft pretzels are.

I upgraded to a room with a Disneyland view and they allocated a corner room. Amazing. The uninterrupted view allowed me to see the mountains in the distance. Not a single cloud sat in the blue sky.

The formalities, including a visit to CVS for breakfast supplies, took two hours. Then back to Disneyland between the two parks until midnight. I had a hotdog for dinner and a churro later as a snack.

I rode fifteen rides with the relaxed approach and larger crowds, then sat in the forecourt again to see the fireworks. I missed out on a Fast Pass to the fireworks, but the forecourt view proved an excellent alternative.

I walked the longer walk home with a full moon lighting the way. I took 34,675 steps over the day.

Food and drink cost $46.90, Max Pass $10, Uber $6.07, hotel resort fee $3.87, and breakfast supplies (and scissors) $25.83. The breakfast supplies included cereal, milk, apple juice and applesauce.

18th October (2018) Los Angeles, CA, USA

My room must have surprised housekeeping as I followed strict anti-bed bug rules (after they hitch-hiked home from Peru). My luggage sat in the bathtub where bed bug's legs can't grip, and I hung clothes on lamps rather than the wooden wardrobe where bed bugs love to hide. I always keep my bags in the bathroom now in case.

Conference day one. I consumed breakfast in my room while looking at the view. Our first session started at 8:00 am and continued until 6:30 pm. A light lunch and snacks at the last session formed enough food.

By 2018, I had attended four ANN Conferences which stands for Academy of Neonatal Nurses. This was my first NANN conference. I assumed they'd be similar, but I didn't approve of the NANN layout. We sat in chairs without tables. How do you take notes? And where do you put your water bottle, cup of tea, etcetera? I struggled with my belongings and to make it work.

I loved my room view, though. A spectacular sunset filled the non-Disney window. Again, not a single cloud in the orange and yellow sky. From the comfort of my bed, I observed the illumination of Disney while browsing brochures and pamphlets from the conference exhibits. I took a photo of my toes brandishing red nail polish, with my floor-to-ceiling windows and Disney in the background. What more can you ask for?

No fireworks tonight, but I'd view them from my window on other nights. Watching from a floor-to-ceiling window was spectacular, the burst of colour filling the sky.

Zero money spent today.

19th October (2001) Wellington, New Zealand

This trip has a long background story after a seed planted in July. The background will help you understand this trip, a greater understanding of the Jamaica trip, and a future story at the 2002 Commonwealth Games. This is where they started.

In the middle of June, they removed the cast from my broken ankle, fitted me into a boot brace, and sent me to physiotherapy. I'd broken the dome of my talus playing netball and had worn a cast for four weeks. The talus bone is part of your ankle joint connecting your leg to your foot. The physiotherapist said, "I can't guarantee you'll get full use of your ankle again."

What? Without my ankle, I thought I'd have to stop nannying, and being my accelerator foot, I couldn't drive, losing my dream of driving across Africa.

> 15th June: I felt deformed, like my life was never going to be the same again, and all alone. The tears just poured out. I was sobbing... two games of netball televised got me through... Sharelle McMahon (Aussie GA) [Goal Attack for the Australian team] excellent shooter.

The Netball Tri-Series was being televised. I watched games between Australia, New Zealand and South Africa. International netball at its best and how I discovered netball legend Sharelle McMahon. Her athleticism and shooting prowess left me in awe. I played goal attack and inspired by her play. They've recently placed a statue of her in Melbourne's sporting precinct.

I became a member of Sharelle's Melbourne netball club, The Melbourne Phoenix. Only two home games remained in the season, but I joined to attend the after-match functions, hoping to meet Sharelle.

I went to my first game on the 21st of July, where I introduced myself to Barry, who I'd conversed with to organise my membership. Most unlike me, but everything cascaded from there. It was worth any internal angst. Barry introduced me to his wife Sue, one player's parents and three players, but not Sharelle. She was there, though, and I watched her play live.

A few days later, I toured a local gym and sports centre. I'd put on weight since breaking my ankle. The guy who gave me the tour seemed familiar, but it took me a few hours to work out where I'd seen him. He was at the Phoenix after-match function. What are the odds?

I joined a different gym, but was not wasting a potential netball contact. I walked to the gym to say I'd seen him at the match. He said he had a friend in the team. Which player? He didn't say. I'd seen him chatting with Sharelle, so confident she was the friend. He said he'd say hello at the next match.

I became obsessed with netball and travelled to interstate away games to see extra games before the season ended. I visited Adelaide twice, where I had friends to catch up and stay with.

As the season reached an end, I wasn't ready to lose netball, so looked into an international series I'd heard mentioned in July. In had three games between Australia and New Zealand in New Zealand. I'd left it too late with one game sold out and the remaining two only back row seats.

Do players get tickets for family and friends? Maybe my gym contact could help me get tickets. Brave. Throughout the walk, I contemplated aborting, but I strode through the gym door and asked. I lied and said I'd be in New Zealand anyway, so thought I'd attend the games to find sold out and wondered if his friend had access to tickets. To my surprise and embarrassment, he rang Sharelle. I was mortified. I meant if he remembered next time he saw her. To my relief, she didn't answer, but he left a message for her to call back. At the end he said, "It's urgent." I was dying. It wasn't urgent. But. Oh. My. Goodness. He was going to ask Sharelle McMahon to get me tickets. I couldn't believe how the circumstances unfolded. Little coincidences adding up to this.

Three weeks later, still no word. I found an Australian team training session open to the public. Off I went. There was no one there, embarrassing, but I overheard one conversation that made it worthwhile.

As the players stretched, I heard them chatting. They mentioned players' tickets and who may be using theirs. Sharelle says, "A friend of a friend is going over and wants tickets. One for each match."

Music to my ears. The tickets had been requested.

> I am on Cloud 9. I'm on top of the world.

Sharelle commented she was unsure if the tickets were still wanted.

> I wanted to jump up and say they were for me and yes, I still wanted them. [But I didn't] I was smiling all the way home in the car. I was beaming!!!

I felt confident I'd get the tickets, booking flights three days later. I'd fly into Wellington and out of Christchurch on Qantas for $658.

Eight days later, on the 4th of October, I had heard nothing about the tickets, so walked to the gym. He rang her. This time she answered and confirmed I had the tickets.

> I'm so happy!! Oh so happy! One ticket to each game, more if I wanted. I'm smiley, happy singing.

A month had passed, but it turned out in my favour. They'd be waiting for me at the venues.

I returned to the gym with a thank you gift of a small bottle of champagne. I bought Sharelle a pedicure gift voucher. The netball tickets cost $40 each, so I saved money even after spending $97 on presents.

Before departing, I looked at the netball ticket availability to discover seats available. I'd be mortified if the games weren't sold out as that was the premise for requesting player tickets. I wouldn't have asked if could buy them myself. But I don't regret asking.

> 1:35 pm New Zealand Time. I'm on the plane... I didn't get to bed till after 11 pm and the taxi booked for 5:40 am. Basically, I got

no sleep. I just went to the toilet and my eyes are red and pretty bloodshot and my face is awful showing every blackhead, pimple, red mark, etc. Not at all in good shape to see Sharelle.

At least I've got my disaster done with for this trip. I arrived at the airport with no passport. It did not occur to me even once. I could not believe it. Luckily, I rang Rebecca, and she had my car and spare car keys to be able to drive straight out to the airport. I arranged for an e-Tag over the phone as soon as I hung up from Rebecca. Pretty easy really. Lucky I was early. The taxi cost $50. It was nowhere near that last time. I think I got duped. I couldn't even see a meter. I wasn't going to argue at 6:00 am. I'm totally exhausted. Hopefully, I can sleep well tonight. I need to be bright and chirpy for tomorrow night.

To this day, I am flabbergasted I forgot my passport. New Zealand's not a separate country. It's part of Australia, right? Oops. It didn't feel like overseas travel. Hence the forgotten passport. I was lucky I knew where my passport lived to tell my flatmate Rebecca and explain my spare car keys' whereabouts. Rebecca didn't have a car, but she'd used mine during the four months I couldn't drive because of my ankle injury. Being early allowed time for Rebecca to drive to the airport via the toll road shortcut, and leave time to check in. If I'd driven myself to the airport, there wouldn't have been sufficient time to drive home and return. I paid $50 for a taxi and my car still drove to the airport. But it worked out in the end. How stupid did I feel, though? My memory says I realised the instant I walked through the airport doors from the taxi. I did not make the check-in line. It's as fresh in my memory as if it happened yesterday.

While waiting for my passport, I exchanged Australian dollars into New Zealand dollars. $1000 Australian became $1141 New Zealand. I love making money out of an exchange.

My 8:10 am flight had three and a half hours of flying time, but with Wellington three hours ahead, I arrived at 3:00 pm local time.

I caught a shuttle from the airport, dropped my bags at the hostel after paying $40 for a two-night stay, and explored Wellington. I bought "lunch" in a kiwi fruit, an apple and a banana, eating said fruit as I walked to the cable car. It transported me to a vantage point, affording a panoramic view of the city and the water. I wandered the streets taking photos, but I have lost the photos. Frustrating.

While returning to the hostel, I had McDonald's for dinner and made a supermarket supply run. As usual, I bought a weird collection. The receipt has faded but with a well-placed torchlight I deciphered extra apples, bananas and kiwi fruit; tinned apricots; apple juice; Ribena; tinned corn and spaghetti; a bagel; a muffin; and pop tarts for $17.70.

Total spend came to $80. Plus the taxi and tolls.

20th October (2001) Wellington, New Zealand

I visited the Te Papa Museum today a few blocks from the hostel. I surprised myself by spending the whole day there. At this stage of my life, I hated the old style museums with labelled objects behind glass. Te Papa was unique as my first interactive museum. It even had rides similar to the audiovisual attractions I liked, but with museum pieces.

I enjoyed the current temporary exhibit called *Body Odyssey: Journey through the human body*. The brochure explains.

How many kilometres of blood vessels are in your body? How do Kiwi kids deal with asthma? Why do you get "butterflies" in your tummy when you are nervous? What causes farts? Come to Body Odyssey and learn hundreds of weird and wonderful facts about your body.

Doesn't that sound fun? I even confirm my blood group while here. I'd been told I had a rare blood group. The information here stated only one per cent of the population had B negative blood. The exhibition was worth its separate fee.

I paid to ride "Future Rush", an eighteen minute experience to Wellington in the year 2055. You laid on a reclining lounge looking up at the future.

I came away from my time here happy and wanting to return. If museums had been interactive in my earlier travels, I'd have frequented more. I'm a real museum person now.

But this trip was about netball with the first match tonight. The stadium was a ten-minute walk on the waterfront at Queens Wharf.

I presented at the ticket collection counter and asked for tickets under my name which were handed to me. Excellent seats too. Row E none the less. Any player tickets should come with a prime view.

I sat next to one player's parents, Alison Broadbent's. They introduced themselves but being nervous, I forgot to listen, so couldn't remember their names. They called me Fran all night and I couldn't call them anything.

They enquired who I was here for, assuming I knew someone in the team. I promise you this is what I said, "I got tickets through Sharelle." I did not say I was friends with Sharelle, but they presumed based on my answer.

I'd taken an Australian flag to help cheer. Alison's, or Ali's, parents proved fabulous partners in crime in flying the flag. They were enthusiastic cheerers, and we cheered together against the might of the New Zealand crowd. Australia won, but the last few minutes were hair-raising, with New Zealand making a comeback.

We held it together with the final score of 51-47 but Australia gave up a ten goal lead.

> I was worried we'd lose, but if we did, it would have been only by one which would have been heartbreaking.

Ali's parents hadn't told their daughter they were there. Several events were occurring in Wellington, making accommodation options difficult for them. I didn't pre-book the hostel and had no trouble.

Ali's parents had low expectations of her potential court time, being her debut in the Australian team. When she did take the court, pride filled her father's face. It was gorgeous to witness.

After the game, they were heading to the change rooms. They didn't know the team's hotel, so unable to reach Ali by any other means. They asked if I was coming.

Netball was relaxed, inclusive and geared towards children. It was easy for children to approach their idols and get players' signatures. So, we weren't the only people heading towards the change room corridor.

I spoke to Nicole Richardson first with an easy introduction by mentioning we had a friend in common, helping the conversation to flow. Get this. My trainer at the gym I joined was friends with Nicole Richardson. These little connections still blow my mind. It was meant to be. Nicole offered me tickets and said to follow them to the after-match function.

I had Sharelle's thank you present, so waited for her to come out. Once the kids had finished, I left Nicole to see Sharelle on her own. I said, "Hi Sharelle, I was the one who got the tickets."

"Oh hi. So you got them?"

"Yeah, after all the back and forwards."

"Yeah, I said 'well I'll need a surname,' and he's like, 'I don't know it.'"

How embarrassing that we're supposed to be friends, and he didn't know my surname. When my surname came up, Sharelle said she replied with, "Oh, I know Fran Heap."

Hearing that made my belly flip.

I gave her the present. "I got you a little something to say thank you for the tickets."

"Oh. You didn't have to do that." And she took the gift bag containing the voucher.

We talked for awhile until the next wave of kids arrived in search of autographs. We ended with, "I'll see you at the next game." No complaints from me. I watched international netball and met the players, including my favourite, who helped me through a difficult time with my ankle. Watching the games on television back then, I could never have imagined it would lead to New Zealand outside the change rooms.

I walked home happy with plans of buying a netball to get signed by the team at the next game. I didn't attend the after-match function.

At some point I talked to Ali, saying I was a friend of a friend of Sharelle's. For the record, I did stick to the truth.

I spent $31.45 all at the museum, including a dust-able souvenir; a colourful standing Kiwi bird wooden puzzle.

21st October (2001) Arthur's Pass Village, New Zealand

Today was a relocation day. I flew from Wellington on Freedom Air at 1:00 pm to Christchurch; a short forty-five-minute flight. I collected a pre-booked hire car and drove out of town. I didn't take a photo of the car but I wish I had because the rental agreement under colour says pink. At least I'd stand out in the snow.

I'm unsure how far I drove today and thus where I stayed. The spectacular scenery was memorable, but hard to appreciate while driving. I'd turn to the side but have to watch the road. I'd glance in the rearview mirror to see what I missed. It would be phenomenal as a passenger.

I was in Fox Glacier by the following day, but the nearest hostel in Franz Josef required a six-hour drive from Christchurch Airport. I signed the car rental agreement at 3:30 pm. Would I have driven that far, knowing I'd arrive after dark?

My diary is sparse. I've commented on scrap paper while waiting at the airport:

> I hope I can manage all this driving and not bitten off more than I can chew. The staff at the hostel were a bit surprised. Okay, time to board.

It's dated the 22nd of October but it must be wrong as flew out on the 21st.

I have a Hostelling International map showing the official hostels. I believe I used it as a driving and accommodation map. Only one hostel lay between Christchurch and Franz Josef, so it had to be Arthur's Pass, a two-hour drive, or Franz Josef.

Comparing my photos with Google Images after searching "Arthur's Pass hostel", I found an exact match. I must have stayed there and not driven through to Franz Josef.

Based on the photos, the sun shone in a deep blue sky with the occasional cloud. Snow blanketed the mountain tops, but not the roads. It was dramatic and exceptional.

With food, newspaper, petrol and accommodation, including paying Invercargill accommodation in advance, I spent $83. Plus $200 for the car.

22nd October (2001) Wanaka, New Zealand

From Arthur's Pass, I had a four-hour drive to Fox Glacier for a heli hike. I'd have three hours on the ice after a helicopter ride. It costs $499 now. I paid $195.

The information said to dress warmly but in photos in front of the helicopter, and on the glacier, my jumper is around my waist, my long sleeves are pushed to my elbows and no speciality gear in sight.

The helicopter landed on an immaculate white landscape in a remote corner of the glacier. From here, we sported crampons and explored. We wondered at ice caves, arches and tunnels with brilliant blue and green hues.

My ankle was still healing and nervous about how it would cope with deep exploring. If it gave out leading to a fall, I might start a domino effect and take everyone with me. I looked into the caves and tunnels but didn't enter. Maybe I should have done a different activity given the ankle issues, but it was breathtaking. I was thrilled just standing on a glacier. It's remarkable up close. The shining sun made the ice sparkle.

I overnighted at Wānaka, a three-hour drive from Fox Glacier.

An expensive day with heli hike, plus sunscreen $13.50, dinner at $14.80, hostel $18 and for the first time doona hire $3. I don't recall previously ever paying for a doona, but I did here. Total $244.30.

23rd October (2001) Te Anau, New Zealand

I've commented in my diary that today's drive was hard because of tiredness. It's a three-hour drive to Te Anau, but I'd not been sleeping well and the lack of sleep had accumulated. I got a single bed for tonight, as opposed to a bunk, which I hoped would allow better sleep without someone's disturbing movements.

I arrived at Te Anau at 2:00 pm and booked an 8:15 pm glow worm tour. With the afternoon off, I did laundry and a supermarket shop. I bought fruit, bread, water, toiletries, milk, pasta, pesto, chicken, salads and chips. I hoped the supplies covered two or three breakfasts and lunches, and three or four dinners.

> I have an easy dinner tonight but the others I have to cook, but it's just boiling up pasta and stirring in pesto, so I think I can handle that. Tonight I have deli salads and cooked chicken.

The glow worms were spellbinding. I relished every moment. First, we caught a boat across the lake to the cave entrance. We alternated between walking and floating in boats. We encountered rock formations, whirlpools, waterfalls and the ethereal glow worm grotto. You float in silent darkness so the blue-green of the glowworms, or larvae, display their silk threads hung from their nests. Bewitching. It's better than a star filled sky as more colourful and closer.

The spend for tonight's accommodation, food, petrol, laundry, tour and a puzzle (?) totalled $101.55. It must have been cheaper to pre-pay accommodation as I've pre-paid $80 for four nights in Christchurch.

24th October (2001) Invercargill, New Zealand

On arrival at Invercargill, I scoped out the stadium. The small carpark would not hold a 4100 strong crowd. This confirmed my plan to go early. I bought a netball and permanent marker for tonight's netball game.

My diary made me laugh when I read how I rummaged through bins for newspapers from throughout the week to find information about the games. I don't have physical tickets, so I don't know what time the game starts and the doors open. And I don't have a mobile phone let alone one with the internet. But it's reported in the newspapers. I learnt the doors opened at 6:00 pm, entertainment starts at 6:30 pm and the game kicks off at 7:50 pm. I planned to arrive at 6:00 pm to secure a carpark and soak in the atmosphere.

The problem was I had no access to the bedrooms and showers until the hostel office opened at 5:00 pm. I worried an hour would not be enough time to shower; dress; cook and eat dinner; and drive to the stadium. I had access to the kitchen so decided to cook the pasta before 5:00 pm; check in; shower; reheat the pasta; brush my teeth; and be at the stadium as close to 6:00 pm as possible.

The hostel staff arrived early, muting the forward planning.

When walking through town, I saw two New Zealand players: Temepara George and Linda Vagana. No Aussies.

I hoped to get a second chance at Ali's parents' names to greet them by name in Christchurch. I looked forward to cheering with them.

An Australian working at the hostel was happy to use the extra ticket in tonight's envelope, but I don't recall her sitting with us. I sat with Ali's parents and Ali's husband arrived in time for this match. We had brilliant seats in row B. Another player's family and friends joined for this game too. With careful listening, I believe Ali's parents' names are Jan and Kurt. Cheering with people is more enjoyable when you know their names. I threw myself into tonight's game, yelling more than the previous game. Maybe because we lost, 47-58. It will increase the stakes for the third match with either team able to claim the series.

After the match, I got the team's signatures on the ball, including coach Jill MacIntosh. When Peta Squires, the best WD [wing defence] specialist player ever, signed, I mentioned my friend in Adelaide who she went to school with. Peta remembered her and said my friend should say hello next time at a game. All these little connections. When Liz Ellis signed, I mentioned I'd read her book, which she appreciated. Ella Southby was friendly but showed no recognition, even though we'd been introduced. Sharelle knew my name and had full recollection. She came straight over, smiling, and signed the ball without me asking. A terrific souvenir.

Yes, I have the netball. And yes, it may contain dust. I don't know why, but it has lived on my bathroom bench since moving into my current house ten years ago.

A welcomed cheap day today. Milk 70 cents, newspaper 70 cents, parking 60 cents, netball and pen $15.45, so only spent $17.45.

25th October (2001) Christchurch, New Zealand

Another relocation day. The biggest drive of the trip. Google says it's a seven-hour drive from Invercargill to Christchurch.

> I've made it to Christchurch and I'm exhausted. I handled the drive well. I made it in 8 hours...It was great having the netball in the car today. Just like in Oz with it rolling around, but this time it has extra special meaning seeing all the signatures.

Petrol became today's main expense, filling up twice. Otherwise I bought food and a newspaper totalling $69. The food included PG Tips tea bags. One of my nanny mums had mentioned you could buy them in New Zealand. I bought a box of a hundred hoping it would last until in the UK for the Commonwealth Games the next year. In 2001, PG Tips had to be sent over from the UK. Now my local supermarket sells them, albeit at a premium price.

At the hostel, I posted an advert for the spare netball ticket.

AUS vs NZ
FREE TICKET
Netball
Sat 27th (in Christchurch)
Loud Aussie supporter
only
See Fran room 107

26th October (2001) Christchurch, New Zealand

I had a free day in Christchurch with two activities in mind. First, the Antarctic Centre and second, making extra green and gold paraphernalia for the final netball match. I also returned the hire car.

    I bought a combo ticket at the Antarctic Centre for $26, which included a Hägglund ride. I was most excited about the Hägglund as it combined my desire for an awesome 4WD vehicle for Africa with my wish to traverse the Antarctic ice. The ride is a tour of the wider complex and you complete an assault course fording water and so forth. It was bright yellow to stand out in the snow, with two carriages. It has tank treads so no wheels to dig out like on African sand. I beamed with joy. It was worth the extra payment.

    The interactive museum section held my interest. You tried on arctic clothing, entered a room with snow, watched movies on the Antarctic animals and learnt about the living conditions. It made me want to visit Antarctica.

    I frequented the supermarket, and it's the worst receipt yet for readability. I photograph receipts now, but that concept never crossed my mind during the film era. From what I can decipher, it included bread; chicken; pasta; pasta sauce;

a Mars bar; more PG Tips tea bags while available; plus other unreadable items for $20.80. I also bought yellow and green crepe paper and sticky tape for $2.55.

While out, I saw New Zealand players in Bernice Mene, Donna Loffhagen, Vilimaina Davu and Belinda Colling. Then the whole New Zealand team through the windows of the Copthorne Hotel. My first tickets in Wellington were in a Copthorne Hotel envelope, so I'm guessing both teams stayed at local Copthorne Hotels. No Australian players seen. I don't believe they were allowed out.

At the hostel, I made myself at home, taking over the lounge room floor. I spread out my Australian flag and decorated it with green and gold streamers and a green and gold braid. This made everyone curious, and I talked with pride about the Australian Netball Team with each passing person.

The Australian team was nameless in 2001. The New Zealanders have always been the Silver Ferns. In the match programs, the Australians are called the Kellogg's Cornflakes Australian Netball Team. I'm guessing Kelloggs sponsored them, but what a terrible name. No supporter will yell, "Go Kelloggs," but the New Zealand supporters scream, "Go Silver Ferns," or, "Go the Ferns." We needed a team name. We became the Diamonds in 2008.

With parking, final car hire costs, transport and extras, I spent $70.35.

27th October (2001) Christchurch, New Zealand

9:30 am. Already had a few pangs of nerves. I should keep myself busy to help the nerves and make the time go faster. I'm just in lazy mode right now. I'm sitting in the lounge with breakfast and a cup of tea in my pyjamas. Ah, I love hostels. If in a hotel, I couldn't do this. I can't believe how early I've been getting up–still not sleeping brilliantly, but getting some, I think.

Still had no Aussies wanting the ticket. There's a Canadian guy, Brian, who's interested if I don't find an Aussie. He's never heard of netball until here but can see from watching a bit on tv that more skill involved than basketball and really interested in seeing more. What better way to be introduced to netball than seeing the 2 top teams in the world play out a tied series in front of over 6000 people! I'd love to take him. I hope I can find him when I'm ready to go. There just aren't any Aussies around. There's a Kiwi who'd like it, but no way. More tea...

I've been getting a few looks from other hostellers about my bare footedness and rough appearance, but I don't care one little bit. If they have a problem with it, it's something they have to deal with, not me.

I miss the me from those days.

Eventually, I had a shower and left the hostel. I treated myself to a jet boat ride and a haircut. I hope in that order. The jet boat ride had been on my must do list and I loved it. The speed and turbulence. It's a 4WD on water.

Then time for the deciding netball match. Brian and I had superb front row seats over a tunnel to the stadiums' behind-the-scenes area. A railing in front made for the ideal location to attach the flag. I'd packed the sticky tape in case of emergency repairs. Brian wasn't embarrassed by the Australiana.

More family travelled for this match. The flag made us noticeable and Sharelle waved and acknowledged me as introduced onto court. Awesome. But to show I wasn't part of it, I didn't receive an invitation to the after party. Ali's parents got invited. The invites were in the ticket envelopes, but no invite in mine. That was disappointing and embarrassing. Ali's mum said to sneak in, but I said, "If she'd wanted me there, she would have invited me." I avoid places I'm not wanted.

I was on fine form in the cheering department, getting us the win, 50-46. A tough match goal for goal with no substitutions. There were speeches and presentations. Australia won the series with two games to New Zealand's one. They presented Captain Kath Harby-Williams with the shield.

Once the formalities done, the players hung around the court signing autographs. I had no excuse to go, but I chatted to Sharelle over the railing. I reiterated my thanks for the tickets. She said thanks for coming. They had an early flight home, so we discussed whether to sleep or stay awake. We ended with, "I'll see you back home." And it was over.

> It was a good night, a great trip. I don't regret it for a second. It's been worth every penny.

I flew home two days later.

My original cash stash of $1141 had dwindled, so I exchanged another $50 Australian, adding $57 New Zealand to the budget. With the jet boat costing $49 and a $20 hair cut, the days spending totalled $76.30.

The netball games were televised on Australian television and I'd arranged for someone to videotape them for me. When I watched the last match, my flag appeared at every centre pass, and at the end, the camera zoomed in on Brian and me. My diary from the 2nd of November:

I finished watching the netball video and after the game there is a whole section on me!!! A great view of me and my flag (with Brian) smiling, laughing, waving. It's brilliant. I watched it about 5 times. I'm so vain.

I searched for my old videos and I have netball ones but not the New Zealand games, unless it's unlabelled. YouTube had the match, but it stops at the final whistle. I enjoyed watching the game and seeing my flag, but my starring role ended up on the cutting room floor. I'm glad I mentioned it in my diary.

28th October (2005) Wonga, QLD, Australia

The job in Far North Queensland didn't work out. Lottie the Arkana and I stayed in a caravan park nearby. The way it ended hadn't given me time to plan. I didn't want to lose my stunning beach and starry sky, so packed and moved next door.

The Pinnacle Village Holiday Park had an exquisite location for beach lovers. I don't understand why it wasn't busy. Full beach frontage doesn't happen often. The campground sat on the beach save a few mangroves, palm trees and ferns. Yet I was the only camper. Others stayed in cabins further inland.

I set up the full camping paraphernalia: I erected my tent with the fly; I unrolled my table; and unfolded a chair. With Lottie in the background, it looked professional. I had pride in my camp, and it took me back to Africa. I paid for two nights ($24) allowing time to figure out a plan.

I continued my daily ritual of walking on the beach, having it to myself apart from a single jogger. I'd walk near the water's edge and the jogger on the sand. We'd wave to each other every afternoon, even though we'd never met. I wandered how long it would take him to realise I'd left.

The expansive beach had not one structure in sight. Mangroves lay to the left, the ocean on the right, and the Daintree River ahead.

The best phone reception had been on the beach, so in the evenings I made my calls with a glittering scene of a thousand stars above me. You were guaranteed a shooting star every five minutes. People got annoyed during phone calls as I gasped at each one. How could I give this up?

29th October (1999) Mackinac Island, Michigan (MI), USA

This weekend involved extensive planning. One of my favourite childhood movies was *Somewhere In Time,* starring Christopher Reeve, Jane Seymour and Christopher Plummer. The romance, the time travel, the costumes, what's not to love? I discovered a *Somewhere In Time* fan club with a yearly gathering at the hotel from the movie. I joined the club to learn more. At $769 for a single, I considered it too expensive.

I advertised in the club newsletter for someone to share the double cost with me at $435 each. A woman called Sue from Indianapolis got in touch and we made arrangements. We met on the day after planning via snail mail.

The Grand Hotel on Mackinac Island, in Lake Huron, Michigan, is a stupendous hotel. The hotel's so prominent it can be seen from the mainland; a stretch of white in the distance with a distinctive cupola.

A horse and carriage greeted us at the ferry as our hotel transfer. It would have been quicker to walk, but a treat I relished. No motorised vehicles are allowed on the island except those used by emergency services. Horse and carriages were the norm or walking or cycling.

The Grand Hotel was resplendent in its size and Victorian majesty. At the time, it was the world's largest summer hotel. It retains its record for the world's longest porch, creating a masterpiece of white Victorian grandeur. The porch overlooks gardens and the water beyond.

Our baggage made its own way. We were early, so unsure what to do, check in-wise. We walked the red carpet into the parlour, as in the movie. Exquisite. I couldn't believe I was there. A couple of people already wore period clothing, which made me jealous. I wanted to dress in authentic clothing. How magical to be dressed up the entire weekend. Sue was a period dressmaker and brought me a dress for Saturday night. With the movie set in 1912, the women's clothing could be spectacular. And how often does the opportunity to be transported to another era present itself?

We found *Somewhere in Time* (*SIT*) registration downstairs. You could pick up the weekend program; sign up for activities; buy souvenirs; enter a raffle for a Grand Hotel music box playing Rachmaninoff; join INSITE (International Network of Somewhere In Time Enthusiasts); buy CDs of music inspired by the movie; and look at books on historical clothes and Maude Adams, on whom Elise McKenna was based. Elise is the character played by Jane Seymour. It was over crowded making me torn between soaking it in and running away.

Despite being early, we attempted to check in to find our room available. We were at the back on the ground floor for the sold-out event. Three hundred and forty-three rooms, occupied by *SIT* enthusiasts. Others stayed off site and came in for the events. Our price included food and horrified when I heard off-site guests paid $70 to join dinner at the hotel, not including any drinks. Yikes!

I delighted in our room. The photos show chintz, which wouldn't pass muster in a historic hotel now, but I thought my luxury historic dreams had come true. We each had a double bed, complete with four posts and a floral material canopy, which matched the wallpaper. I was ecstatic with sleeping under a canopy that nothing else mattered. Despite the plush decor, I didn't sleep well over the weekend because of a busy mind about returning to Australia.

After settling in, we walked into town, discovering the old buildings and quaint shops. I acquired a Christmas ornament depicting the Grand Hotel.

We bought lunch completing an expensive but worth it day.

I returned to the hotel before Sue to partake in the activities. I toured the hotel kitchens, who use 210,000 pieces of cutlery and crockery per day. Their dishwashers have conveyor belts.

I attended a slide show by the movie's cinematographer showing film techniques used in the movie with stories. Izzy Mankofsky told entertaining tales. They held an INSITE member's meeting, then time to dress for dinner. I relished dressing for an occasion.

I didn't see Sue from leaving her in town until dressing for dinner. We joined the cocktail reception together, but once she had her drink, she disappeared. I was self-conscious by myself, in a short blue dress; the shortest I have ever worn. I found a seat. Someone else sat, and we talked. She invited me to join them for dinner. I was relieved. Sue later joined us.

We had a table of eight. Clark, Darlene, Maureen, Julie, Rosslyn, Peter, Sue and me. We got along and made plans to eat together the next night. It worked out in the end.

Dinner contained five courses with at least three choices. My choices:

Appetiser: fruit cocktail (melon balls).

Soup: mushroom.

Salad: I skipped.

Main: roast veal.

Dessert: white chocolate mousse cake.

I drank a cola and later presented with a bill for it. I had no money with me. Clark paid the check. Thank goodness. I assumed drinks were included–at least soft drinks. The main reason I had no money was I didn't have an evening bag to carry it. I noted I'd have to buy one.

After dinner, we watched *SIT*. The studio spent over $10,000 for a never-before-seen print and gave it to Jo Addie, the Editor of INSITE. I'd never seen the movie on the big screen. It made for goosepimply moments, and I fought back tears multiple times. I loved every second. I'm glad I hadn't watched it before coming. It meant more after not seeing it for years.

I peeked in on the dancing, wishing I had someone to dance with. Without a key, I waited for Sue but never found her. I presumed she'd returned to the room. I knocked three times before she opened the door. She'd felt unwell and gone to bed. I woke her. Sorry. Another repercussion of not having an evening bag. I'm a mess fashion-wise.

30th October (1999) Mackinac Island, MI, USA

We rose early to join an 8:30 am movie location tour. Breakfast didn't impress me. The French toast bread contained raisins of which I did not approve. I added two fried eggs, a sundry of miniature pastries, orange juice and tea. I could have eaten more, but the French toast tainted the entire meal.

> The location tour was really good. We went to all the spots in the movie. The "Is it you?" tree, park they walked in, the gazebo, the stables, the theatre, the sound stage, Laura Robert's house, building used for outside the theatre. There were lots of stories and background information, oh the coin shop as well. We had re-enactments of some of the scenes too. It went for 2 hours and I loved it all. We were late for the next event.

After an initial interest in the antique clothing talk, my attention waned and left for lunch.

They called it the "Grand Buffet Luncheon" held in the main dining room. The dining room was magnificent in size and decor. The rear of the restaurant was barely visible from the entrance. A central corridor flagged by white and mirrored columns added elegance, light and space. The chairs were a bold green on the front and a green and white stripe on the back, and given their number, created an alternating level of colour and extra grandeur. Throw in white linen tablecloths with green and white crockery and it was a scene I never expected to find myself. Usually, a rope in the way showed it was not for me.

Despite the sumptuousness, or because of it, I felt uneasy requesting a table for one.

> Anyway started lunch by myself and it was terrible. Felt awful saying just one and so on. It was a beautiful big buffet. While getting food, I found Clark, Darlene and Sue at a table for four, so I moved with them. I didn't eat it all properly because they had been there longer and I didn't want to hold them up.

I also didn't want to be late for the autograph signings.

> I got everyone's from Arthur to the grown up man (very cute) who played little Arthur. To the set designer, to editor. It was great. I got a photo with both old and young Arthur.

I didn't enjoy the waiting in line part of the autographs, but being with Darlene helped pass the time.

Next on the agenda, the celebrities held a panel discussion where I asked a question and received an answer. The movie version we watched last night didn't include a scene where Richard, played by Christopher Reeve, tries on the old suit he wore to travel back in time. I remember the scene from when a child. I asked if countries had different cuts and although the editor couldn't answer, one panellist, an actor in the movie, had the script with him. He let me read it and the scene I pictured was in the script. I thought I must have imagined the scene, but I have a good memory.

I have the DVD and watched it while writing this. The scene was not in that version either. I wonder how it was in my childhood version?

I stayed for the trivia contest despite not registering, assuming I wouldn't know the answers. But I could have done well.

Time to dress for dinner. I love announcing that! Tonight was the program highlight with most attendees in period dress.

Sue wore one of her creations each night and brought one for me to wear tonight. It happened to be a redhead's perfect colour of baby blue. She dressed me completely with full length gloves, a necklace and headdress. I was in heaven. A little long, but manageable if careful. My princess moment.

> Felt so good. I felt beautiful. I loved every second in that dress. I tell you the gloves made a huge difference. They made it feel real. It was magical. Going down into the parlour with nearly everyone dressed in old clothes really felt like going back in time. I didn't want the night to end.

Being close to the *Titanic* movie release, also set in 1912, I recognised costumes from that movie. Patterns for the *Titanic* movie costumes were available to buy, thus any sewer could make them. It added an additional, but authentic period aspect to the night. I was torn, though. I love both movies in their own rights and didn't want them merged together.

Imagine this, you are in a historic building with everyone around you dressed in period clothing and you hear horses' hooves clip-clop. I cherished every moment, knowing it was my only chance to travel back in time. A dream come true. As a child, I tried to wish myself back in time like Christopher Reeve in the movie. This weekend made that wish come true.

Once our entire group was present, we took photos and entered the dining room to be seated for dinner. Not everyone on our table had dresses in Sue's calibre, but everyone dressed as best they could, attempting to be less modern. Peter wore a top hat and tails and extra wax in his styled moustache.

The dinner menu:

Appetiser: Sparkling Michigan Raspberry Juice (scrumptiously delicious)

Soup: Tomato Bisque

Salad: none

Main: Muscovy Duck

Dessert: real (unbaked) cheesecake

Clark and Darlene adopted me this weekend. Clark bought me a second glass of the raspberry juice after seeing how much I loved it, as a surprise.

During dinner we toasted wishes. We each made a wish with the potential to materialise by the next year. We planned to return to the next *SIT* weekend to tell everyone how our wishes came true. A marvellous sentiment which wasn't followed through. But we clinked glasses, as in Rosslyn's words, "We are making magic here."

Even in my diary a few days later, I was muddled as to what I'd wished for, but I settled on returning to Space Camp, which I did. Maybe magic was in the air.

After dinner, we watched the parade ogling the magnificent dresses. People suggested I should parade, but I wanted to see the costumes. Right near the end, I had a burst of desire to take part. I grabbed Darlene, and we paraded together in front of the crowd.

It was a great feeling. We were second last, but I'm glad I did it.

After dinner, they held an auction and presentations, followed by a genuine apology video message from Jane Seymour.

> That was nice. I still can't believe she was all booked to come and then only three weeks ago cancelled because had to work on another movie. I was so close to meeting her. Can you imagine that? That would have been awesome.

With the formalities over, I utilised the business centre to check e-mails. I checked and replied to e-mails stretching out the night before returning the dress to Sue. In a later diary entry, I wrote:

> I wish I had a photo of me all dressed up Saturday night typing on the computer, gloves and all. That must have looked really funny. It felt funny typing in gloves.

Hilarious. Nothing like skipping out on 1912 for a 1999 activity.

When I returned to my room after the fairytale evening, I still didn't want it to end. I lay on my luxurious bed in my finery, writing my diary.

> I felt so exquisite. I felt genteel and ladylike. The gloves got really hot at one point, but I wanted to wear them as they would have. I can't tell you how much I love this dress. I'm still wearing it, as I don't want to take it off. She's selling it but I think it's best not to buy it, not that I can afford it...Well to bed now. Unfortunately, time to take the dress off.

31st October (1999) Indianapolis, Indiana, USA

Today, we bid farewell to our wonderful hotel. At 7:00 am we ate a breakfast of pancakes and potatoes. We readied our bags for an 8:00 am pick-up. The goodbyes started and check out completed. We walked to the ferry terminal for the 9:00 am departure. Half of our bags did not make it. We waited for the next ferry. One more bag arrived. The bag holding Sue's dresses hadn't come. She arranged for it to be sent to her house rather than wait. At least Sue was semi local. If it had been my bag, it would have been trickier given I was leaving the country in a week.

The plan had Sue drop me off at East Lansing Train Station in Michigan, like on arrival. However, I stayed overnight with Sue and her husband in Indianapolis instead. This saved me from spending a night in Chicago. And it helped keep the weekend alive while saving money.

The following day I travelled west via train towards Los Angeles and Australia.

INSITE remains active and continues to hold *SIT* weekends at the Grand Hotel. 2022, being the forty-second anniversary, had Jane Seymour in attendance. I wish I'd met Jane Seymour, but I was enamoured by my weekend regardless of who didn't make it.

November

1st November (1998) New York, NY & Princeton, New Jersey, USA

I celebrated my first Halloween in America, starting with trick or treating with the family I worked for in the early evening. It wasn't as exciting as television shows made it look.

Afterwards, I headed into Manhattan from Princeton Junction Train Station to meet friends. We tried to watch the Greenwich Village Halloween Parade, but I proved too short. One friend, Martin, put me on his shoulders for ten minutes. I took photos, but none came out being night-time.

We had plans to meet others at a bar nearby, which I loved. I sat at the bar enjoying a hot apple cider. Live jazz music played and candles lit the room.

Our friends didn't arrive, so we left for Times Square. Martin took us to an Irish pub, but unimpressive after the previous place. Being after 10:30 pm without eating dinner, I was starving. I needed somewhere to sit and eat, neither of which were options at the pub.

> We got two beers into Caroline and then found a restaurant where I had some fries and a piece of cheesecake.

We called the night a bust and headed to Penn Station to catch our various trains home. We shared our subway carriage with a sleeping devil. An older lady wore devil horns on her head as she slept away.

I caught the last departure to Princeton at 1:40 am arriving at 2:50 am. Others alighted in need of a ride home. We'd assumed we'd get taxis, but they'd finished for the night.

> In the end, the Police felt sorry for us and drove us home. I was with 8 Princeton Uni students, so at least I wasn't there all by myself. So I rode home in the back of a Police car–that was cool. It's very small–no leg room and of course you can't open the doors or windows. So anyway, I got home at 4 am.

The highlight of my night was a ride in an American police car; an unexpected end to the night. I'd always wondered why they help arrested people into the car. Now I can tell you. There is no leg room. Your feet are under the front seat. You need to move your body in specific ways to get your feet in and under. It would be difficult with your hands in handcuffs. The easiest way is to sit sidewards, watching your head as the officers say. You'd balance yourself if you had free hands and place one leg in at a time. It makes sense once you do it. At least I didn't do it in handcuffs. I'm not sure what would have happened without the police; a long, cold walk.

A local Princeton friend woke me with a phone call at 9:45 am and picked me up soon after to attend church. She went every week, and I'd asked to join her on this date as hoped for familiar readings.

It was seven years since my Year 12 final school mass. I did a reading so had an affinity with this particular mass, even though it had been years since I'd attended mass regularly. I wanted a trip down memory lane. But wished I'd had more sleep. We arrived late, missing my 1991 reading, but it was the correct mass and memories flooded back.

So that was my mini Halloween and 1st of November adventure in New York and New Jersey, on the seven-year anniversary of finishing high school.

2nd November (2005) Cape Tribulation, QLD, Australia

After two nights at the campground, I extended my stay to a week to qualify for the cheaper weekly rate. I paid $48 to make up the $72 weekly fee. Beach front property for $10 per night. I was paid up to tomorrow morning.

I had relaxing days of enjoying the beach, reading books, and taking stock of my life. Every day at 1:00 pm I'd stop and wait for my neighbour to walk by. A goanna of the enormous variety swaggered through my campsite at the predictable hour each day. He never bothered me. I never bothered him.

But time was running out. I explored this part of the world before heading to Melbourne and reality. I packed Lottie, but didn't have to leave at any particular time with tonight being paid for.

Every morning I filled my thermos at the kitchen and brought it back to camp, allowing multiple cups of tea without repeated trips. Today I packed while I drank, then said farewell to my beachside home.

I headed north to cross the Daintree River and make the Cape Tribulation pilgrimage. We shorten the name to Cape Trib. When I mention long drives I've done, I say Melbourne to Cape Trib, as opposed to Melbourne to Wonga.

I drove ten kilometres to the ferry, the scariest part for me. I worried about getting Lottie on and off the ferry. When alighting, it's a short but steep hill. I was nervous Lottie wouldn't make it. But we both survived crossing the Daintree.

The rest of the drive proved easy. The hardest part was deciding where to stop with constant signs to lookouts, boardwalks or places to eat.

My first stop was lunch. I don't recall where, but I can tell you it cost $18.50, which sounds expensive, but everything became expensive once you crossed the river.

Everyone stops at the Daintree Ice Cream Company, so ice cream formed my afternoon tea. This also sounds expensive at $9.50. Talk about blowing the budget at the last minute.

I made it to the end of the sealed road and walked to the Kulki Lookout. The breathtaking beauty of the World Heritage listed Cape Tribulation greets you. Tropical rainforest meets the sand and sea with Thornton Peak and Mt Sorrow in view. It is spectacular. To make it better, some Danish tourists were at the lookout. I had the magnificent scenery in front of me, accompanied by the comforting sound of Danish. Bliss!

I walked to the beach at low tide, and the sand stretched on forever. I turned my back to the water to see the tree-covered hills. With few people milling around, it felt like the end of the world. It was getting harder to leave.

I stayed the night in a nearby campground for the bargain price of $7.80, less than the cost of an ice cream.

3rd November (2005) Cairns, QLD, Australia

Today I meandered along the boardwalks through the tropical Daintree Rainforest. I love these places. I'm a sucker for a boardwalk, and the tree roots are mind-blowing. The roots are so fascinating I could stare at them for hours. How they entwine around each other, creating braided trees. What root belongs to what tree? Throw in roots strutting out everywhere and you've encountered another planet. A tangled web of trees and roots.

I headed to Cairns, taking in the coastal road ocean views one last time. Lottie's door had been fixed, so it wouldn't fly open on the twists and bends.

I caught up with friends in Cairns and organised the transport of Lottie home by truck. I wasn't ready for another long drive, so flew home a few days later. My Far North Queensland experiment/adventure had finished. No regrets. It wouldn't have been possible without Lottie.

4th November (2002) Canberra, Australian Capital Territory, (ACT) Australia

The previous day I had driven from Melbourne, arriving at the hostel at 10:30 pm. I'd requested an early finish from my nanny job and we agreed to 2:30 pm as opposed to the usual 4:00 pm. I left at 2:45 pm but the mother gave me glassware and fragile items she was throwing out and I didn't want to take them to Canberra. So I had to return home before starting the drive. I'd arranged a late arrival with the hostel giving me until midnight, but made good time taking under eight hours. I remember arriving disappointed when the drive finished.

In my diary before leaving:

> There shouldn't be any traffic as not peak hour and freeway all the way. I'll stop for toilet stops and dinner at McDonald's and that's all. 8 hours of driving and singing. Can't wait. I found all my tapes, so have a great selection.

The main reason I snuck in a trip to Canberra was I'd become obsessed with fitness in order to improve my netball playing. My international netball viewing had made me want to become the best player I could and for that, I needed to be fit and eat a good diet. Where to get the best advice? The Australian Institute of Sport in Canberra, of course.

I was ecstatic to be visiting. You were taken on a tour by an elite athlete and shown the training areas, including swimming pools, gymnastic equipment and netball courts. I hoped to meet a netballer, but that didn't happen.

They have simulators to test yourself on, like virtual golf and rowing. Being a Tuesday, it was quiet, so tried everything in relative solitude. I loved the vibe.

I bought two recipe books from the shop to fuel my sport, called *Survival For the Fittest*, and *Survival From the Fittest*. Although I only cooked a handful of the recipes, I recall the excitement of the books. I expected them to turn me into a champion. At least I tried.

I also bought a netball training manual which I put into action.

5th November (2002) Canberra, ACT, Australia

I had a few hours before driving to Albury to stay with friends. I visited the Canberra Space Centre to fuel my space passion. Here you gawked at space suits, rocks collected from the moon and the Deep Space Communication Complex. They have huge antennas to pick up signals from the space shuttles. The largest dish is seventy metres in diameter and weighs over three million kilograms. They are ginormous up close.

I copied a web address informing me when a space shuttle would fly over Melbourne. There was a mission from the 10th-20th of November, so I may see one cross the night sky soon.

I drove back to Melbourne on the 6th, with a detour for dinner at my father's in Echuca. That was the toughest drive day. But there's nothing like a mid-week mini adventure.

6th November (1999) Melbourne, VIC, Australia

After seven years of travelling and working around the world, on the 4th of November, I departed Los Angeles Airport on a flight to Melbourne, Australia. I was slated to arrive on the 6th of November at 10:20 am, seven years after flying to Los Angeles on the 7th of November 1992. That was not planned. It naturally unfolded that way, but I love the symmetry. It wasn't the ten years I said as I waved goodbye in Albury, but pleased I'd achieved seven years.

When checking e-mails while dressed up at Mackinac Island, friends Chris and Jason said they'd pick me up from the airport. I met Chris and Jason in a house share in London in 1997 from which they'd returned to Australia. I was grateful my first introduction to Australia after seven years would be from people I'd met overseas; a transitional bonus.

I went through Immigration and Customs in Sydney, and relieved they let me in. They also let in my treasured wooden African souvenir. I was nervous they'd take it off me and remember blurting out, "I've had it for over a year and nothing has ever grown out of it." The customs officer said she'd seen nothing like it. She let it in without an issue. My beautiful Dogon door from Mali.

I arrived late in Sydney so missed my Melbourne flight. The next flight was full, so had to wait an extra few hours. I felt bad my friends had to wait. The plan was they'd pick me up and take me to lunch with another mutual friend.

I sat at Sydney Airport writing my diary, confused about the snack options.

> Samboy Chips seem to have been pushed out by the American Lays. I really feel like some right now, but only have Smith's and Lays. I didn't even know you could get Smith's in salt and vinegar. I guess that might help my craving.

In my absence, my favourite potato chips, Samboy Chips, disappeared from the everyday shelves. I'd been so looking forward to seeing Samboys everywhere but Smith's sat in their place. It confused me. I have adjusted to Smith's Chips now, but I will always consider Samboys the ultimate salt and vinegar chips.

I stressed over money. I arrived with US$36 exchanged into AUS$49.50. That's all I had until they refunded my American working visa deposit. They returned the money after you'd left the country. I had contacted a couple of Australian nanny agencies before arriving and arranged an interview for Monday in two days' time. Not knowing the state of the Australian nanny jobs market, I was anxious about what the future held.

Everything was weird and unfamiliar and a big adjustment. For the past seven years, moving to a new country hadn't fazed me, and now hesitant about my native country.

> I'm worried I'm not going to make it back here, well like it. Just hearing the Aussie accents and seeing Australians. I don't know. I guess it's natural for it all to seem weird and have apprehensions. It's a big change. A big culture shock.

I was also having trouble resisting buying chips. Then I landed in Melbourne.

I'm here. It's freaky, freaky, freaky. I guess it still hasn't sunk in.

My dear friends Chris and Jason had waited through the delay and greeted me. It was the best welcome home I could have asked for. As planned, we drove to another friend's house, where even more people waited. Such a surprise. I'd met everyone overseas, which eased the transition. I was home.

Who know's what's going to happen. Anything's possible.

About the Author

Fran, currently living in Melbourne, Australia, has travelled to 57 countries and will be adding three more soon to make an even 60. Her life is travelling and caring for other people's babies as a nanny and neonatal nurse. By her own admission, she's a terrible redhead with a penchant for quirky data collecting. Her favourite motto being "Curiosity killed the cat, *but information brought her back.*" She loves ancient ruins and drains, hates dusting, loves going behind the scenes, can't smile in photos and detests selfie sticks. In her younger days, she wanted to be an actress, an astronaut, a hostel owner, a department store owner, and a writer. When she was ten, she wrote in her diary: *Tonight I vowed I will get a story published at some stage before I die.* This book series fulfils that vow. And she now proclaims to be the happiest she has ever been her whole life!

My Books!

Thank you for reading!
I hope you have enjoyed my book.

Amazon Australia

If you have, *please* consider **writing a review** so I know what you enjoyed the most or what you would like to see more or less of in future books. (Scan the QR codes to the left and below for direct links to Amazon reviews for the Australian and American sites.)

Even a simple, "I really enjoyed this book!"
is *super* helpful.
Or even a simple star rating!

Thank you!

Amazon America

Sign up

If you want to be notified when I publish new books
or
be part of my ***advanced reader team*** for a future book, you can sign up to my monthly newsletter by scanning the QR code to the left or at my website:

https://franheapwriter.com/sign-up/

For more behind-the-scenes information of the stories, and writing about the stories, listen to my **podcast** titled "365 Dates of Travel with Fran Heap" wherever you get your podcasts or:

https://franheapwriter.com/podcast/

Podcast

Future Travel Books!

Stand alone trips

For example:

America 1992

Czech Republic, Slovakia, Hungary, Greece and Turkey 1995

Africa 1998

Index

This index allows you to choose your own adventure across both books. Trips in italics are in *The first six months* book. QR codes on page 341, will direct you to other themed indexes.

Chronological Order

1984
- *January 25th – Flying from Europe to Australia (aged 9)*

1988
- *April 17th – Australia (aged 14)*

1992
- *November 7th – USA (aged 18) (7th-10th, 12th-13th, 20th-21st, 25th-30th; December 2nd, 9th-20th, 30th-31st; January 7th, 14th; February 5th-6th)*

1993
- June 23rd – Uk, Hampton Court Palace

- August 26th – UK, Buckingham Palace

1994
- August 2nd – Italy (2nd-5th & 7th)
- August 27th – France (27th-28th)

1996
- *January 3rd – Canada, Vancouver*
- *April 5th – Norway (5th-6th)*
- June 5th – Denmark (5th & 22nd)
- September 23rd – Ireland (23rd-26th)
- *December 21st – Israel & Egypt (21st-29th; January 1997 1st-2nd, 4th-5th; extra information January 16th-17th)*

1997
- *January 15th – Denmark (15th-18th)*

1998
- *January 12th – UK, England (12th-13th)*
- *February 7th – UK, England (7th-11th, 14th, 17th-18th)*
- *March 11th – Africa overland via Europe (11th-13th,15th-27th; April 3rd-4th, 13th-14th, 18th-22nd, 27th-30th;* May 15th-16th, 29th-30th)

- July 31st – UK, Scotland

- November 1st – USA, Manhattan and Princeton

1999

- July 23rd – USA, Woodstock 99 (23rd-25th)

- August 21st – USA, Statue of Liberty crown visit

- September 12th – USA, Space Camp in Alabama (12th-17th)

- October 2nd – USA, Boston

- October 29th – USA, Mackinac island (29th-31st)

- November 6th – Australia, arriving home after 7 years overseas

2001

- October 19th – New Zealand (netball) (19th-27th)

2002

- *February 15th – Australia, Newcastle (netball)*

- August 8th – UK, England

- November 4th – Australia, Canberra (4th-5th)

2003

- July 17th – Jamaica (netball) (17th-18th)

2004

- May 10th – Australia, Perth to Melbourne via the Nullarbor Plain (Lottie) (10th-14th)

2005

- June 18th – Australia, Warrnambool (Lottie)

- July 3rd – Australia, Seymour (Lottie)

- August 29th – Australia, Melbourne to Far North Queensland (Lottie) (29th-3rd September)

- October 28th – Australia, Far North Queensland (Lottie)

2010

- *January 6th – Libya & Egypt (6th, 8th-11th, 19th-22nd, 24th)*

- *November 14th – Syria & Jordan (14th-19th, 22nd-24th)*

2012

- July 6th – East Africa (6th-13th, 15th-16th, 19th-20th, 22nd, 26th-30th; August 1st)

2013

- *March 7th – Finland (7th-9th, 14th)*

- October 11th – European River cruise (11th-15th)

2014

- September 6th – Africa, South Africa

2015

- *January 28th – UK, Germany & Romania (28th-31st; February 1st-4th, 12th-13th, 19th-25th, 28th)*

2016

- *April 23rd – Turkmenistan & Italy (23rd-26th; May 1st-8th)*

- May 23rd – Australia, Victoria & South Australia (after Italy) (23rd-25th)

- October 3rd – Australia, Melbourne to Gold Coast for Netfest (3rd-7th)

2017

- *March 29th – Poland (29th-31st; April 1st-2nd)*

- September 8th – USA, Las Vegas, National Parks & New York (8th-11th, 19th-22nd, 27th-1st October)

- October 9th – Australia, Melbourne to Gold Coast for Netfest (9th-10th)

2018

- *April 7th – USA, Los Angeles & Charlotte (7th-12th, 15th-16th)*

- June 6th – Peru (6th-17th)

- September 4th – USA, New Orleans (4th-5th, 7th)

- October 16th – USA, Los Angeles, Disneyland (16th-18th)

- *December 1st – England & Germany (1st, 3rd-5th, 7th-8th)*

2019

- *March 10th – USA, Los Angeles*

- May 9th – New Zealand, Auckland

- May 17th – USA, storm chasing in Tornado Alley & Las Vegas (17th-22nd, 26th-28th, 31st-4th June)

- August 9th – USA, Los Angeles to Rhode Island via Washington D.C. & New York City (9th-15th, 17th-18th, 20th-25th)

- *November 11th – Lebanon (11th-12th)*

- *December 6th – Australia, Sydney*

2020

- *February 26th – Portugal (26th-27th; March 1st-6th)*

2022

- June 19th – Australia, Wilson's Promontory (19th-20th)

- June 24th – Australia, Tasmania (24th-30th; July 1st-2nd, 4th-5th)

Other themed indexes include:

By Country

Unique Experiences

Trains

Christmas Themed

Disney

Packing

Flights

Lottie the Arkana Tales

Nanny Stories

Netball Stories

Access extra indexes by scanning the QR code or going to https://franheapwriter.com/indexes/

365 DATES of TRAVEL
The first six months

A story for each date of the year

Fran Heap

The first book in this series:
365 Dates of Travel: The first six months.

www.ingramcontent.com/pod-product-compliance
Lightning Source LLC
Chambersburg PA
CBHW020314010526
44107CB00054B/1834